INTERNATIONAL TOURISM

Identity and Change

edited by
Marie-Françoise Lanfant, John B. Allcock
and Edward M. Bruner

SAGE Studies in International Sociology 47
Sponsored by the International Sociological Association/ISA

© International Sociological Association 1995

First published 1995

SAGE Publications Ltd
6 Bonhill Street
London EC2A 4PU

SAGE Publications Inc
2455 Teller Road
Thousand Oaks, California 91320

SAGE Publications India Pvt Ltd
32, M-Block Market
Greater Kailash – I
New Delhi 110 048

British Library Cataloguing in Publication data

A catalogue record for this book is
available from the British Library.

ISBN 0 8039 7512 0
ISBN 0 8039 7513 9 (pbk)

Library of Congress catalog card number 95-069619

Typeset by Mayhew Typesetting, Rhayader, Powys

Contents

Contributors

John B. Allcock, Research Unit in SE European Studies, University of Bradford, UK

Anath Ariel de Vidas, Office de Recherche Scientifique et Technique Outre-Mer, Colegio de México, Mexico

Claude-Marie Bazin, Unité de Recherche en Sociologie du Tourisme International, Centre National de la Recherche Scientifique, Paris, France

Edward M. Bruner, Department of Anthropology, University of Illinois at Urbana–Champaign, USA

Malcolm Crick, School of Social Sciences, Deakin University, Geelong, Australia

Suzy Kruhse-MountBurton, Griffith University, Brisbane, Australia

Marie-Françoise Lanfant, Unité de Recherche en Sociologie du Tourisme International, Centre National de la Recherche Scientifique, Paris, France

Jean Michaud, Groupe d'Études et de Recherches sur l'Asie Contemporaine, Faculty of Social Sciences, Laval University, Quebec, Canada

Meaghan Morris, freelance writer, Bundeena, Australia

Michel Picard, Laboratoire Asie du Sud-Est et Monde Austronésien, Centre National de la Recherche Scientifique, Paris, France

Danielle Rozenberg, Institut de Recherches sur les Sociétés Contemporaines, Centre National de la Recherche Scientifique, Paris, France

Shelly Shenhav-Keller, Department of Sociology and Anthropology, Tel-Aviv University, Israel

Wendy Williams, Centre for Environmental Design and Research, University of California, Berkeley, USA

Preface

It seems important to begin by explaining the choice of title. Many tourism studies have examined such topics as flows, costs/benefits and location, often to help developers and policy-makers carry out decisions. This is not yet another book aiming to update these data. The title itself points to another approach. What distinguishes this book is the angle from which the analysis is undertaken. Tourism transcends individual societies and has become an international fact, yet the local and the global must be understood simultaneously.

Although the localities studied in this volume are in different areas of the world (Bali in Indonesia, the Andean Cordillera, Ladakh in India, northern Thailand, the Balkans, Périgord in the French countryside, Palaia Epidhavros in Greece, Ibiza in the Balearic Islands of the Mediterranean, Australia and Israel – truly an international sample), there are many similarities in tourist development owing to the trans-geographic, cross-cultural character of international tourism. Tourism operates on a world scale, crossing many boundaries.

In this volume we recognize that the local cannot be understood independently of the global and that the global is never independent of the local setting within which it operates. The problem we struggle with in these studies is essentially one of bringing tourism research within the ambit of a truly international sociology. The chapters in the book develop themes of change, identity and tourism. In particular each author contributes to an integrated collection by reflecting upon tourism from the inside, from the perspective of insiders or 'natives', and from the outside, from the viewpoint of the traveller or the 'foreigner'. By making a deliberate connection between change, identity and international tourism, by abutting questions of identity against those of change, and by simultaneously making questions of change reflect back on identity, this work moves on a terrain fertile with paradoxes and contradictions.

For the most part the case studies in this collection deal with regions far removed from the centres of industrial power: they are island societies, territorial enclaves, communities in the rural hinterland, peninsulas, frontier zones, and regions that have become marginalized. Previously classed as traditional societies, they were condemned to a slow death. Because of their 'discovery' by circuits of international tourism, however, they have been propelled into the firing line of the project planners. They have been salvaged, recast in the forges of development and thrust on to the world stage, and have become tourist societies. There is an inflow of money, enormous economic upheavals, and confrontation with the foreign hordes, yet these societies are asked in the name of tourist activity to conserve and reconstruct their traditions. They are encouraged to open their frontiers and their dwellings to foreign visitors and are pressured to engage in commercial transactions of a very particular type in which they offer their culture, their heritage, their traditions and even certain members of their population.

In this context identity is put to the test, and becomes an object of exchange. International tourism compels local societies to become aware and to question the identities they offer to foreigners as well as the prior images that are imposed upon them. Processes involved in the reworking of identity include the displacement of the local, the disruption of systems of reference, the endowment of heritage with new affect, the processes of mirroring, reflexivity and transitivity, the recovery of forgotten memories, and the revealing or concealment of self. Identity is always in reformulation, a constant site of struggle for those involved.

A fundamental contradiction is that from the inside, from the native point of view, tourism is a route to economic development; but from the outside view, the natives are a traditional object of desire. From the inside, tourism means modernity and change; but from the outside, the tourist object is seen as exotic, primitive and immutable. The locals are called upon to preserve a purity that never existed. Once again we encounter the age-old Western prejudice which sees change as a mark of corruption and identity as a purity which must be preserved.

This book results from an international collaboration and is not simply a collection of chapters provided by authors from different countries. The project matured within an international network of researchers who have been working and meeting regularly since the mid 1980s. In 1990, under the impulse of URESTI (France), international tourism was, for the first time, officially recognized as an area in the scientific programme of a World Congress of the International Sociological Association (ISA). At the last World Congress in Bielefeld, in July 1994, this group became a permanent Research Committee of the ISA.

It was at the end of the 1990 Congress in Madrid that the project for the writing of this book really took shape. This was enhanced by the rich contents of the field work presented by researchers, most of whom had spent several years on location learning local languages and customs. The book was also strengthened by integrating themes and questions from an array of disciplines, especially anthropology, economics, geography, semiotics and sociology.

This ambitious project has only been realized thanks to the efforts of many people whose work is not directly represented in this book. We want to record our thanks to all who have contributed to its completion. Above all we want to express our gratitude to Jacques de Weerdt (URESTI, France) for his valued help over many years. Without his energetic and dedicated support it is unlikely that our efforts would have reached fruition.

Marie-Françoise Lanfant
John B. Allcock
Edward M. Bruner

Introduction

Marie-Françoise Lanfant

General orientation

From the outset it is necessary to avoid any misunderstanding: this book is not strictly speaking a book on tourism. For anthropologists and sociologists who have participated in this collection, tourism is a difficult subject and object to delimit, even though the field of research is widening, deepening and reaching a kind of maturity (Graburn and Jafari, 1991). This book intends first to clear the ground and gather data in order to pave the way for a comprehensive understanding of a phenomenon which holds enormous potential for social and cultural change, greatly affecting the future of societies. But how can such an analysis be conducted?

The approach advocated here fits with an epistemological perspective stressing diversity in sociology. It engages what Geertz (1986) called 'outdoor sociology'. Researchers in the field, working simultaneously in numerous parts of the world, with tools appropriate for their respective disciplines and demonstrating a great variety of techniques of investigation, observe the changes taking place in relation to tourism in different societies. These analyses are all conducted from the point of view of the locality. This is a major step.

The local focus in an important factor owing to its scale, its dissemination and the multiplicity of inductive questions it raises. In this sense, tourism is perceived as being within society and the tourist as being an actor in society. In this book we distance ourselves from a methodology dominated by what is commonly called the study of social and cultural 'impact', which tackles tourism as an exogenous force, assessing its effect (positive or negative) on some targeted milieu.

Local research

The word 'local' carries various meanings. First of all it is important to get away from any association between unity of observation and fixed geographic unity. For the anthropologist, the point of observation can be an ethnic group, an informal living environment, a centre of initiative, a journey, a transfer and so on. The place is in some sense always in motion. But as far as this work is concerned the local is above all a methodological choice. The 'locality' is the place itself, which both provides the data for the research and mediates the questions posed by science and its results. And if, within the structure of this work, the places – the names of the places and the geographical regions – take on a certain importance, it is because at some point in their history they have been singled out as having 'a tourist vocation', and in this respect they carry with them a demonstrative force. Bali, Ibiza, St Pantelejmon, Sydney Tower, Savignac-Lédrier, Taquile, Titicaca and the Himalayas are not simply diacritical marks but signposts to scientific examination.

By building bridges between series of facts springing from different local situations, one forms the dominant impression that international tourism is a powerful lever operating on a world scale. We are confronted by a dynamic that brings together regions of the world normally placed by social discourse in significant opposition to each other: post-industrial society and underdeveloped society; modern society and traditional society; urban society and rural society. Little by little we begin to glimpse the extent to which international tourism has become a force for integration on a world scale. This approach allows us to grasp at which point tourism is fundamentally at the heart of the exchange, a 'total social phenomenon'.

I have developed these arguments in Chapter 1, where I explain why I use the term 'international tourism' without dissociating the word 'tourism' from the word 'international'.

From global to local: identities in the logic of world integration

For researchers interested in its study, international tourism is fertile soil for the understanding of our age. At the end of the 1960s numerous regions in the world, deprived and far removed from the great centres of industrial development, were simultaneously transformed into resorts for thousands of holiday-makers from the great metropolises of the industrial world. One cannot understand the triggering of such a process without considering the politics of tourist promotion which was then being organized on a global scale, under the direction of international organizations. Operating in accordance with the great powers of the Western world, these processes are organized with the help of multinational enterprises for transport and amenities and with the scientific and technical support of international experts.

At a local scale the tourist option (in most cases) arrives in the wake of a global strategy. Decisions which affect local societies are adopted at a level which not only is politically superior to the state, but more specifically lies within the context of plural and/or supranational institutions. Upheld by an official doctrine which makes international tourism a factor of economic development, the 'system of action' for tourism gains a foothold in numerous regions of the world which are declared as underdeveloped. Frequently this happens in geographical areas where no other economic option seems possible. Tourism is often presented as the last chance. Thus, through international tourism, poor regions which have been removed from any focus of activity, closed in on themselves, and condemned to certain death by economists find themselves rediscovered and thrust into the path of development, linked to the international market and propelled on to the world scene.

During the 1980s and 1990s large industrial countries (LICs), faced with the world economic crisis, also became resolutely involved in tourist policies on a national scale, with a view to resolving the economic difficulties cropping up in certain areas of their own territory. They adopted for themselves a doctrine which had originally been reserved for the Third World. Tourist promotion is becoming a universal model for development.

The objectives which inspire it do not concern, as one might suppose, the strict domain of the organization of pleasure trips or the development of leisure areas. They spring from a policy of global development which intends, by means of developing tourism, to model the environment, structure territories, and link outlying barren regions with urban metropolises. Moreover, with the new trend to 'sustainable tourism' that is asserting itself in high places, this policy fits into strategies for the conservation of the planet and the preservation of local cultures. Economic, political and cultural strategies work closely together (Lanfant and Graburn, 1992).

It is necessary to realize that as international tourism generates globalization in economic, socio-cultural and socio-political processes, it also raises the 'question of identity' to a new prominence in global analysis. By bringing together in this work studies conducted in places as different as Bali in Indonesia, the Balearic Islands in the Mediterranean, the Andes Cordillera, the high plateau of the Ladakh in the Himalayas, the hills of northern Thailand, the

Balkans, Israel, Greece, south-west France and Australia, we aim to advance step by step in an analytical procedure which links the global to the local.

There is obviously a big gap between generalization and the local realities we study but, from the viewpoint which is taken here, the important thing is not to lose sight of the global strategy which is imposed at local level. This is why one of the recommended rules for following the development of the chapters is to situate or resituate the place of observation in a process which transcends local characteristics by referring the interior to the exterior and vice versa. From this viewpoint, the social causality will no longer be understood as unidirectional – from north to south or from the centre to the outlying areas – but can be analysed in terms of a circular process.

Identity and world-wide exchanges

The process of the internalization of exchanges and the movements of individual self-affirmation are occurring in a world where the economy dominates. In this respect international tourism constitutes incomparable analytical ground. It must be remembered that international tourism is already considered as one of the primary economic activities in international exchange under the heading of external trade and that, according to the World Tourist Organization, by the year 2000 it is destined to become a 'first world industry', a 'driving force' of global development (OMT, 1992a; 1992b). The study of international tourism throws us into the core of the problems which occur within contemporary societies in economic, political and cultural domains in relation to the extension of the market economy.

Through global integration, those peoples who previously remained behind their frontiers are now invited to consider themselves part of great multi-cultural units, sometimes alongside former enemies. And tourism, particularly 'cultural tourism', is often considered by international organizations as a pedagogic instrument allowing new identities to emerge – identities corresponding to the new plural-ethnic or plural-state configurations which are forming. It is necessary to distinguish, however, between a desire to construct new identities which is basically motivated by ideology, and those identities which emerge naturally from the working of societies. The task of sociologists and anthropologists is to clarify the second of these.

From local to global

With tourism, what enters a country is not only passing tourists but also the apparatus of tourist production, a model for planning development and all the incentives which lead a society down the road to change under the influence of what we, along with the anthropologist Georges Balandier (1969), will call 'a dynamic from without'. Economic and cultural strategies become progressively bound together with the aims of the tourist industry. Imperceptibly the place becomes determined by external forces and reconstructed from a tourist point of view. As Meaghan Morris concludes in Chapter 10, planning for tourism leads to actions at all levels and effects 'the series of relations by which cultural identity is constituted' and consequently legitimated. Everywhere the pressure for tourism is strong, whether it be in an LIC like Australia or in remote and economically weak regions where the territorial stakes are of quite a different order. In Bali, Ibiza or Cancún the reports are the same: researchers observe changes which disturb all the components of the environment upon which identity rests. The pressure of tourism leads a society progressively to open itself to the facts of the world economy and to consider its dynamism and place in the world according to allogenous criteria. This is most certainly a challenge to identity.

Methodological orientations

In this research field one could easily be inclined to treat tourism as a force of social change coming to destroy territorial and local identities. Tourism as an agent in the destruction of cultures is a banal theme. Literature in this field, which comes under the heading of 'social and cultural impact' is relatively plentiful. As we know, such literature has given rise to numerous criticisms of a methodological nature: for our part, we have rejected such a conceptual model where local society and tourism are presented as being in relations of exteriority (Lanfant, 1987).

However, it is not a question of us moving away from the problems which have been created in local societies by the massive intervention of machinery for tourist production and consumption – intervention which can give natives the feeling of foreign interference. The tourist system of action is not a monolithic force. It would be pointless to seize upon it as if it were a hegemonic and imperialist power perpetuating disguised neo-colonialism. This system is a network of agents: these tap a variety of motivations which are difficult to define and which in concrete situations often contradict each other. It should not be forgotten that governments planning for tourism have to answer to strategic interests in the structuring of the territory and even in its security. Strategies for conquering the market cannot be dissociated from political strategies to conquer resources, to exploit lands and to occupy territories. We know that in numerous cases the local population is presented with a *fait accompli* but, as we will demonstrate through the studies presented here, there is a range of choices in attitudes. The important thing from our perspective is to restore to the local society its rightful status as actor. This status itself is not homogeneous. The undertaking of a tourism project always involves a multiplicity of local and non-local interests which can compete with each other.

In all the cases presented, tourism appears as a powerful lever for social change, carrying with it contradictions at every level of actual experience. In the large territories with linguistic and cultural diversity, international tourism is often deliberately exploited by nation-states in order to deal with internal ethnic problems manifesting themselves in border or insular areas (India, Indonesia, Spain, Thailand and Mexico). Within emerging states, central power uses or has used tourism in order to achieve national unification (Yugoslavia, Israel). Similarly in the LICs tourism is called upon to thwart conflicts of identity which manifest themselves in regions of depopulation (the French case).

For their part local communities are not passive, and often seize upon tourism as a means of communication in order to display their existence and to establish their own power. Certain ethnic groups have been marginalized and excluded by central power, and through tourism they acquire recognition on the international scene. International tourism becomes an important factor to take into consideration in the analysis of what Hechter and Lévi (1979) have called 'ethno-regional movements'.

Tourism is a double-edged sword. In certain cases it contributes towards repressing, marginalizing and neutralizing autonomous or resistance movements. In other cases it allows ethnic minorities that have been cut off from international decision-making to claim and assert their identities. As we can see as we read each chapter, the authors of this book, one after the other, observe extremely diverse movements. There are a multitude of interests at play; and according to one's angle of observation, different aspects are brought to light. There is no one way of tackling identity, but several ways. It would be dangerous to claim to discover a uniformity which does not exist. On the contrary, I find it necessary to show the multiplicity of processes for affirming identity which are in use and which the development of tourism in the world exacerbates at all levels of actual experience.

Conceptual orientation: what is identity?

As we know, researching the concept of identity demands caution (Benoist, 1977). I shall guard against defining it, as doing so risks halting the progress of our thought. Identity cannot be reduced to a number of identifiable characteristic traits by which individuals belonging to a whole should be able to recognize themselves or, worse, to which they should conform. For us identity has sense when it is supported by a subject. Identity is the test to which all human beings living in society are constantly subjected. This test is enhanced when the individual is attacked, weakened, marginalized, placed in awkward situations or torn between conflicting interests. It is only by linking together different studies that little by little the reader gets some idea of the conflicts, illusions, utopias and false obligations which punctuate the processes of constructing, deconstructing and reconstructing identity. So fragile is identity, continually being called into question in an ever more mobile universe, and always under threat of alienating itself in processes of identification using models of reference as guarantees.

We are trying to understand the way in which the actors at all levels of experience face the problem of their identity objectively and rationally, and how subjectively they take on the metamorphoses and, particularly, the images of themselves which they receive from others. At the heart of our preoccupations is the way in which social groups and individuals assume the change which affects them in their capacity to move towards their choices, and here we enter another field of analysis. We touch on the subjective components of identity concerning others, concerning the central values of the society in which we live, and concerning universality: for in a world where circulation becomes the norm, the world-wide spread of exchanges becomes the sought-after horizon. It becomes impossible to build up identity without abutting it against the identity of others. Challenge to identity is an experience of alterity.

Specific problems in this field of research

With the world-wide spread of exchanges our field offers one remarkable thing: the society ordained to be a tourist destination is called upon not only to open its frontiers and its homes to foreign visitors, but also to engage in a very particular trade, which is a question of culture, heritage, traditions and identity itself. Certain parts of the population become merchandised, as Meaghan Morris says in Chapter 10, making 'life' itself a 'tourist object'. With international tourism, identity as such is at stake in world trade.

What happens to a society which sets out to become a tourist product? How does a society become a tourist society? These questions run right through this work, and the data gathered in each chapter emphasize their poignancy.

In this field of research the problematics of identity cannot be dissociated from the process of commoditization. Identity is a product to be offered to the consumer, a product manufactured and packaged according to marketing procedures. The past – history and memory – are seen as 'tourist resources'. Cultural heritage becomes capital to make a profit, ethnicity a resource to exploit. Thus the system of the promotion of tourism indirectly intervenes in cultural references, in the definition of the values, signs, supports and markers of identity.

Appeal to identity

By linking identity, change and international tourism, by pushing the question of change on to that of identity, and by making the question of identity react on that of change, this work advances into a terrain fertile in paradoxes. The spread of tourism in the world economy leads to the internationalization of cultures and the extroversion of societies. Along this path the most firmly anchored identities are weakened, torn from their moorings and broken up. Heritage, tradition and memory are misplaced. The line between the inside and the outside becomes blurred. The identification traits by which individuals recognize themselves as being part of the same community are manipulated and lose their legitimacy. And at the outset it is the very notion of identity which becomes obsolete and inadequate. With international tourism we enter the domain of mobility, displacement, discontinuity, separation and transience.

That is why the way in which the question of identity emerges in discourses on international tourism is surprising. This question is omnipresent, and what is intriguing is its insistence in relation to the demand for it. Appeal to identity has the effect of a double meaning when one realizes that it comes mainly from inside the system for the production of tourism: from international organizations, from national and regional tourist offices, and from the tourist operators themselves, who in their publicity aim to motivate tourism. This appeal, echoed at the local level in tourist communities, creates a sense that there truly is a demand to supply.

Far from breaking with tradition, tourism allies itself with cultural identities. All official rhetoric on international tourism supposes that there are identities to preserve, maintain, seek out and celebrate. This is not the least of the paradoxes. Tourism presents itself as supporting a return to sources, a journey towards the roots and natural untouched regions. In a version of history oriented primarily towards economic considerations, tourism presents itself as one of the most powerful levers for global exchange, and this at the outset might seem to be a factor likely to make for cultural homogenization of societies. Hence the resurgence in this field of research of what Karl Popper (1979) called 'the influence of Plato': that is to say, in contemporary societies the attraction for a system of values where any change means degeneracy and corruption, and where identity is an immutable purity which is near to perfection and must be preserved.

It has often been said that the appeal of identity in traditional societies meets the demand from Western tourists for authenticity. Anthropologists in the field – Danielle Rozenberg, Shelly Shenhav-Keller, Jean Michaud, Michel Picard, Edward Bruner and Anath Ariel de Vidas – talk about those tourists seeking authenticity who choose to visit a place in order to rediscover in themselves an identity which they cannot find in their everyday lives. Ethnic tourists who go to Ladakh or who cross the Andean Cordillera, the hippies who seek another life in Ibiza, Jewish tourists from the diaspora who go to Maskit, and Australian men who go on sexual trips to South East Asia, all have something in common: an interest in an authentic other place. Should tourism lead to another possible life, a real life where for a time the individual can meet his or her 'true' self (Meyer, 1988)?

If we want to indicate a conceptual direction for studying identity in the frame of our field of research, it is necessary to put into perspective two processes which develop simultaneously and which can seem to be contradictory. On the one hand, the spread of tourism in the world economy leads to extroversion, internationalization and deterritorialization. On the other hand, it works towards the retrenchment of identities in a territory, a system of filiation and patrimony, all acting as a fulcrum. There is a constant tug-of-war between mobility, which is motivated by a zest for modernity, and an appeal to identity, which takes for granted the equality of cultures on their own terms.

On a scientific level one observes a similar double polarity. While one trend asserts itself within sociology, which places emphasis on the world-wide spread of social phenomena (Archer, 1991), a new tendency is becoming apparent which boasts the 'indigenization' of sociology. Celebrating diversity, on behalf of the right to be different, this new tendency thus aspires to better defend cultural specificities and ethnological heritages (Akiwowo, 1988; Park, 1988).

The sociology of international tourism cannot ignore these two sides of the analysis. It must take into account the fact that international tourism, through a series of actions, fits into a process of globalization, without ignoring the local approaches to which this book bears witness.

For some people this double polarity, which asserts itself simultaneously in the field of sociology, seems like an opposition which puts globalization and indigenization back to back. It is not for us to oppose these two trends, to make rivals of an integral sociology and a differential sociology, a macro-sociology and a micro-sociology, a holistic model and selective studies. Sociology observes the phenomenon of homogenization, of uniformity, whilst at the same time recording the creativity of the social field. There is no reason to contrast unity and diversity, or to oppose global and local, identity and change. Rather we must fasten on to the tension between these poles in two respects: the global world which encompasses all the individual 'particles' in motion; and lively differentiation governed by universal exigencies. In fact the trickiest problem for the sociologist studying international tourism is to grasp the analysis at both ends and to know how to master it. The sociology of international tourism is a sociology of 'communication and of complexities' (Morin, 1991). It is not a new anthropology establishing itself in the web of international tourism.

Contributions to this book

Several studies in this work are situated in outlying regions: insular communities, territorial enclaves, rural hinterland communities, peninsulas, ethnological niches, border regions and escheated regions. The majority are traditional communities, the chosen ground of the ethnologists who try to gather knowledge that is disappearing. This is what also gives them value as a tourist product. The idea of primitiveness attached to these places makes them attractive.

But what a paradox! At the very moment that tourism makes communities emerge from their isolation and set out on the road to modernity, they have to reinvent their past and keep alive their traditions in order to maintain the image that tourists have of them.

Since McKean (1973) targeted his theory of cultural involution on the island of Bali, it has become without doubt the most enlightening example of such a paradox. Since the discovery of the island and its artistic treasures by colonial administrators, European artists and anthropologists, Bali has had a badge of its own identity bestowed upon it by foreigners who have functioned within the frame of reference of academic culture. This fixing of an image has made the society a 'living museum'. 'Bali must look like Bali!', extol its admirers, 'May Bali stay true to herself!'

However, at the end of the 1960s, by virtue of the doctrine that makes international tourism a factor in the economic development of developing countries, the Indonesian government, with the aid of the World Bank and foreign consultants, decided to make Bali the greatest focus of tourist development in the Indonesian archipelago. This decision was taken without any kind of local consultation.

As soon as the project to initiate large-scale tourism was mooted, however, the question of its negative impact was raised. It was clear to the experts that tourism would be a source of wealth in this predominantly agricultural, underdeveloped region, but at the price of the destruction of Balinese culture. This is why the concept of 'enclave tourism' was proposed for the Nusa Dua peninsula, in order to maintain a clear separation between the native people and the foreign tourists, and to avoid the contamination carried by the latter.

Faced with this project, Bali distinguished itself. To the formula of 'enclave tourism' conceived by the experts, the Balinese opposed another conception. To the dilemma of tourism – without tourism Bali is condemned, with tourism it will be destroyed – Bali found a solution: the doctrine of 'cultural tourism'. In this particular situation such a doctrine took on an exemplary value: by means of this device Balinese identity could be preserved. However, Bali accepted confrontation with the tourists, accepted the test of otherness, and moreover deliberately chose this part, refusing to withdraw in on itself.

Research by Michel Picard, which was to continue for several years, begins at this significant moment (Chapter 2). The doctrine of cultural tourism was profoundly ambivalent, in that it involved a movement between terms that appeared to be in opposition: us and them; the inside and the outside; the Balinese culture and the cultural demands made by tourists. It sought to reconcile objectives which at first appeared to be incompatible. This doctrine implied that culture could in some sense be detached from the daily life of the Balinese and thought of as capital which could be put to use within the framework of market transactions. Picard exposes the processes by which Balinese culture progressively came to be transformed from within, in order to satisfy the needs of the tourist market, and thus became a 'tourist culture' (to use an expression invented by the Balinese themselves).

This hybrid culture, shared with the tourists, is difficult to live out in practice. It blurs the distinction between native and foreign. Furthermore, under the pressure of the religious elite in particular, the Balinese were tempted to reimpose a frontier within this mixed culture, between things which could be shown to the tourists and things which had to remain reserved from them. Attempts at discrimination of this kind, because they were rooted in reference to conceptual categories which were alien to the Balinese (sacred/ profane), could not possibly be realized concretely within daily life. What is more, the points of orientation became fuzzy, and the references to identity clouded. One could sense the onset of a crisis of identity. 'Are we still Balinese?' they asked in 1990.

In contrast, by putting herself in a position to see things from the native's point of view, Anath Ariel de Vidas (Chapter 3) comes to see tourism as a new opportunity for survival and revaluation for a marginalized minority ethnic group within a national society, itself dominated by foreign powers. The author, trained as an anthropologist, takes the side of those who analyse the permanence of ethnic groups in the context of internationalization not as a predicament of history but as a sign of its dynamism – as long as these groups consider their ethnic tradition as a resource. And in this sense her work distinguishes itself from many ethnological discourses which point out the devastating effect of tourism on traditional societies.

According to the author, the Indians of the Andean Cordillera, who are geographically distanced from each other (the island of Taquile in the middle of Lake Titicaca; Otavalo in Ecuador; Salasaca in Ecuador; and Jalq'a in Bolivia) have no difficulty in following a path which unites the expectations of the tourist market with popular arts and traditions. Since the height of Inca civilization, weaving has always had an economic value. Thus, the Indians from the Andean Cordillera adapt very naturally to the tourist market. Andean textiles, which carry within their very substance the distinctive mark of their identity, have always fulfilled the function of internal and external use. Textiles provide a means of communication between ethnic groups spread out along the Andean Cordillera. They have a role to play in terms of memory, of archives and of texts. They form the link between past and present. One can trace, in the light of history, the evolution of their motifs as a function of events, of Indian contacts with the outside world and the development of the techniques of production.

Trade which supports tourism leads to a continual destructuring and restructuring of the medium of ethnic identity. The latter is not a fixed phenomenon to which members of the group must conform in order to be part of the community. It is constantly at work, and that is what allows the group to assure its continuity. In the light of foreign exchanges the evolution of Inca history can be followed. Trade is an incentive to create new designs but also to reuse old ones and, by doing so, to revive long-forgotten know-how, sometimes through the impetus given by foreign ethnologists. Ethnic tourists also provide this impetus: they like to feel the permanence of the past, to buy what is original and carries the mark of a craft tradition. In such a situation, the local knowledge of Andean societies fulfils the demand for authenticity from tourists in search of all that is Indian. Life in the community is regulated by cycles of activity connected to the international markets. With the sale of the textiles that they weave, the Indians buy materials, looms and land; they dress in the traditional way for foreign visitors, and in Western clothes when they want to look like the tourists. There is movement and dealing both ways.

By becoming aware of these new systems of production, the Andeans can resist assimilation and can find a certain new independence which was bitterly disputed in colonial times. They find a certain legitimacy. From a state point of view, the renaissance or maintenance of Andean ethnicities plays an important role in the process of national independence. This know-how is sublimated as a symbol of resistance to colonial rule. Andean ethnicity takes on the value of a national symbol demanded by the state which is itself in search of recognition on the international scene in the context of Latin America

In the Antipodes, Jean Michaud, who works as an anthropologist in the mountainous regions of Ladakh and the north of Thailand, comes up against similar problems where the respective Indian and Thai governments are pursuing aims of integrating ethnic minorities into national areas (Chapter 4). Michaud explains why the state uses international tourism to settle nomadic populations that move around strips of territory on contested borders.

In these mountainous regions it is not a question of mass tourism but of ethnic, ecological tourism amongst the inhabitants, which corresponds to what is newly termed 'alternative tourism', promoted by the international organizations as being more respectful of the environment. The state finds the opportunity, through the promotion of ethnic tourism, to intervene in the process of cultural change, while at the same time pandering to the sense of identity of the minorities. In the framework of promotional images, ethnicity, marked with the objective attributes of authenticity, takes on an exceptional character. Furthermore, tourist activity favours new economic alliances between young villagers and brokers from outside the communities: travel agents, wholesalers, hoteliers, guides. These new relationships forcibly break their elders' opposition to change – an opposition upon which rests the balance between these communities and their feudal and lineal traditions.

In these somewhat inaccessible regions, tourism is on a small scale, but is nonetheless controlled by transport and promotion companies. In Ladakh, it is the tourist guide or the travel agent who contacts the local inhabitant likely to host the ethnic tourist. The emissary already has a certain concept of the authenticity his client will expect: the wearing of traditional dress, building in natural materials, no electricity. Nothing should be present to indicate that symbols of Western technology have penetrated these supposedly untouched places.

But the encouragement of this ethnic assertion is a double-edged weapon. It is a means of national integration, but also an opportunity for local societies to enter into new systems of international exchange and perhaps to reinforce regional power, and at the same time to relativize state supervision.

The observation of the transformation of historical and folk monuments in two sensitive areas of the former Yugoslavia inspires John Allcock to reflect on current events (Chapter 5). He takes us to Macedonia, to the old city of Ohrid, where under all the superimposed layers of successive transformations rest the remains of St Pantelejmon. Tourists who go there, guidebooks in hand, are very surprised to find themselves in a building which appears to be a mosque, but which is presented as a Christian church. This example has allegorical value. It is not by chance that one part of the history of the monument has been brought to light at the expense of another. The group which claims political power over this territory, which takes the name of Macedonia, is searching for an anchorage point which can provide a foundation for its own identity.

The inherited object in question is a church originally associated with St Clement, which has been elevated to the function of providing an identifiable marker in order to permit members of the ethnic community to recognize themselves, both individually and through the same filiation. Hence the quasi-logical necessity to eradicate a part of the monument's past. By dedicating it as a foundation for a particular group, the present inhabitants have removed all traces of the multiplicity of its historical past. Tourism allows this place to be elevated in value and to be consecrated as a founding place. But, by doing this, an act of symbolic violence is committed against others.

The second example chosen by John Allcock is in contrast to the first. In the former Yugoslavia, where the federal state is trying to construct national unity within the framework of a multi-ethnic nation by adopting from the outset the principles of equality, the question of the choice of an identifying trait which makes sense to everyone is posed in a peremptory fashion. Hence there is the temptation to blur this one trait, which only one group can recognize, in order to allow everybody to invest in it.

The presentation of folk dances at national festivals or tourist gatherings, appealing to everyone, must flatter the feeling of identity within each community that is being integrated into the national whole. In order to portray a coherent image of national heritage, elements are borrowed from several folklores descended from the rural past of different provinces. A new synchronic model has been created, but it does not find a common denominator from specific differences: these cease to be decipherable because they have been cut from the source from which they take their primary significance, a means of denying the specificity of each difference.

In this case, tourism is not a simple catalyst for the movement to affirm an identity. It legitimizes the argument of the pretenders and for this reason peddles an ideology. What was the prerogative of a particular group becomes, in the eyes of anonymous foreign tourists who do not know how to tell the difference, the distinctive mark of a nation. Tourist exploitation of historic monuments confuses the play on memory. But it may happen that the tourist, like the sociologist, is not duped, and does not adhere to the incomplete and shortened history on offer. Tourists sometimes lift the veil to reveal the story concealed beneath. Entire segments of history, which yesterday were repressed, could tomorrow be new springboards for legitimizing new pretenders.

How is a disappearing world returned to the path of economic development by its transformation into a tourist product, and how does tourism come to hold the key to its future? Claude-Marie Bazin takes us to the heart of France (to Aquitaine and the depths of the Périgord) and to the ruins of a dying industrial civilization (Chapter 6). Known for its prehistoric painted caves, the most famous of which is Lascaux, the region was prioritized in the 1980s for a new effort in the promotion of French tourism abroad. This is a very interesting case since, as we know in recent years, France has been classified as one of the most popular destinations in world tourism. Together with archaeology, a declining industry is now becoming the springboard for the economic relaunch of the region.

The example presented by Bazin is particularly significant: it concerns a medieval forge belonging to one family for centuries, which had continued to work, despite its age, until the 1970s. This forge, which has been transformed with state funding into a museum of industrial archaeology, has become one of the stepping stones for the promotion of regional tourism in an international context. The collective memory, idling in neutral gear and hesitating between preservation and construction, has been voluntarily redirected towards construction/reconstruction. In the course of this conversion, the industrial heritage, which had been the property of one family, became public property to be made profitable as tourist capital. The place and the memory attached to it change in significance. The change affects not only the operative function, but also the symbolic content and more precisely the way in which the local population, the social group and the individual relate to this place, in as much as it is considered as an anchorage point for identity. In favour of the debate which opposes those responsible for preserving the place, the tenants for its reassignment more or less accepted the demands of tourist development: the discourse does its work. The reconstructed history of the place, and its transformation into a tourist product, are closely linked. Numerous points of view contest the memory and each claims a true origin. But by changing its belonging, this heritage loses its connections with the place. The reference system for identity is modified; and moreover, because of the confusion which surrounds the notion of heritage, this change is unnoticed by the social actors who are the most affected.

By making apparent the new meanings which the notions of heritage and inheritance take on in private and in public law, and by linking these conceptual changes to the transformation of places into tourist attractions, the author questions the paternal reference which lies at the heart of the notion of heritage ('heir' from *heres*) and patrimony ('father' from *pater*). Could the latter be losing its founding value? In fact, another reference system is being imposed, as it is now no longer a question of ensuring the perpetuity of a family by means of handing over goods, but one of absorbing the diversity of perspectives forged through singular strategies into a common and democratic vision of history. Between its former status as an item of inheritance and its latter status as heritage lay a shadowy region within which local identity underwent a more or less confused process of redefinition aimed at a clientele drawn from all corners of the world.

With the case of Palaia Epidhavros in Greece we touch on other mechanisms which concern the relationship between societies and mythical traditions (Chapter 7). Palaia Epidhavros is a Peloponnesian village situated near the archaeological site of Epidaurus, the last stage on the road to Trizina before reaching the famous theatre, which provoked a cry of admiration from Pausanias in ancient times. This site, which is one of the prizes of world heritage, attracts thousands of tourists annually.

The rapidly growing population of the locality, which makes its living from links with the towns (it is not far from Athens) and from contacts with international tourism, finds it hard to tolerate the pressure imposed upon it to conform to town planning regulations and the architectural norms which these lay down. These aim to preserve a degree of local consistency, but conflict with the community's own aspirations for development.

To some extent these norms are hard to tolerate because they are imposed from outside by experts according to their idea of Greek tradition. As a result, conservation becomes conservatism. Behind the enforcement of these norms for town planning lies a certain image that the experts have of the identity of the place; a fixed identity, clothed in a sort of Platonic ideal, allotted to a population who, by being exposed to these annoying aspects of officialdom, will no doubt sooner or later be obliged to abandon the site. This will ultimately be for the benefit of the functional planning of an archaeological site that has been transformed according to an aesthetic notion of the environment. Is this a conflict of values and/ or a conflict of interest?

It is from the point of view of the tourist that Shelly Shenhav-Keller takes up the question of authenticity, and does so in a critical situation, since the author deals with the Jewish tourist in Israel (Chapter 8). The journey takes on the aspect of a pilgrimage to a spiritual centre. In this sense, Shenhav-Keller's study is in agreement with the works of authors who see in the practice of tourism the form which the appeal of the sacred takes in our modern society. The Jewish tourist who goes to Israel fulfils a sacred duty.

Measured in this way, the satisfaction that the author observes the Jewish tourist gains from the trip itself seems derisory. It is in the purchase of souvenirs from Maskit that people find confirmation that the journey had an aim. For tourists from the diaspora, possession of an object stamped 'Maskit' is like receiving an assurance of their belonging to the Promised Land.

Maskit, the centre of the Israeli craft industry, was founded by the government in 1954 under the auspices of the Minister of Employment, with the aim of perpetuating past and present local know-how in the new environment of the state of Israel: it is an element of the national ethos. To buy an object from Maskit – the word itself means 'sacred ornament' – assumes a particular significance when Jewish identity is at stake.

We go into Maskit with our researcher at the moment when she is recording the words and commentaries exchanged between vendor and customer. The customer asks for an authentic object. The vendor, through her discourse, adheres to this demand. Maskit presents itself as being able to offer guarantees of Israeli authenticity. However, an ensemble of ambivalent attitudes accompany this made-to-measure guarantee of identity. The criteria of authenticity are dependent upon relationship between the subjective meanings deployed in the interaction. The negotiations which take place between sales assistants and their customers reveal the desires upon which these exchanges are based. It is not so much the authenticity of the object that must be questioned, but the demand for authenticity. It is not the certificate of authenticity which is to be considered but the process of authentication. Authenticity is not a property inherent in the object. Neither is it an essence.

In Ibiza, one of the Balearic Islands of Spain, Danielle Rozenberg asks: 'What was the influence of the hippies in transforming the island?' (Chapter 9). At the beginning of the 1970s hippies were arriving by the dozen on the boat from Barcelona each week, and for this generation of young people, revolting against consumer society, the island of Ibiza symbolized another life, 'real life'. Rozenberg cleverly describes how this fringe group, whose journey she followed, was carried along by a utopian dream which they tried to put into practice: a return to nature, manual labour, craftsmanship, community life, moral freedom, a certain kind of dress and a self-sufficient vegetarian life.

In this insular area which was predominantly agricultural, people lived in self-sufficient manner until the 1960s, when large-scale tourist resorts were established. Then within this society, which was being rapidly led down the road to modernization, a fringe group of the developed world sought a return to rusticity, and valued a traditional way of life which was foreign to them but to which they attached themselves. The author takes advantage of this paradoxical situation in her analysis. Between the two extremes of the inter-cultural confrontation expressed in the dualism of tourists and host population she introduces a more subtle form by placing a third presence on the scene, that of the hippies – a presence which marks a turning point between two worlds which seem to be turning their backs on one another. How do these contradictory points of view manage to become reconciled in the same place? And, 20 years later, what has become of this fringe group and their dream?

They are to be found assimilated into a tourist society which mixes modernity and tradition. Moreover, these anti-modernists work together to establish the tourist image of the island. Not only have the majority of them become economic partners in the local tourist industry, but it is from their utopian values, codified by Western ideals of leisure, that the island community sees its own identity redeveloped in order to be represented abroad as a lethargic and permissive world that is mixed and pluralistic and in which the local population comes to recognize itself. The author describes the community on Ibiza as being extrovert. It becomes internationalized and in so doing becomes a pluralist society. A new system of values made from flexibility, adaptability, cohabitation and tolerance, which our ethnographer likes, is becoming established.

In the body of this work the text by Meaghan Morris provides a turning point (Chapter 10). Australia is the land of the Aborigines, the original people; it is the place of the primitive society, of an elementary form of religion which, at the turn of the century, attracted ethnologists, sociologists and psychoanalysts in search of true foundations for their scientific speculations. This land presents itself on the world economic stage as a new country, figuring among the 10 or 12 LICs which send tourists abroad. The Australian case seems exemplary in the sense that it allows us to note that the doctrine which made tourism a factor in the development of poor countries can be applied to a large rich country which is in economic difficulty. The observations of Meaghan Morris turn this doctrine back upon itself, showing that rich countries can share the same fate as poor countries, and find in tourism even greater relief.

From the height of the observatory atop the Sydney Tower, Meaghan Morris gradually deciphers the many mirrored images in which her own society is reflected. This famous tower, erected to the glory of modern Australia, destined for all its own citizens and constituting the place where the country can recognize its identity, has been transformed into a space for foreign tourists. It has become a 'place for others'. The initial references which exalt the idea that this young state had of its arrival on Australian soil are pushed back into the wings, and in their place have appeared utilitarian and functional signs to facilitate the circulation of tourists in the tower.

The other is everywhere, not in the form of foreigners but as a gaze, a witness, a warrant of judgement and of legitimation. Society seems inhabited physically and mentally by the presence of the other.

While celebrating its Bicentenary, a ceremony precisely to reinforce national feeling, Australia became aware of its dependence on a foreign power, in this instance Japan. She realized her own vulnerability and came to ask herself whether or not she had an underdeveloped economy. She was led to wonder about the influence of foreign images of herself on feelings of national identity – images that were sometimes upsetting, offending the grandiose idea she had of her excellence – while she struggled to present to the world an identity in the form of a first-class product. Australian society internalized the gaze of the other with mixed feelings: fear, and the desire to appear and to be recognized as an ideal model.

With Meaghan Morris, we undertake a symbolic journey in the Sydney Tower. The centre of observation not only pivots on its own axis, but moves around until it settles in one's mind the viewpoint of the other: multiple and alternate viewpoints which rebound on one another. The variation in perspectives favours the permutation of places. The differences fade between tourists and inhabitants, between societies which provide tourists and those which receive them, between rich and poor societies, and between futurist and aboriginal societies. Each has embarked on systems linked by reciprocal causalities.

Between tourists and local inhabitants, between societies providing tourists and those receiving them, there sometimes exist disturbing correlations. By organizing exchanges, travel agents appear as go-betweens who impose an infinity of love. The societies sending tourists experience backlashes which are sometimes unexpected.

The taste for sexual tourism in South East Asia among Australian men is connected with the evolution of the family in Australia. Suzy Kruhse-MountBurton, who adopts this working hypothesis, has done valuable work in a field in which moralizing discourse is the rule. In this young society which is at present changing, women are becoming emancipated. Men are finding their male status unstable; couples break up; men go looking for women elsewhere. In South East Asia they find women haloed with the emblems of femininity that sexual tourism subtly offers them – and this results in what may be termed a mixed marriage!

This fact is so important that it takes on the allure of a true social movement, of an offensive/defensive reaction by men who want to preserve the attributes of their masculine identity. At the very least it is surely a trait outlining the sexual difference between man and woman.

It is also the case that in this world in turmoil, the anthropologists themselves are disoriented. For researchers, observation of this shifting phenomenon, which draws meanings from the cultural transfers between contrasting universes, poses problems that are not only conceptual and methodological but also practical. For, in order to fully grasp what is at stake in international tourism, these researchers are expected in some way to circulate in adjoining spaces, where in turn they can encounter the confrontation between identity and otherness.

Malcolm Crick and Edward Bruner tackle these questions in the two concluding chapters to this work. Their contributions complement each other. Tourists and anthropologists are circulating in the same place. Tourists armed with cameras encroach on the territory of ethnologists, and very often the tourists themselves inform Western societies about what is happening away from home. It is not uncommon for students, having presented their first findings as tourists, to be transformed into ethnologists. Is it not right that there should be a reciprocal relationship between tourism and anthropology? Now wherever anthropologists are working in the field, tourists interfere, attracted by ethnic differences and objects of curiosity, so that the natives do not always know how to tell the difference between the two.

Malcolm Crick (Chapter 12) expresses his unease as somebody who is dedicated to a career as an ethnologist but has to justify not being a tourist. The painful experience of this misunderstanding within his field of research leads the author to pose two provocative questions. 'What is the difference between an anthropologist and a tourist?' 'What is the meaning of the fear that an anthropologist has of being mistaken for a tourist?' This subject gives full scope for the author's wit. The determination with which the author sets out first to unearth all the arguments put forward by different anthropologists to distinguish their role and practices from those of the tourist, and then to destroy them, shows that here is a sensitive issue which torments the discipline. Tourism and anthropology are difficult to dissociate. With each desire for differentiation, it becomes evident that those anthropologists who seek to dissociate themselves have not solved their own problem of identity, since the boundaries between anthropology and tourism have become clouded.

Crick proposes the following hypothesis, which is loaded with consequences: it is the absence of any outward separation between tourist and anthropologist which makes the anthropologist reject the relationship with tourism and the tourist as if he or she had taken on board something that cannot be assimilated. Anthropologists cannot talk about tourism for fear of speaking about themselves and of seeing their own identity dissolve by becoming assimilated into someone else's. They cannot shake off their subconscious identification with an idealized model of themselves.

When working on the blurred boundaries between anthropology and tourism, Ed Bruner leads us to the heart of some incongruous situations which may be embarrassing for the anthropologist, but provide many new tracks of research (Chapter 13). By choosing, as a means of being able to study the tourist, to accompany a group of American travellers in Indonesia, Bruner boldly tests this contamination in a binary experiment by adopting the dual roles of tourist guide and ethnologist. Working as such, on the turbid boundaries between anthropology and tourism, the anthropologist feels the ambiguity of his or her role. It is precisely this median position, however, oscillating between two roles, and chosen deliberately, which allows him to understand the relationship between the anthropologist or the ethnographer and the tourist. He takes up Malcolm Crick's question: 'What is the difference between an ethnologist and a tourist?' By comparing his various experiences from his stays in Indonesia as an anthropologist and as a tourist guide, where each time the ethnographer/tourist is alone or with the tourists means taking on a different role, the researcher draws the demarcation line which differentiates them. His own experiences are intersected in the account as in an experimental model constructed according to the principle of an orthogonal matrix, and this allows the significant differences and the common points to appear without confusion. The style contrasts sharply with the classical scientific discourse where the 'subject of enunciation' disappears behind the 'subject of the enounced'. The author puts himself personally into the narration. He implicates himself subjectively in his account. Through the others' viewpoints – those of the group of tourists watching Indonesian society – the anthropologist comes face to face with his professional point of view. He cannot avoid questioning the desire which compels him. Thus he is led to ponder the responsibility the anthropologist has in constructing the description of identity of the native society. This is why he concludes: 'writing is a political act.'

(Translated by Alison Steele and Nelson Graburn.)

References

Akiwowo, A. (1988) 'Universalism and indigenisation in sociology theory: introduction', *International Sociology*, 3(2): 155–60.

Archer, M.S. (1991) 'Sociology for one world: unity and diversity', *International Sociology*, 6(2): 131–47.

Balandier, G. (1969) 'Réflexions sur une anthropologie de modernité', *Cahiers Internationaux de Sociologie*, XLVIII: 197–210.

Benoist, J.M. (1977) *L'Identité: séminaire dirigé par Claude Lévi-Strauss.* Paris: Grasset.

Geertz, C. (1986) *Savoir local, savoir global: les lieux du savoir.* Paris: Presses Universitaires de France.

Graburn, N. and Jafari, J. (1991) *Tourism Social Science*, special issue, *Annals of Tourism Research*, 18(1).

Hechter, M. and Lévi, M. (1979) 'The comparative analysis of ethnoregional movements', *Ethnic and Racial Studies*, 2(3): 260–74.

Lanfant, M.F. (1987) 'L'impact social et culturel du tourisme international en question: réponses interdisciplinaires', *Problems of Tourism*, 10(2): 3–20.

Lanfant, M.F. and Graburn, N. (1992) 'International tourism reconsidered: the principle of the alternative', in V.L. Smith and W.R. Eadington (eds), *Tourism Alternatives: Potentials and Problems in the Development of Tourism.* Philadelphia: University of Pennsylvania Press. Chapter 5, pp. 88–112.

McKean, P.F. (1973) 'Cultural involution: tourists, Balinese, and the process of modernization in an anthropological perspective'. PhD dissertation, Brown University.

Meyer, W. (1988) *Beyond the Mask.* Saarbrücken and Fort Lauderdale: Breitenbach.

Morin, E. (1991) *Communication et complexité.* Paris: La Découverte.

OMT (1992a) *Forum international du tourisme, année 2000: perspectives et défis.* Organisation Mondiale du Tourisme.

OMT (1992b) *Évolution du tourisme d'ici l'an 2000: tendances 1992, évolution, perspectives de la politique touristique.* Organisation Mondiale du Tourisme.

Park, P. (1988) 'Toward an emancipatory sociology: abandoning universalism for true indigenisation', *International Sociology*, 3(2): 160–70.

Popper, Sir K. (1979) *La Société ouverte et ses ennemis. Vol. 1: L'Ascendant de Platon.* Paris: Seuil.

1

International Tourism, Internationalization and the Challenge to Identity

Marie-Françoise Lanfant

International tourism and world integration

What is international tourism? The expression 'international tourism' makes for confusion. Some think that it refers to one particular aspect of the general phenomenon of 'tourism', and that one can lighten the text by deleting the word 'international'. The term is used here, however, as a single conceptual entity without dissociating the word 'international' from the word 'tourism'. This choice of terminology is fully intentional, however, and not a matter of the simple spatial extension of a phenomenon which has hitherto been confined within national limits.

The word 'tourism', as it is defined in dictionaries or operationalized for example in statistics, has grown out of an idea which was forged within industrial societies. This idea has become attached to a phenomenon which is actually global in scale, although rooted in an explanatory framework which is characterized by Western ethnocentrism, univocal and reductive.

It has often been said that modern tourism was born in England during the eighteenth century, in the form of the Grand Tour. A series of factors have been put forward to explain its subsequent development, which include the existence of a class which enjoyed conspicuous leisure, the reduction of the working day, the democratization of holidays, the desire to escape from the towns and the rise of consumer society. This list is by no means exhaustive. Thus a framework of explanation which was constructed in order to think about the growth of leisure in industrial societies has been transposed into the study of the phenomenon of tourism to the point at which tourism, leisure and holidays have become equivalent and interchangeable terms.

In the same vein, 'international tourism' has been defined very narrowly in relation to the 'demand' which is experienced in the 10 or 12 large industrial countries which are the principal countries sending international tourists. It is seen as a geographical extension of a migratory movement whose initial causes are to be found at the specific point from which it originates. We thereby fall into a unidirectional mode of explanation, which is the vehicle for an ideology sustained by ideas of leisure which are current within industrial societies; but we overlook those factors which have strongly shaped the world expansion of tourism. I have developed this analysis in several earlier works (Lanfant, 1972; 1989).

A history which is aware of the way in which civilization has actually developed would associate tourism with a whole series of factors which were already operative in many different cultures even before the word 'tourism' made its appearance in the dictionaries (Graburn, 1983). Anthropologists, geographers, ethnologists, economists, sociologists and semiologists all travel in the real world; and having undergone these experiences they are now reconsidering the criteria adopted by the first theoreticians of tourism. We are now beginning to compile a general history of this phenomenon within a world context, and to repudiate those points of view which in the past have provided rather glib explanations of the rise of tourism in terms of the particular cultural context of industrial societies (Baretje, 1981–7; Boyer, 1980; Towner and Wall, 1991).

In order to escape from the trap set by these definitions we propose to approach tourism as an 'international fact'. In doing so we locate ourselves squarely within the perspective adopted by the founders of the French school of sociology:

> It is not appropriate to internationalize all social facts . . . There are some phenomena which reflect more exactly the character of a group, a people or a nation, and others which are better associated with the *exchanges* between peoples. These overflow the bounds of a national territory, and take on a life which is in some sense supranational. (Durkheim, 1969: 681–5, my emphasis)

> It is possible to divide social phenomena into two groups. One kind does not travel well: the other does. On their own account they overflow, so to speak, the *boundaries* of any given society, boundaries which themselves are often difficult to define. (Mauss, 1969: 243, my emphasis)

By presenting tourism as an 'international fact' we break with all those approaches (such as marketing) which analyse tourism as the consequence of a demand for leisure within the industrialized societies. It overthrows the barriers which have been set up between areas of research. While the sending societies have been preoccupied with the motivations of tourists, the receiving countries have concerned themselves with the profound changes produced by tourism planning. Our approach to tourism as an international fact is reminiscent of what Marcel Mauss called a 'total social phenomenon', understood in the strong sense which he gave to that expression in his 'Essai sur le don' (Mauss, 1980), namely, 'a phenomenon which sets in motion all society and its institutions' (Cresswell, 1975). Tourism on a world scale makes itself felt at every level and in all sectors of collective life – economic, political, geographical, ecological and technological – as well as in the less visible and tangible areas of social reality, such as its systems of signs and symbolic processes. Tourism furnishes our conversation, and its discourse fills our fantasies. There is nowhere *a priori* which might not be brought into its embrace.

In directing attention to this international dimension we are made aware of certain facts which are rarely emphasized. During the 1930s the states which participated in the League of Nations became aware of the impact on the balance of payments of expenditure by international travellers. Yielding to the temptation of protectionism during the years of depression, they were inclined to place limits on expenditure by their citizens beyond their national frontiers. The Economic Commission of the League of Nations declared itself to be in favour of a liberalization of international tourist movements, however, and it was at this time that the distinction was created between 'internal' (or domestic) tourism and 'international tourism' as an economic activity indissolubly linked to foreign trade (League of Nations, 1936).

This was a turning point in the development of the concept of tourism. International tourism was assimilated within the economic study of markets, given the status of a branch of import/export trade, and judged solely in relation to its monetary value in international exchanges. This priority given to the economic dimension, which became accepted especially after the Second World War, legitimated a whole series of practices in the field of planning as well as in the general way in which tourism was conceptualized.

The number of foreign tourists who each year enter national territory has now become an index of the state of the market. International organizations and consultancy firms regularly calculate the balance of receipts and expenditure of countries on the tourism account, and countries are classified according to these results. Ministers or their representatives sound off about the level of performance achieved nationally, and urge the regions to vie with each other in competition. That the development of tourism is a good thing has become axiomatic.

Generally speaking, in official publications, international tourism is defined in terms of those individuals who cross national frontiers in order to travel or stay for non-professional reasons in a country other than their own. Measured in these terms, since the 1960s statistics have recorded an uninterrupted growth in the movement of international tourists. Accelerating sharply between 1960 and 1967 (at more than 9.4 per cent per annum and then slowing a little, although still reaching appreciable rates between 1967 and 1980 (6.8 per cent per annum), this growth continued at a rate of 6 per cent per annum between 1983 and 1990, following its only period of stagnation between 1980 and 1983. In spite of some slackening since, the most recent projections agree that international tourism will sustain growth rates of 3.7 per cent per annum from now until the year 2000. In 1990 it was estimated that 415 million people crossed frontiers; and the most conservative projections indicate that at least 600 million, with an upper limit of 750 million, will do so by the year 2000.

Tourism has become a major economic factor which is growing world-wide. Few industries can hope to attain growth rates of between 4 and 5 per cent per annum during the next decade (Hawkins and Ritchie, 1991). These statistical data provide a rough indication of the scope of the phenomenon of the international spatial mobility of people.

In the early 1960s, the idea was mooted that international tourism could be of benefit to developing countries. Kurt Krapf, one of the pioneers of the economic theory of tourism, spelled out this doctrine (Krapf, 1961). In 1963 the United Nations Conference on Tourism and International Travel in Rome solemnly declared that tourism made a vital contribution to the economic development of developing countries. This thesis was enunciated at a time when the better-off nations, at a high point of economic growth, had decided to extend aid to the less well-off nations, and in a period during which many former colonial countries were attaining political independence.

In the following years an intense campaign aimed at persuading the less developed countries (LDCs) to adopt this orthodoxy was orchestrated by the international organizations. Foreign capital was solicited, which the LDCs were invited to accept. The latter threw themselves into this enterprise enthusiastically, hoping to find in it a solution to their endemic poverty. Between 1969 and 1979, 24 projects supported by the World Bank got off the ground in 18 countries. Huge tourism centres were created, worlds set apart on the margins of everyday life, in diverse regions around the world, including the Caribbean islands, Spain, Indonesia, the Maldives, Mexico, Sardinia and Thailand.

The opening up of the LDCs to international tourism compels us to look at this phenomenon from an entirely new angle. We are dealing here not just with a change of scale, but with a complete change of direction. It would no longer be possible to describe international tourism simply as an extension across international frontiers of domestic tourism, driven by some irresistible propensity to travel, or to reduce its economic significance simply to its contribution to external trade. Tourism had become a transmission belt between two worlds, unequal in their development: the post-industrial sending societies, and the developing countries.

At the same time, the function of tourism was being redefined within the developed societies, which themselves were experiencing symptoms of crisis following years of euphoric economic growth. An activity which had hitherto figured only as a branch of the export trade acquired a new significance. In addition to the advantages which had already been claimed for it – such as the creation of new employment, the multiplier effect as a factor for growth, and the relief of external indebtedness – tourism came to be seen as one, and in some cases the only, treatment for the growth of unemployment.

Formerly considered as secondary in many industrialized countries, tourism was now viewed as the economic activity of the future, and its development as a prime necessity. Consequently we see these countries embracing for themselves the very doctrine which they had formerly directed at the underdeveloped countries. Nowadays almost every government is trying to derive advantage from this activity, vying with each other in avaricious competition to bring in the maximum number of currency-laden foreign tourists.

At the international level, the tourism policy of the large post-industrial countries draws together aims which they hope are convergent. With respect to their own populations, they adopt a policy of free time, holidays and recreation, which they hope will articulate with the aspirations for development of the economically weaker countries. The consequences of these political choices are considerable. The free time of their own employed populations is reinserted into an economic calculus of productivity. Meanwhile, societies which know nothing of industrialization are reoriented towards the process of modernization by their incorporation into tourism.

Tourism thus constitutes a vector of political and cultural integration on a world scale. It occupies an increasingly central place within the North–South dialogue, and is coming to be a constituent part of the new world economic order, the debate about which is a matter of growing current concern. 'Tourism cannot be omitted from those factors which will contribute towards the building of the new social and economic world order', according to the Secretary General of the World Tourism Organization (WTO) (Lonati, 1980).

International tourism has not been the result of spontaneous generation. Its development has been impelled by a powerful apparatus of tourism *promotion*, which has been supported within the highest reaches of the international organizations – the UN, the ILO, UNCTAD, UNESCO, the IMF, the OECD and the World Bank. The influence of these international institutions has been evident not only in the discussion of policy, but more concretely in the enactment of global strategies of planning and the movement of people. These organizations have worked in close cooperation with the bodies which make up the international tourism industry, such as the transport companies and the hotel chains.

It is in the very nature of tourist activity that a large number of connections link actors working either in apparently different fields, or in countries which are a long way from each other. The tourism transnationals (that is, the multinational companies of the tourism industry, emerging from the play of takeovers and mergers) have turned into a network of agents whose economic power extends well beyond their touristic function in the narrow sense. This network of firms has become involved in economic systems at regional and local levels whose interests have nothing in common *a priori* with tourism. At the international level such networks are ever more effectively coordinated by, and integrated within, a movement of the centralization of decision-making (Buckley, 1987; Dézert and Wackermann, 1991; Tremblay, 1990).

International tourism is deployed within a space shaped in large measure by advanced technologies. Information technology confers upon this industry powerful means of organization and management, accelerating the rationalization of the demand for tourism, and making possible the progressive refinement of market segmentation. Thanks to their capacity for the storage and processing of vast bodies of data, the computers which provide the basis for decision-making facilitate more and more subtle compartmentalization of the behaviour of consumers. Information science, electronics and telecommunications are all integrated into the functioning of these organizations, involving transport, accommodation, catering, recreation and entertainment.

This apparatus of production has come to extend across the entire planet, progressively transforming societies and cultures into 'tourist products'. In this respect the thesis which Edward Morin (1962) developed in his *L'Esprit du temps*, on the prospects for a planetary culture, is completely apposite. Through the agency of commercial transactions other links are formed between national or regional societies and certain categories of their populations. Since they involve the exchange of people, these essentially symbolic exchanges are of greater and greater interest to sociologists.

Tourism draws together social groups with contrasting modes of social discourse: developed countries and developing countries; urban populations and rural populations; technological societies and traditional societies; hot societies and cold societies. It establishes new social bonds which one might paraphrase in a famous sentence: 'Exchange is not an effect of society; it is society in motion' (Merleau-Ponty, 1960).

We are faced with a phenomenon which participates in that process of globalization which Margaret Archer (1991) rightly considered as offering one of the challenges confronting the modern world.

> What has changed is that the global process is now partly constitutive of social reality everywhere, and constitutes that part which cannot be understood in strictly local terms, for its origin and impact stem from outside localised 'forms of life'. This in today's world is what supplies international sociology with its new brief.

Along with international sociology we are also entering a 'new world' at the level of epistemology. Here too we have lost our fixed points of reference, and we see-saw within

> a kind of decentred thought, without reference, where the essential thing is not to open up a path towards a point of anchorage which is presumed to exist, as it has always been supposed to exist in some way, but to call into question the path itself, along with that which is transferred, and the means of transport . . . identity is overthrown by the same stroke, because the spatial pair Here/Elsewhere is no more than the spatial representation of the pair Same/Other. (Serres, 1972: 144–5 and 147)

This, we claim, is also the special domain of international tourism.

The challenge to identity

The field of problems relating to the question of identity associated with the development of tourism in the world is of enormous significance. During the 1980s the question of identity became a hackneyed theme within the social sciences to the point at which its value became suspect. Nevertheless, the theme of identity is omnipresent within discourse about tourism. It figures in the discourse of the international organizations which have been preaching the development of tourism; in that of the marketing people who have fashioned the product; in that of the states which have orchestrated promotional campaigns on behalf of tourism in their own countries; and in that of regions which have aspired to assume their proper place in tourism development (Ascher, 1984). It is a theme which is dear to the hearts of those who work in the planning of tourism; and it is discovered equally in the writing of numerous sociologists and anthropologists (Crick, Chapter 12 in this book; Bruner, 1991a; 1991b; Chapter 13 in this book). 'Identity' is on the lips even of the tourists themselves (Allcock and Young, 1991; Urbain, 1991). A theme with so many different facets is difficult to disentangle, but demands research precisely because of its recurrence in those discourses which refer to tourism.

The problems that appeals to identity raise within the discourse of tourism are irregular in form, but nevertheless implicated in each other. We have tried to locate the different motives which give rise to such appeals at the international, regional and local levels, as well as within institutions and individuals.

We encounter the question of identity first of all at the level of the attempt to evoke it. Within the decision-making circles of tourism the attempt to evoke identity has taken on the character of a plea on behalf of *cultural identities*: that is, a demand that other cultures be respected. This principle is generally recognized within the intergovernmental organizations (IGOs), which rarely lose the opportunity to remind us of this necessity on every solemn occasion, and of the hope that tourism might become a factor making for mutual recognition between peoples (WTO, 1980; Przecławski, 1990). Within this context the concern to preserve identities takes on a normative, prescriptive value.

This particular appeal cuts in two directions. It is directed to the local population, that they should conserve their own culture, and also at the citizens of all countries, that they should become mutually respectful of the culture of others. In this 'dialogue of cultural identities' (Gallet, 1982) tourism makes a particular offer: to place the *citoyen du monde* (the international tourist) directly into the presence, *in vivo* and *in situ*, of these other cultures.

The IGOs support and attempt to promote every show or display which allows the receiving societies to demonstrate to foreigners their own original contribution to world civilization. In the universalist vision of humanity to which they are firmly attached, every culture is worth the same as every other; and it is necessary to make a place – its own place – for each of them in a world in which they are multiplying. According to this approach, every society will have acquired a singular character, and by displaying this will provide a guarantee of its own authenticity.

This demand for universalism, however, is not accepted unanimously by sociologists and anthropologists (Dumont, 1983; Lévi-Strauss, 1973; 1983; 1984; Todorov, 1989; Balibar and Wallerstein, 1988). Claude Lévi-Strauss, for example, has expressed his own doubts on several occasions: 'It serves no purpose to protect the originality of cultures against themselves' (1973: 403–4). Recruited by UNESCO in 1971 to open the International Year against Racism, he took the opportunity to make his audience aware of the limits of universalism: 'I invited the audience to have the wisdom to doubt the advent of a world in which cultures, seized by a shared passion, would aspire to do nothing more than to celebrate each other' (1983: 16). Addressing the World Congress on Cultural Policies in 1982, he stressed that it was an illusion to 'want to overcome antinomian propositions by means of well-intentioned words', such as those which 'counsel faithfulness to oneself and openness to others', or which 'are in favour at one and the same time of the creative affirmation of every identity, and the drawing together of cultures' (1983: 16).

The practices of marketing have allied themselves with these preoccupations of the IGOs. Within the framework of the market the demand for identity involves the instrumentalization of identity for economic ends. In order to commercialize a country it must be turned into a tourist product.

The international promotion of tourism demands that every place should have its own specific character. In order to give a country the best chance in a competitive market it must have some trade mark which emphasizes both its originality and its superiority within a given domain. According to this promotional logic every country and every region is invited to produce, affirm and label itself with an identity in the form of an affirmation of itself on behalf of others. These others are the tourists, who project on to their hosts their own demands, motivations and wants.

Throughout the world there has been a frantic forging of signs of identity with a view to their manufacture as tourist products. These signs of identification which societies offer for the approval of foreign visitors might include: memorable places, historic monuments, the heritage of traditional societies, and craft skills. Their populations are enjoined to draw the attention of foreigners to their character traits or their creativity by means of visible and accessible signs. Everybody is being exhorted to prepare representations of themselves.

On the basis of information gathered in surveys, tourism marketing shapes the image of a place, and then correlates the motivational systems of potential clients with the components of its identity. In this process of manufacture, the identity of the society is described in terms of seductive attributes, and crystallized in a publicity image in which the native population is insidiously induced to recognize itself. An encounter with the inhabitants of New Guinea is sold by presenting them as the last remnants of a cannibal society (Bruner, 1989). Some African peoples are presented as societies which are close to savagery (Bruner and Kirshenblatt-Gimblett, 1994). The receptive femininity of young women and girls from Thailand is sold (Kruhse-MountBurton, Chapter 11 in this book), as is the traditional orderliness of the Amish. Thus the identity of a human group is framed and becomes fixed in order to meet the needs of the market, and the image of the identity of the natives then becomes a norm which has to be respected (Harrison, 1990).

The task of promoting the publicity image of a territory falls to the state in the form of the Ministry of Tourism (WTO, 1985); and the state, through its representatives, exploits that tourist image in order to reinforce national cohesion. An image is presented which flatters national identity. To boast about the resources of the country means to praise the idea of the nation. This kind of discourse is common, whether in countries which have recently acquired political independence, in those which are experiencing movements for regional autonomy, or in large industrial countries which have begun to integrate themselves into larger social groupings, as in the case of Europe during the construction of the Europe of the Twelve.

On other occasions, however, international tourism is presented as an alien power which is in conflict with national interests. The national and the international come to be thought of in terms of an opposition between contrary interests. Tourism is presented in the guise of the foreigner, and the foreigner as an intruder. Consequently it is experienced as an undesirable presence and an interference, rather than as an opportunity to be open towards others.

One can detect contradictory processes at work here in the form of a gap between discourse and practice. Often state governments which follow a policy of promoting the country's tourism challenge national autonomy through their own alignment with strategies of internationalization. Actors often argue on the basis of a narrowly national perception of problems without reference to the imperatives of the international market, whether that market is limited to a region beyond the confines of the state, or extends to large structures which operate at a global level. They argue as if the state was able to exercise complete sovereignty, whereas its decisions are often restricted by the place which it occupies within a network of transactions. The structures of such networks develop in such a way that national societies are identified no longer essentially in terms of their place within hierarchies of domination/subordination, but by variable roles and functions (Dézert and Wackermann, 1991). Relations between the transnational companies and centres of state power are defined less in terms of relations of force than in terms of systems of power within which the public and the private are intermingled (Perroux, 1982).

At the regional level one comes across problems which illustrate even more clearly the socio-political issues which underlie discourse about identity. Problems become complicated at the regional level as the demand for identity springs from several places, both internal and external. Representatives of the state, professionals, temporary or permanent residents, both those who are long established and those who are newly arrived in the region, all project upon the region itself a variety of demands which give rise to controversies. These demands denote an attachment to the place, and convey the wish for its symbolic appropriation, for mastery over it or for a share in it (Bourdieu, 1980).

Once the choice of tourism is imposed upon a region, however, its integration into new systems of power and influence begins (see Chapters 2, 4 and 9 in this book). The changes which are produced within the framework provided by the major operators of tourism planning, especially in peripheral areas, can sometimes be drastic. An appeal to regional identity which is expressed from outside the region can appear as part of a superficial, ideological discourse. If it is motivated by political aims, and addressed more particularly to the cultural level, this kind of discourse can defuse the subversive component of the demand for identity. Expressed from within the region, however, the appeal to a regional identity can take on both a defensive and an offensive character, and give rise to a variety of social movements (Touraine, 1980).

The region can quickly lose a part of its autonomy, in that through tourism its development is suddenly grafted on to factors which are external to it. Local elites can come to be dispossessed of a part of their powers to the benefit of external actors. These changes can be experienced in terms of degradation or corruption, and give rise to various movements of protest, defence, protection or conservation. In each case socio-cultural dynamics are re-oriented, and we are called to witness processes of the recasting of identity.

Tensions, struggles and conflicts between interests are all characteristic in general terms of the relations between a tourist region and the central state. Very often, before coming to be exploited for tourism, a region will have had at its disposal meagre resources, and will have depended upon state aid. With the arrival of tourism it discovers the capacity to make its own impact upon the economic scene, and possesses a standard against which to measure its own value in a world which is becoming internationalized. Through the presence there of the multinationals, the region acquires a capacity for decision-making which extends beyond the state. With the touristification of the area there is a slow but irresistible process of the redistribution of national and regional powers within the context of international totalities.

An appeal to identity presupposes allocutors (Wittgenstein, 1981). It suggests a model of communication in which social relations are conducted implicitly via roles. The society to which the message is addressed is targeted as a subject, and is thereby located within a relationship of mastery and subordination. The master assures the Other that by responding it will become an object of enjoyment for tourist consumption. The agent of this discourse proposes, insists, incites, prescribes, recommends, implores, ordains. The entire gamut of imperative, deontic and performative utterances is found within this discourse (Bourdieu, 1982).

These attempts to evoke identity tend to conjure up a place of the other which is a shelter from change: peasant societies which are supposedly profoundly rural, or archaic societies in which it is supposed that the traces of primitive humanity have been preserved. It has often been remarked upon that tourists, through their own displacement, are looking for that which they feel their own society has lost – nature, purity, wisdom, childhood, originality, freedom (Krapf, 1964; Morin, 1962; Bruner, 1989). The search for identity rekindles the Platonic ideal of an archaic society, which is uncorrupted, close to perfection, the guardian of Truth, Beauty and Goodness (Popper, 1979).

Primitive society survives in the imaginations of modern people in the form of an unrealized ideal, the quest for which also draws in sociologists and anthropologists. Stimulating archaic, traditional or peasant societies to produce an ideal identity is tantamount to asking that they construct an imaginary place for an Other, and an image of self which seduces both self and Other. Host societies are invited to sublimate themselves in the form of a superlative me (Kohut, 1974).

What is it that makes tourists choose to go to these other kinds of places? And what becomes of these traditional societies when they do try to resemble this ideal identity? Tourists find themselves in a position where they encounter, in the guise of an ideal identity, the idealized identity which they have in their own heads. They approach places of this kind without ever having had to ask themselves what really happens there. The visited society itself imagines that it is offering to its guests an authentic image, a fair face (Meyer, 1988), in spite of the fact that this authenticity, this beauty, this transparency, exists only in the eye of the beholder, who happens to stand in a particular relation to the focal point (Lacan, 1975). Tourists and the receiving society are thus engaged in a process of reciprocal misconstruction.

Rereading the work of anthropologists, one is struck by the change which has come about in the way in which they have come to look at traditional society. Not long ago they were asking about the erosion of tradition under the impact of modernization. It was practically taken for granted that 'tradition' and 'modernity' were terms which stood in polar opposition to each other. The debate excited both modernists, who were partisans of change, and traditionalists, who were attached to the permanence of a past. Although debate today resorts to the use of the same terms, it tends to eliminate the gap between them. By 1974 Georges Balandier was already proposing a new way of examining this opposition between tradition and modernity: 'Every examination of modernity, and not only in the case of the so-called advanced societies, calls into question those things which appear to be authentically novel, by which these societies bring about their own dislocation' (1974: 250; cf. Balandier, 1985). With international tourism the discontinuity between modernity and tradition is overcome. Modernity presupposes no longer a break with tradition, but its absorption. Inversely, tradition is not reanimated by a protest movement against modernity, but is embodied within modernity.

The modern tourist is fed upon and invigorated by tradition (Jules-Rosette, 1990). The receiving society, in this respect, comes to reflect upon its own traditions and values through the confrontation with otherness signified by the presence of tourists. The reconstruction of its identity begins with the gaze of the foreigner, and finds within this gaze a point of reference which guarantees that identity. So the evaluation of the affirmation of its own identity can only be accomplished by reference to the Other.

Theoretically, interior and exterior form no longer two separate worlds, but a single continuous surface with one edge but two faces. The tourist, the *citoyen du monde*, just like the small ant moving over the surface of a Möbius strip, passes from one to the other without being aware of having made the jump, or of any kind of break or discontinuity.

The principal change which tourism has introduced in the relation between tradition and modernity is that the archaic and the traditional are to be understood and exploited primarily from an economic point of view. It is not so very long ago that societies classed as traditional were condemned by development economists to certain death, although the ethnologists affirmed their disappearance with a degree of sadness. These same societies have now discovered in international tourism a means of survival and even of advancement. Tradition has been re-evaluated, integrated into the mechanisms of economic production and incorporated into the cultural systems of modern society.

Traditional societies are vigorously encouraged to retain their own cultures intact for the sake of tourism. Tradition has come to be a resource for publicity in the market. The same process can be seen at work everywhere in the world where the pressure of the tourist industry is experienced. This process is not the prerogative of traditional societies. It affects any kind of society in which tourism provides one of the bases of its economic development.

An important part of this process is that, in becoming a tourist product, 'heritage' changes its meaning. It becomes a capital to be used profitably and made to yield a return. The assaying of heritage and its conversion into a tourist product imply that its cultural value is transformed into a commercial value. In the course of this operation it undergoes several semantic changes and transformations (Bazin, Chapter 6 in this book). It is restored in conformity with both rational scientific criteria and the norms of commercial promotion. Heritage has become a tourist object, part of a 'package of services'; and a visit to a heritage site can be sold as just one component within a circuit made up of many and various attractions. Throughout the world we can see a frantic movement towards the restoration of heritage associated with the development of tourism.

Heritage, or the 'spoken track of history' (Merleau-Ponty, 1960), acquires its value by means of a wide variety of procedures: by restoration to an identical form; by relation to a romantic conception of its environment; through scientific and educational presentation within a museum; by redressing the various vicissitudes to which it has been subjected by time. There are fantastic restorations and false constructions which imitate the real to perfection. Contemporary creations are incorporated even into places which people can remember. (In this way we find the columns of Buren in the garden of the Royal Palace in Paris.) Monuments themselves can be decontextualized. Europeans visiting the United States are often struck by their encounters with Gothic churches or Roman remains, or Scottish castles which have been transported stone by stone to American soil, along with more or less fantastic additions.

In presenting its heritage for tourism, society is called upon to participate actively, both materially and subjectively, in demonstrating that things are as they must have been. This is the price of access to modernity. Society has to reinvest in its past, to reappropriate it, having exposed it to the gaze of the foreigner as a diacritical mark of its own identity, and that does not happen of its own accord. In order to engage with the memory of a place it is necessary that there should be a social group which can ensure the transmission of memory (although we might hypothesize that the application of productive imagination here will not only appeal to memory, but also add a fair amount of fiction). Thus in assuming its tourist vocation a place becomes the expression of a collective memory,

> a place in which many exchanges take place, not only between the individual and the collective but also between the past and the present, between that which has already been experienced and life today, between the spoken and the unspoken, the explicit and the implicit. (Amphoux and Ducret, 1985: 201)

This process involves a peculiar inversion of values. The tie with tradition is maintained, but within a completely different context. In the attempt to respond to an external demand for authenticity the inhabitants of traditional societies will willingly indulge the fantasies of the foreigners. They reinvent for them fêtes, shows, costumes, culinary practices or funerary rites in a new spirit of aestheticism. This new tradition is a manufactured tradition, however, which has been recomposed to correspond to the wishes of tourists. It only mimics the old ways, and is reconstructed on the basis of collections of folk-tales borrowed from various sources and mixed in syncretic forms which obscure their relationship to their original reference. When these constructions come to be presented as true, as the most authentic ones, we enter into the region of hyper-reality (Eco, 1985; MacCannell, 1992).

Henceforth the history of the place and tourism live side by side; and the symbolic production of special places takes place through their insertion into tourism (Davallon, 1991). National, regional and local histories are brought up to date, comparing in interesting ways with the accounts which were given formerly. A change of perspective takes place in the way in which historical monuments are presented to foreigners. There is a real anxiety about the past expressed in an interest in tradition and history. This corresponds to a moment when people are being torn from their roots and references, and resembles in some respects the experience of mourning (Jeudy, 1986). Monuments and other things which not so long ago were being consigned to obscurity regain through tourism a contemporary interest. Going beyond this, however, archaic objects are manufactured which take their place alongside those things which still live in the collective memory, or even which remain in active use.

Through this process of creating touristic values, the heritage of Everyman becomes part of the public domain. Even if it is still inhabited by family members who might be expected to inherit it, it will be relocated within a new system of property. It might become the property of the nation-state, or even feature in the inventory of world heritage. The signifying processes of heritage, which can be deciphered by tracing a family tree, come to be re-evaluated and put to use within a new system of interpretation and according to other criteria. These aim not only to allot a place to heritage within a system of consanguinity or descent, but also to incorporate it into a totality.

MacCannell (1989) has described in a remarkable way how a society can be transformed into a 'system of tourist attractions' which functions as a system of signs. The object which one sets out to see during the ritual of a journey is identified in the first instance by a trait, and this trait is signed with a marker by means of which the object becomes *unique*. It is framed, raised up, illuminated, mounted, placed under spotlights, and in this way is exposed and set apart from normal things, detached from the profane world, and becomes in some respect sacralized. The discovery of heritage, by procedures such as restoration, reconstitution and reinvestment with affect, in one sense breaks the very chain of significance which first invested it with authenticity, in that on subsequent occasions it is retouched and elevated to a new status. The object of heritage is reconsecrated through this process of marking, and thereby it certifies the identity of a place for the benefit of anonymous visitors.

Tradition, memory, heritage: these are not stable realities. It is as if the tourists have been invited to take part in a fantastic movement in which social memory is re-created through the celebration of heritage. Collective memory is constructed through the circulation of tourists around the world, justifying the remark of Fernand Braudel (1986) that the collective memory is a dialogue between the distant past and a rapidly changing, evanescent present, which does not always know either where it has come from or what is taking place all around it.

Why is it that in contemporary society heritage is called upon to become the guarantor of identity? Perhaps it is because heritage bears the guarantee of our paternity in the midst of an accelerating process of globalization of the exchanges in which we are engaged, and because in securing its present to its past, every society is trying to avoid being engulfed within some Grand Universal All.

Everything which touches upon heritage is shot through with an irresolvable tension and ambivalence. On the one hand, it is good to be conserved in the same state in which it was bequeathed to us by our ancestors or the recently departed. On the other hand, it is a good which has to be made to bear fruit which we will transmit to our descendants.

Those who work on the conservation of heritage pretend to be unaware of its tourist function, as if heritage and tourism have nothing in common. Typically, however, they are deeply divided in their minds between choices which seem to be contradictory. Conservation agencies are constantly confronted by two strategies which appear to be at loggerheads. The one seeks to conserve heritage in its original state, and restore it in all its integrity: the other is drawn towards giving it a new purpose within a conception of development which is linked to tourism.

On the one hand, there is a return to the past, which identifies it in relation to a line of descent, which renews and reinforces the feeling of belonging to a system of cultural parentage, and gives assurance as to the permanent character of society. On the other, patrimony is endowed with a new purpose, despite its link with the past. In this way all cultures are being pulled up by their roots and relocated within a context which, in the end, could well unite all of them upon common ground.

(Translated by John Allcock.)

References

Allcock, J.B. and Young, A. (eds) (1991) *Black Lambs and Grey Falcons: Women Travellers in the Balkans.* Bradford: Bradford University Press.

Amphoux, P. and Ducret, A. (1985) 'La mémoire des lieux', *Cahiers Internationaux de Sociologie*, LXXIX: 199–201.

Archer, M.S. (1991) 'Sociology for one world: unity and diversity', *International Sociology*, 6(2): 131–47.

Ascher, F. (1984) *Tourisme, sociétés transnationales et identités culturelles.* Paris: UNESCO.

Balandier, G. (1974) *Anthropo-logiques.* Paris: Presses Universitaires de France.

Balandier, G. (1985) *Le Détour.* Paris: Fayard.

Balibar, E. and Wallerstein, I. (1988) *Race, nation, classe: les identités ambiguës*. Paris: La Découverte.

Baretje, R. (1981–7) *Tourisme et histoire: essai bibliographique*. Aix-en-Provence: CHET, Collection Essais, nos 69, 121, 203, 230.

Bourdieu, P. (1980) *L'Identité et la représentation: éléments pour une reflexion critique de l'idée de région*. Paris: Actes de la Recherche.

Bourdieu, P. (1982) *Ce que parler veut dire: l'économie des échanges linguistiques*. Paris: Fayard.

Boyer, M. (1980) 'Évolution sociologique du tourisme: continuité du tourisme rare au tourisme de masse et rupture contemporaine', *Loisir et Société*, 3: 49–81.

Braudel, F. (1986) *L'Identité de la France*, Vol. 1, 'Espace et histoire', Vols 2 and 3, 'Les Hommes et les choses'. Paris: Arthaud-Flammarion.

Bruner, E.M. (1989) 'Tourism, creativity and authenticity', *Symbolic Interaction*, 10: 109–14.

Bruner, E.M. (1991a) 'Transformation of self in tourism', *Annals of Tourism Research*, 18: 238–50.

Bruner, E.M. (1991b) 'The ethnographic self and the personal self', in P. Benson (ed.), *Anthropology and Literature*. Urbana, IL: University of Illinois Press.

Bruner, E.M. and Kirshenblatt-Gimblett, B. (1994) 'Masai on the lawn: tourist realism in East Africa', *Cultural Anthropology* 19(2): 435–70.

Buckley, P.J. (1987) 'Tourism – an economic transactions analysis', *Tourism Management*, September: 190–4.

Cresswell, R. (1975) *Éléments d'ethnologie: huit terrains*. Paris: Collin.

Davallon, J. (1991) 'Produire les hauts lieux du patrimoine', in A. Micoul (ed.), *La Production symbolique des lieux exemplaires*. Paris: Dossiers TTS, Ministère de l'Équipement.

Dézert, B. and Wackermann, G. (1991) *La Nouvelle Organisation internationale des échanges*. Paris: CEDES.

Dumont, L. (1983) *Essais sur l'individualisme: une perspective anthropologique sur l'idéologie moderne*. Paris: Seuil.

Durkheim, E. (1969) 'Note sur la notion de civilisation', in *Journal sociologique*. Paris: Presses Universitaires de France. pp. 681–5.

Eco, U. (1985) *La Guerre de faux*. Paris: Grasset.

Gallet, D. (1982) *Dialogue pour l'identité culturelle*. Paris: Anthropos.

Graburn, N. (1983) *To Pray, Pay and Play: the Cultural Structure of Domestic Tourism*. Aix-en-Provence: CHET.

Harrison, D. (1990) 'Tradition, modernity and tourism in Swaziland'. Unpublished paper presented to the Thematic Group on the Sociology of Tourism, XII World Congress of Sociology, Madrid.

Hawkins, D.D. and Ritchie, J.R.B. (1991) *World Travel and Tourism Review: Indicators, Trends, Forecasts. Vol. 1: UK, USA, Asia*. CAB International.

Jeudy, P.H. (1986) *Mémoires du social*. Paris: Presses Universitaires de France.

Jules-Rosette, B. (1990) 'Simulations of post-modernity: images of technology in African tourist and popular art', *Society for Visual Anthropology Review*, 6(1): 29–37.

Kohut, H. (1974) *La Psychoanalyse des transferts narcissiques*. Paris: Presses Universitaires de France.

Krapf, K. (1961) 'Les pays en voie de développement face au tourisme: introduction méthodologique', *Revue de Tourisme*, 16(3): 82–9.

Krapf, K. (1964) 'La consommation touristique: une contribution à une théorie de la consommation'. Aix-en-Provence, CHET, Collection Études et Mémoires, Vol. 2.

Lacan, J. (1975) 'La topique de l'imaginaire', in *Le Séminaire. Vol. 1: Les Écrits techniques de Freud: 1953–54*. Paris: Seuil. pp. 87–103.

Lanfant, M.F. (1972) *Les Théories du loisir: sociologie du loisir et idéologies*. Paris: Presses Universitaires de France.

Lanfant, M.F. (1989) 'International tourism resists the crisis', in A. Olszewska and K. Roberts (eds), *Leisure and Lifestyle: a Comparative Analysis of Free Time*. London: Sage.

League of Nations (Société des Nations) (1936) *Étude sur les mouvements touristiques considérés comme un facteur économique international*. Geneva: League of Nations.

Lévi-Strauss, C. (1973) 'Humanisme et humanité', in *Anthropologie structurale*, vol. 2. Paris: Plon. pp. 319–422.

Lévi-Strauss, C. (1983) *Le Regard éloigné*. Paris: Plon.

Lévi-Strauss, C. (1984) *Paroles données*. Paris: Plon.

Lonati, R. (1980) 'Note du Secrétaire Général', in *Étude sur la contribution du tourisme à l'échange des valeurs spirituelles et à une meilleure compréhension entre les peuples*. Conférence Mondiale du Tourisme, Manila. Madrid: WTO.

MacCannell, D. (1989) *The Tourist: a New Theory of the Leisure Class*. New York: Schocken.

MacCannell, D. (1992) *Empty Meeting Grounds: the Tourist Papers*. London: Routledge.

Mauss, M. (1969) 'Les civilisations: éléments et formes', in *Essais de sociologie*. Paris: Minuit.

Mauss, M. (1980) 'Essai sur le don: formes et raisons de l'échange dans les sociétés archaïques', in *Sociologie et anthropologie*. Paris: Presses Universitaires de France.

Merleau-Ponty, M. (1960) *Signes*. Paris: Gallimard.

Meyer, W. (1988) *Beyond the Mask*. Saarbrücken and Fort Lauderdale: Verlag Breitenbach, Social Science Studies on International Problems 134.

Morin, E. (1962) *L'Esprit du temps*. Paris: Grasset.

Perroux, F. (1982) *Dialogue des monopoles et des nations: equilibre des unités actives*. Grenoble: Presses Universitaires.

Popper, Sir K. (1979) *La Société ouverte et ses ennemies. Vol. 1: L'Ascendant de Platon*. Paris: Seuil.

Przecławski, K. (1990) 'Le tourisme et ie monde de l'unité dans la pluralité', *Les Cahiers du tourisme*. Aix-en-Provence: CHET.

Serres, M. (1972) *L'Interférence, Hermes II*. Paris: Minuit.

Todorov, T. (1989) *Nous et les autres: la réflexion française sur la diversité humaine*. Paris: Seuil.

Touraine, A. (1980) 'Les deux faces de l'identité', in P. Tap (ed.), *Identités collectives et changements sociaux*. Paris, privately printed. pp. 20–6.

Towner, J. and Wall, G. (1991) 'History and tourism', *Annals of Tourism Research*, 18(1): 71–84.

Tremblay, P. (1990) 'The corporate structure of multinational enterprises in tourism: transactions costs and information'. Unpublished paper presented to the Thematic Group on the Sociology of Tourism, XII World Congress of Sociology, Madrid.

Urbain, J.D. (1991) *L'Idiot du voyage: histoires de touristes*. Paris: Plon.
Wittgenstein, L. (1981) *Investigations philosophiques*. Paris: Gallimard.
WTO (1980) *Déclaration de Manille sur le tourism mondial*. Manille.
WTO (1985) *Rôle de l'état dans la sauvegarde et la promotion de la culture comme facteur de développement touristique et dans la mise en valeur du patrimoine national de sites et de monuments à des fins touristiques*. Madrid: World Tourism Organization.

2

Cultural Heritage and Tourist Capital: Cultural Tourism in Bali

Michel Picard

> The touristic dilemma is clear: to freeze or not to freeze, to maintain boundaries or to remove, to assimilate or to segregate, or in short – the sword cuts with both edges.
>
> J. Jafari, 'Unbound ethnicity'

In the early 1970s, when the news spread that the Indonesian government had decided to launch mass tourism on Bali, tourist experts and lovers of Bali alike anxiously started asking the question: would Balinese culture survive the impact of tourism? For most of them there was little doubt that, sooner or later, the island of Bali would be overwhelmed by the flood of tourists who were sweeping her shores: inexorably, business would get the better of culture.

The first expression of concern came from an American historian, Willard Hanna, who published an inflammatory article on the impending ravages of tourism on Balinese culture. He wondered whether the Balinese could profit from tourism without losing their culture:

> How to exploit the tourist potential of the Island of Bali for the benefit of the culturally rich but economically poor Balinese, without at the same time inducing vulgarity or commercialization ... In other words, the intent is to maximize the benefits (profits) and minimize the detriments ('social and cultural pollution') and thus to preserve Balinese values by acquisition of desperately needed foreign valuta.[1]

In his opinion, the problem was not likely to be resolved, and if tourism in Bali were to prove to be a commercial success, it would become a cultural tragedy, as authentic traditions were being packaged to conform to tourist expectations, legendary Balinese artistry was being harnessed to create souvenir trinkets, and age-old religious ceremonies were being turned into hotel floor shows: in short, Balinese culture was becoming a tourist commodity. Consequently, he foresaw the not so distant days when the

Balinese would start mistaking the commercial by-products they sell to tourists for the genuine manifestation of their artistic traditions.

While Willard Hanna was giving vent to his concern that undiscerning tourists would spoil Balinese culture, the American anthropologist Philip McKean was challenging the charge of corruption commonly laid against tourism by foreign observers. According to him, the joint effect of the admiration evinced by tourists for Balinese culture and of the money they brought to the island was to renew the Balinese's interest in their cultural heritage while stimulating their artistic creativity. So much so that by patronizing Balinese culture, tourism would contribute to its preservation and even to its revival, to the extent that it was turning it into a source of both pride and profit for the Balinese: 'The entertainment, education, and care of international visitors would then pay the Balinese to do what they have learned to do so well for their own satisfaction – perform their arts and religion, their crafts and ceremonials.'[2]

Two decades later, pros and cons are still being deliberated as to whether tourism has a beneficial or a detrimental effect on Balinese culture. Thus, when one glances through the academic literature on the so-called 'socio-cultural impact of tourism', one finds some authors for whom tourism has helped preserve the cultural heritage of Bali, and others who accuse tourism of destroying Balinese culture and turning it into a commercial commodity.[3]

In this chapter, my intention is not so much to contest the conclusions of such studies as to challenge the very question they address as being misleading. In my opinion, the question is not whether or not Balinese culture has been able to withstand the impact of tourism, but rather what is entailed by talk of 'the impact of tourism on Balinese culture'. What conception of culture, of tourism and of the way tourism affects culture is implied by such a phrase?

As a matter of fact, the question of the socio-cultural impact of tourism is an attempt to solve a problem facing the tourist industry, that of the so-called 'sustainable development of tourism' – which is to develop a kind of tourism which does not destroy the resources it exploits, be they 'natural' or 'cultural'. Here is how a well-known tourist expert formulates the problem:

> Tourism can destroy tourism. Tourism as a user of resources, can be a resource destroyer, and through destroying the resources, which give rise to it, make the resource-based tourism short-lived. Impacts, benefits and costs can and should therefore be evaluated in advance of tourism development.[4]

The solution to this problem is generally sought in a cost–benefit analysis, involving some sort of trade-off between cultural and economic values. This way of tackling the problem is not just a matter of convenience, it is structurally determined by a recurrent set of oppositions: on the one hand, between that which relates to *culture* and that which concerns *economics*; and on the other hand, between that which is located *within* the host society and that which comes from *without*. As such, tourism is signified by economics whereas society is signified by culture: tourism brings money to a society in exchange for exploiting its culture.[5]

This approach – while congruent with the prospects and vested interests of the tourist industry – does not clarify the process of *touristification* of a society. Indeed, the mere fact of talking about the impact of tourism entails something of a ballistic vision, which amounts to perceiving the host society as a target hit by a missile, like an inert object, passively subjected to exogenous factors of change, with the subsequent problem of assessing the ensuing fallout.[6] On the contrary, I contend that, far from being an external force striking a native society from without, touristification proceeds from within. Or, to be more precise, it blurs the boundaries between the inside and the outside, between what is 'ours' and what is 'theirs', between that which belongs to 'culture' and that which pertains to 'tourism'.

It should thus be clear that what I call the touristification of a society amounts to much more than just developing an area and equipping it with the facilities necessary to accommodate tourists. In the process of touristification, it is not only the landscape and the local colour but also the cultural traditions of a society, and the distinctive markers by which its members acknowledge their being part of it, which are being severed from their context, serialized and combined with a view to composing a tourist product. As soon as a society offers itself for sale on a market, as soon as it attempts to enhance its appeal to the eyes of foreign visitors, it is the very consciousness that society has of itself which is being affected. Thus the native populations are not passive objects of the tourist gaze, but active subjects who construct representations of their culture to attract tourists. Therefore, behind the commonly stressed risks entailed by the commercialization of culture, one should pay attention to what is at stake with the new meaning a culture acquires for its bearers by being promoted as a tourist attraction. In other words, to the extent that it alters the view that a society takes of itself, tourism reveals the way the native population relates to its memories, to its traditions, to its values – in short, to its identity.

As to Balinese culture, my point is that it was neither destroyed nor revived – nor even simply preserved – by tourism. This is because tourism cannot be conceived of outside culture at all: it is inevitably bound up in an ongoing process of cultural invention. In other words, I contend that tourism should be viewed as an integral part of Balinese culture.

Consequently, instead of asking whether or not Balinese culture has been able to withstand the impact of tourism, I shall investigate here why it is that Balinese culture inspires such concern in Westerners, Indonesians and Balinese alike. This I shall attempt mostly by submitting to a discourse analysis what various sources – from Bali as well as from abroad – say about Balinese culture when they speak of tourism. And rather than focus on the commercialization of culture, as in impact studies, I shall pay attention to the dialogic process through which culture has become Bali's defining feature.

The living museum

If today Bali is internationally renowned as a tourist paradise, it is not due solely to the charm of the Balinese or the beauty of their island, or even to the extravagance of their ceremonial pageants. What appears nowadays to be the *touristic vocation* of Bali is the result of deliberate decisions not originally made by the Balinese themselves but made by others beyond their shores.

When the island of Bali was finally subjected and incorporated into the Netherlands Indies in 1908, it had already long been viewed by Dutch orientalists as a 'living museum' of the Hindu-Javanese civilization, the one and only surviving heir to the Hindu heritage swept away from Java by the coming of Islam. This view also prevailed within government circles, with the result that the enlightened colonial policy designed for the island was to preserve the Balinese cultural heritage. In fact, the island of Bali not only had to be rescued from the onslaught of modernization, but furthermore its inhabitants had to be taught by their new lords how to remain authentically Balinese: such was the aim of the cultural policy known as the 'Balinization of Bali' (*Balisering*). Once restored to its pristine splendour, Balinese culture could then be presented to the appreciation of the outside world.[7]

Tourism in Bali took off in 1924, with the launching of a weekly steamship service connecting the island with Batavia, Surabaya and Makassar. After the opening of the Bali Hotel in 1928, the number of visitors increased steadily from a few hundreds to several thousands a year before the war. Among these visitors, special mention should be made of the small party of foreign artists and connoisseurs who established the reputation of Bali. The accounts, paintings, photographs and films which recorded their sojourn on the island contributed to forging a sensational image of native life, an image which would be relayed in due time through the promotional services of the nascent tourist industry. And indeed, the island of Bali has consistently been described ever since as the Island of the Gods, as the homeland of a traditional culture insulated from the modern world and its vicissitudes, whose bearers, endowed with exceptional artistic talents, devote an out-standing amount of time and wealth to staging sumptuous ceremonies for their own pleasure and that of their gods . . . and now in addition for the delight of the tourists.[8]

After the artists came the anthropologists who – like the tourists at that time – were mostly American and belonged to the 'culture and personality' school.[9] Their studies comforted the Dutch colonial policy of cultural preservation while providing academic credit to the image of serene harmony bestowed on Bali by the artists. Reading them, one gathers that the Balinese were too busy performing their culture to bother with the presence of a foreign administration. And indeed, once the matters of government had been appropriated by the Dutch, the Balinese were left with not much else to do but to cultivate their arts and celebrate their religious festivals, further elaborating their expressive culture.

Despite the Dutch government's claim to preserve Balinese culture, the colonial occupation of the island provoked the dis-integration of its traditional order, while the requirements of a modern administration prompted the formation of an indigenous intelligentsia, which mediated between the Balinese population and its foreign masters. On the one hand, Balinese intellectuals started questioning themselves about the relationship between religion, art and social order, with the aim of bringing to light the foundations of their cultural identity; whereas on the other hand, they were in the novel position of needing to explain what it meant to be Balinese in terms comprehensible by non-Balinese.

Thus it is that *culture* – in the case in point, mostly narrowed down to artistic and ceremonial manifestations – became Bali's defining feature, providing the common ground on which Dutch orientalists and American anthropologists, artists and tourists could encounter each other and the Balinese.

No sooner had culture become the emblematic image of Bali than foreigners started fearing for its oncoming disappearance. Indeed, when one reads the accounts of inter-war Bali, one realizes how firmly their authors were convinced of witnessing the swan-song of a traditional culture miraculously preserved from the contagious corruption of modernity. In fact, since the 'discovery' of the island by an avant-garde of artists and anthropologists, it is as if the mere evocation of Bali suggested the imminent and dramatic fall from the *Garden of Eden*:[10] sooner or later, the *Last Paradise*[11] was doomed to become *Paradise Lost*. And one could surmise that the appeal exerted by the island of Bali over its visitors rested to a large extent on the premonition of the impending demise of its culture.

Among the perils seen to be threatening Balinese culture, the most conspicuous was none other than the coming of tourists themselves. Hence the ambivalent attitude evinced by the colonial authorities with respect to tourism. On the one hand, Balinese culture was the major asset for the tourist promotion of the island. On the other hand, if the cultural heritage of Bali was to be preserved, measures had to be taken to protect it from the corruptive contact with the modern world through the presence of foreign visitors to the island.

The war spared the colonial government the necessity of defining a consistent tourist policy for Bali. After Indonesia's independence, tourism on the island remained very limited, visitors being dissuaded by the rudimentary state of the infrastructures together with the political turmoil and the xenophobic orientation of the regime that marked the period. Yet, President Sukarno made Bali – now a province of the Republic of Indonesia – a showplace for state guests. Eager to use the fame of the island to attract foreign tourists, he undertook the construction of an international airport and had a luxury hotel built on the beach. The Bali Beach Hotel was completed in 1966 just when Indonesia closed its doors to foreigners, following the mass killings of 30 September 1965.

Only after the 'new order' regime installed by President Suharto began opening Indonesia to the West would tourists start coming back to Bali in significant numbers. More precisely, one can date the launching of mass tourism in Bali from 1969, the year of the inauguration of the international airport.

The master plan for the development of tourism in Bali

Earlier that year, the first five-year development plan had stressed the importance of international tourism as a factor of economic development for Indonesia – and more specifically, as a means to curb the ruinous deficit of the country's balance of payments – while laying the foundations of a national tourism policy. Banking on Bali's prestigious image as a tourist paradise, the government decided to make this island the showcase of Indonesia as an international tourist destination. Furthermore, Bali was to serve as a model for future development of tourism in the archipelago.

Following the advice of the World Bank, the Indonesian government commissioned a team of French experts to draw up a master plan for the development of tourism in Bali. Their report, published in 1971 and revised in 1974 by the World Bank, proposed to confine the bulk of the tourists to a luxury beach enclave, while providing for a network of excursion routes linking the new resort with major attractions on the island.[12]

Now, why should tourists be confined to an enclave? According to the market study on which the master plan was based, these tourists were expected to be wealthy Westerners touring Bali with the idea of vacationing a few days on the beach. Yet, for prospective visitors Bali was not just another tropical island with beaches and white sand bordered by palm trees; it was the Island of the Gods, a place teeming with temples and ceremonies, vibrating with music and dance. But if they expected to find in Bali a traditional culture preserved until now from the undermining attacks of modernity, the tourists themselves were active carriers of this modernity spreading across the planet, so that their presence might well smother what they strove to embrace. Therefore the problem faced by the French consultants was to develop tourism in Bali without damaging Balinese culture. Consequently, by keeping the tourists well away from Balinese residential areas, they tried to shield Balinese culture as much as possible from the frontal shock of tourism.

The rationale underlying the master plan was thus to warrant a sustainable development of tourism on Bali by ensuring the preservation of the resources upon which its success was seen to depend: primarily, the cultural traditions which had made the island famous the world over.

With the official promulgation of the master plan by presidential decision, tourism ranked second only to agriculture in economic priority in the province. Meanwhile the number of tourists multiplied from fewer than 30,000 in the late 1960s to over one million in the early 1990s; this did not take into account the growing numbers of Indonesian tourists visiting Bali, for whom there are no statistics available. During the same period, hotel capacity increased from fewer than 500 to about 30,000 rooms. As for the Balinese themselves, they are approaching three million on an island which is only 5,600 km^2 in area.

While for the last two decades tourism has been the most visible factor of economic growth in Bali, its actual contribution to the regional economy is difficult to assess accurately. Most experts tend to agree that tourism has conferred considerable financial gains on Bali, even though their uneven distribution within the population and throughout the island, as well as the growing encroachment of foreign interests, remain a matter of concern. On the other hand, the Balinese authorities appear to display an ambivalent attitude towards the implications of tourism for their society and culture.[13]

Cultural tourism

To tell the truth, the Balinese authorities did not actually have any say in the decision of the central government to trade in their island's charms in order to refill the state coffers; nor had they been consulted about the master plan. Behind a façade of official assent, the plan advocated by French consultants, finalized by World Bank experts, and imposed by Jakarta technocrats gave rise to undisguised criticism in Bali. For its Balinese detractors, the master plan might be a plan for the development of tourism, but it clearly was not a plan for the development of Bali: witness the fact that it was based on a market study of tourist arrivals in Bali and not on an assessment of the development needs of the island.

Faced with a *fait accompli*, the Balinese authorities attempted to appropriate tourism in order to use its benefits as a tool for regional development, while taking advantage of the fame it was bringing to their island to further their position within the Indonesian nation. In response to the master plan, they proclaimed their own conception of the kind of tourism they deemed the most suitable to their island – namely what they termed 'cultural tourism' (*Pariwisata Budaya*).[14] This conception was formulated in 1971, a few months after the publication of the master plan, when the Governor convened a Seminar on Cultural Tourism in Bali, under the joint aegis of the provincial agencies for tourism, religion, culture and education.[15]

The proceedings of the seminar reveal that the Balinese perceived tourism as being at once fraught with danger and filled with the promises of forthcoming prosperity. On the one hand, the artistic and religious traditions which had made the name of Bali famous the world over provided its main attraction as a tourist destination, thus turning Balinese culture into the most valuable 'resource' for the island's economic development. But on the other hand, the invasion of Bali by foreign visitors originating from different horizons was seen as a threat of 'cultural pollution'. Accordingly, the Balinese regarded tourism as a 'challenge' to be taken up with caution: 'How to develop tourism without debasing Balinese culture?' Such was the task assigned to cultural tourism: to take advantage of Balinese culture to attract tourists, while using the economic benefits of tourism to foster Balinese culture.

Thus one sees that, from the 1930s to the 1970s, the problem facing the authorities in charge of designing a tourist policy for Bali -- the Dutch colonial administration, the French consultants, the World Bank experts, the Balinese government – has been defined in terms of a *dilemma*: tourism relies on culture, but tourism is a threat to culture. Yet the solution favoured by the Balinese differs significantly from the one adopted by their foreign predecessors: instead of trying to keep the tourists at bay, they welcome them.

The rationale underlying this choice is that, in order for tourism to contribute to the development of Bali, the local population must be in a position to participate in the tourist trade and reap its benefits, which in turn implies that the tourists must be allowed to spread and spend their money throughout the island. But this presupposes that the threat hanging over culture owing to tourism should be removed, as the whole idea of cultural tourism rests on the claim that the interests of Balinese culture must concur, in the long run, with those of the tourist industry.

Moreover, the Balinese appear to be genuinely proud of the fame of their culture abroad, and are eager to show their cultural traditions at their best to the tourists. In this respect, they link the success of tourism to the state of their culture -- and thus bind their culture to tourism – to a larger extent than did the master plan.[16] By so doing, they turn to their own advantage Jakarta's decision to promote their island as an international tourist destination in order to acquire hard currency. Indeed, as tourism makes their culture the main economic resource of their island, by the same token it is their main bargaining asset *vis-à-vis* the Indonesian government. Clearly, should the touristic exploitation depreciate Balinese culture, it would diminish the appeal of Bali as a tourist paradise. Thus, not only would the tourist industry have ruined Balinese culture, but it would have sown the seeds of its own destruction as a result. Accordingly – so the Balinese say – once the central government has chosen Bali as the main tourist destination in Indonesia, it is in its own interest, as well as in the interest of the tourist industry, to preserve and promote Balinese culture.

Now, the problem remains that the provincial government has no legal authority to conduct its own tourist policy. Under these conditions, it is not really surprising that, instead of the concrete measures one might have expected, the doctrine of cultural tourism led to a confusing profusion of discourses while arousing impressive fervour in Balinese public opinion. But one should beware of dismissing all this enthusiasm as mere verbal gesticulation, as but an implicit admission of helplessness on the part of the Balinese authorities.[17] For, by defining Balinese cultural identity in reference to the 'challenge' of tourism, these discourses strengthen the social links that bind the Balinese people together in defence of their culture, while their authors can pretend they are actually speaking in the name of Bali.

Promotion of culture and development of tourism

The Balinese doctrine of cultural tourism was elaborated and propagated throughout the 1970s by a series of surveys and seminars dealing with the development of tourism and its consequences on Balinese society and culture.

In 1972, a research programme was launched by the University of Bali in order to assess the 'sociological impact' of tourism. Six reports were published between 1973 and 1978, with results revealing not so much the actual implications of tourism for the Balinese as their perception generally shared among the intelligentsia.[18]

As Indonesian academics, the authors of the reports rationalize the exploitation of the bountiful cultural 'resources' of their island for the purpose of developing tourism, in as much as it is officially recognized to be of benefit to Indonesia. But as native Balinese, they cannot but be disturbed at the thought that the most intimate expressions of their culture are being listed in the catalogues of tour operators, together with hotel services and tariffs. One could surmise that they would rather not have to acknowledge the fact that they are compelled to assess the worth of their culture according to its monetary value, thus to make commensurable that which is not. Whereas for the foreign experts it was only a matter of cautious management of resources, for the Balinese it is an axiological upheaval which strikes them at the very core of their identity.

Nonetheless, they recognize that cultural tourism is basically a trade-off between cultural values and economic values. Even though they do not actually carry out a formal cost–benefit analysis, the balance sheet of their research shows that, by and large, they consider the economic impact as *positive*, whereas the cultural impact is on the whole *negative*. More specifically, they condemn tourism as 'polluting' Balinese culture, a pollution whose symptoms they see everywhere, be it the profanation of temples and the desecration of religious ceremonies, the monetization of social relations and the weakening of communal solidarity, or the slackening of moral standards which results from the pervading mercantilism. For them, it is as if the price the Balinese have to pay in order to raise their 'standard of living' was the violation of their 'rules of life' – a painful dilemma indeed.

How could the Balinese acquire economic values without losing their cultural values? How could they improve their standard of living without contravening their rules of life? In other words, how could they maximize the economic benefits of tourism while minimizing its cultural costs? Such was the issue discussed at no fewer than five seminars held between 1977 and 1979, some convened by the Directorate General of Tourism alone, others jointly with the Directorate General of Culture.

From the proceedings of these seminars, it emerges that the solution of cultural tourism consists in promoting culture and tourism simultaneously, so as to ensure that the development of tourism results in a reciprocal development of culture. This is clearly illustrated by the title of the seminars organized by the Directorate General of Culture and the Directorate General of Tourism: 'Promotion of Culture and Development of Tourism' (Pembinaan Kebudayaan dan Pengembangan Kepariwisataan).[19] Consequently, to make sure that the interests of culture do concur with those of tourism, the cultural and the tourist policies were coordinated by a Commission of Cooperation for the Promotion and Development of Cultural Tourism, jointly created in 1979 by the Director General of Culture and the Director General of Tourism. The objectives of this commission were defined as follows: 'To increase and extend the use of cultural objects for the development of tourism, and to use the proceeds of tourism development for the promotion and the development of culture.'[20]

Since the agreement defining the respective roles of culture and tourism was signed, the enthusiasm initially aroused in Bali by the motto of 'cultural tourism' has waned, while the surveys and seminars on tourism have been few and far between. Not that the concern for tourism among the Balinese has diminished, far from it, but tourism has become part of their cultural landscape. In fact, the Balinese nowadays appear more interested in making the most of their culture in the interest of tourism rather than attempting to assess the impact of tourism on their culture.[21] At the same time, the fears originally raised by the coming of the tourists have given way to a public expression of satisfaction. Indeed, the reversal of opinion regarding the consequences attributed to tourism is spectacular: formerly accused of being a cause of cultural pollution, tourism is now extolled as an agent of the cultural renaissance of Bali. As for justification to back this favourable reappraisal of tourism, one finds continually asserted in the media that tourist money has revived the Balinese interest in their artistic traditions, while the admiration of foreign visitors for their culture has reinforced the Balinese sense of identity.

If one relies on Balinese public opinion, one might surmise that, after an initial period of adjustment during which the rapid spread of tourists on the island would naturally arouse legitimate fears, cultural tourism has achieved its mission successfully. Yet, before rejoicing with the Balinese, one should elucidate what has become of Balinese culture in the discourse of cultural tourism.[22]

Balinese culture: cultural heritage and tourist capital

In less than a decade, between 1971 and 1979, the doctrine of cultural tourism succeeded in merging the promotion of culture with the development of tourism, to the point of entrusting the fate of Balinese culture to the interested care of the tourist industry. By the same token, it managed to reconcile the interests of their respective spokesmen. But for this to happen, the opposition between tourism and culture – which had given rise to the doctrine of cultural tourism in the first place – had to be denied. This was achieved by splitting Balinese culture into two distinct conceptions: whereas before the advent of tourism their culture was for the Balinese a 'heritage' which they had to preserve, it now became, in addition, a 'capital' which they could exploit for profit.

In the discourse of cultural tourism, Balinese culture is invariably defined by referring to three concomitant components:

It has its roots in the Hindu religion.
It permeates the customs of the Balinese community and inspires its traditional institutions.
It is embodied in artistic forms of great beauty.

Thus defined by the interweaving of religion (*agama*), custom (*adat*) and art (*seni*), culture (*kebudayaan*) is presented as the distinctive marker (*ciri khas*) of Balinese identity (*identitas Bali*). In this respect, their culture represents for the Balinese a heritage handed down by their ancestors, and should be considered as a cultural value (*nilai budaya*). Moreover, given the religious character of their cultural heritage (*warisan kebudayaan*), it is admittedly difficult for the Balinese to distinguish that which belongs to religion from that which pertains to custom, and, therefore, to differentiate clearly between the sacred and the profane.

With the coming of tourists, their culture is no longer the exclusive property of the Balinese alone, since it has become the main attraction of their island in the eyes of its visitors. And it is precisely its unique blending of religion, custom and art which represents the trademark (*citra*) of Bali, that which confers on its tourist product a decisive superiority in the competition with other destinations in the area. So much so that, because of its appeal to tourists, their culture has become for the Balinese their main capital, that is, an economic value (*nilai ekonomi*). Now, as a tourist capital (*modal pariwisata*), the Balinese culture is so entangled with tourism that it has become difficult to separate that which belongs to culture from that which pertains to tourism.

By viewing their culture as capital, the Balinese blurred the initial opposition between tourism and culture, between economic values and cultural values. This in turn resulted in reversing the professed relationship between tourism and culture: the warning that obedience to the rules of custom and religion should not be sacrificed to the interests of the tourist industry notwithstanding, it plainly appears that if the provincial government exhorts the Balinese to take good care of their culture, it is to the extent that the economic value of the tourist capital of Bali depends on the cultural value of its cultural heritage: in short, to attract more and more tourists.

But one must push the argument further and ask whether the Balinese view of their culture as a heritage – presented by them as being its original state, going back to before the coming of the tourists – is not in fact the sign that it has already been converted into a capital. For, all available evidence points to the fact that it is only once it had been enlisted as a tourist asset, available for profitable financial transactions, that the Balinese started regarding their culture as an heirloom to be carefully preserved and nurtured. Accordingly, one suspects that the alleged primordial unity of religion, custom and art, in terms of which the Balinese nowadays readily define their culture, far from expressing the intrinsic substance of their identity, is the outcome of a process of semantic borrowing and conceptual adjustment which they had to make as a result of the opening up of their social space to the outside world – via the colonization, the Indonesianization and the touristification of their island.

Boundary maintenance

Now that their culture has become the prime resource of their island, the problem for the Balinese is to decide how far they are actually willing to turn their cultural heritage into a tourist capital, or in other words, to what extent their cultural values may be assessed according to their economic value. Indeed, failing to know their cultural boundaries, what is theirs and what is not, the

Balinese incur the risk of no longer being able to differentiate between their own values and those brought in by the foreign visitors. Such a result would turn Balinese culture into what the Balinese authorities themselves call a tourist culture (*kebudayaan pariwisata*) – that is, a state characterized by an axiological confusion between what belongs to culture and what pertains to tourism.

This is in fact the crux of the matter: is there a clear demarcation line for the Balinese between what they do for themselves and what they do for their visitors, between that which belongs to culture and that which pertains to tourism? As we recall, for Willard Hanna, Balinese culture was becoming a tourist commodity to the extent that the Balinese were mistaking the commercial attractions they present to the tourists for their genuine cultural traditions. And it was on this point precisely that Philip McKean opposed Hanna's conclusions.

He maintained that, far from destroying Balinese culture, tourism was in fact revitalizing it, a conviction based on one of the most deeply rooted assumptions about Balinese culture – its dynamic resilience. Indeed, the Balinese have long been celebrated for knowing their cultural boundaries, and they are praised for their ability to borrow whatever foreign influence suits them while nevertheless maintaining their identity over the centuries. Accordingly, McKean claimed that the Balinese are coping with the tourist invasion of their island as well as they have coped with others in the past – that is, they are taking advantage of the appeal of their cultural traditions to foreign visitors without sacrificing their own values on the altar of monetary profit. And he stated that tourism has reinforced among the Balinese a sense of *boundary maintenance* between what they do for themselves and what they do for their visitors.[23]

This conclusion has been elaborated further by Raymond Noronha, the World Bank's cultural adviser to the Bali Tourism Development Board. 'Why is it that tourism has not destroyed Balinese culture?', asked Noronha. In his opinion, it is because the Balinese have learnt to distinguish their cultural performances according to the audience for whom they are intended, with the consequence that the meaning of a Balinese cultural performance is not affected by its being performed for a tourist audience.[24]

Following the lead of McKean and Noronha, the Swiss sociologist Jean-Luc Maurer devised four criteria to assess the socio-cultural impact of tourism on a host society, among which is what he called its 'degree of cultural functionality', that is the ability to differentiate between the sacred and the profane, between what can eventually be commercialized and what must absolutely not be affected by commercial relations. And when it came to applying this criterion to Balinese society, he discerned the emergence of two distinct and juxtaposed spheres of cultural production, one reserved for internal consumption, the other producing for external consumption. From which he concluded: 'the Balinese know perfectly well where to draw a clear line between the sacred and the profane; between what can be sold and what must be protected at all costs.'[25] Interestingly enough, a decade later, in a reassessment of the socio-cultural impact of tourism on Bali published in 1988, Maurer observes that according to the criteria of internal cohesion, cultural creativity and social solidarity, Balinese society is now threatened by social dysfunction. However, he still contends that 'if there is one criterion that Balinese society appears to have maintained intact, it is the distinction between sacred and profane.'[26]

The sacred and the profane

As a matter of fact, the provincial government has been acutely conscious of the danger of axiological confusion entailed by the commercialization of Balinese culture, and it has endeavoured to provide the local population with specific instructions concerning what they may and what they must not sell on the tourist market. This concern is reflected in the numerous warnings regarding the misuse of traditional symbols and artefacts as decoration for hotels, restaurants and shops, as well as the turning of cremations into tourist attractions. But the topic which has received the most extensive publicity in Bali is certainly the attempt at enforcing the distinction between the sacred and the profane in relation to dance performances.

As one should know, the celebrated dances which have contributed so much to the fame of Bali abroad are not merely a *spectacle* to be watched but also a *ritual* to be enacted. Indeed, dance in Bali is not intended only for human audiences, because present among the spectators are the ancestors, the gods and the demons, who share with the Balinese a keen taste for lively festivals and fine performances. In this respect, Balinese dance is at once an offering to the gods and an entertainment for the people.

As long as their dances were reserved for their own use, there was no need for the Balinese to know where ritual ended and where spectacle began. But when ritual dances were turned into hotel floor shows, the provincial government was faced with the necessity of drawing a demarcating line between religious ceremonies and the commercial attractions which were being derived from them. This was attempted as early as 1971, when the Balinese cultural authorities convened a Seminar on Sacred and Profane Dance.[27] The aim of this seminar was to work out criteria to separate 'sacred art' from 'profane art', in order to distinguish between the dances which might be commercialized for the tourist market and those which should not. This proved to be a very delicate task, judging by the confusion of the participants, a select group of Balinese officials and academics requested to write a paper on that topic. Their embarrassment was not really surprising, bearing in mind that the Balinese language does not have at its disposal the terminology which would permit its speakers to articulate the opposition between the sacred and the profane. In fact, as in any official meeting, the seminar was conducted in Indonesian, a language which also has no terms for 'sacred' and 'profane'. Consequently, the organizers had to resort to neologisms borrowed from Latin languages for the very wording of the problem at hand.

This semantic borrowing resulted in uneasy attempts to create a distinction which was in fact alien to the Balinese. Small wonder, then, that several participants, unable to understand the proposed terms of reference, decided to look for further clarification in their Dutch dictionary, which in turn led them to commit a revealing misinterpretation. Instead of conceiving the problem they had to solve as a matter of discriminating between two domains which had hitherto been left undifferentiated, these Balinese started elaborating about sacred and profane dances as one all-encompassing category, thus conferring the attributes of the sacred and of the profane on the very same dances!

These conceptual difficulties notwithstanding, the Governor of Bali issued a decree prohibiting the performance of sacred dances for tourist audiences. But the fact is that this decree was never really enforced for the obvious reason that it did not make sense to the Balinese – certainly not, in any case, to the performers themselves. The observation of those tourist performances which, building on the fascination of foreigners for possession trance, deliberately exploit the dramatic character of ancient rites of exorcism, clearly confirms this, by demonstrating the difficulty encountered by the Balinese in distinguishing between the ritual and spectacular dimensions of a performance, however commercial its purpose might appear.[28]

In any case, some years later the Balinese authorities had come to a different perception of the problem. Witness the position adopted by one of the former participants of the 1971 seminar, who stated at a conference on Balinese culture in 1985 that the sacred dances were threatened by imminent extinction, as a number of them were no longer performed in the context of religious ceremonies. Accordingly, he proposed that these dances should be 'processed' to become a source of inspiration for the composition of new choreographies, some of which could then be used to renew the tourist performances, which are in real danger of losing their attractiveness by becoming a mere routine.[29]

Culture as trade mark and identity marker

The outcome of this investigation might appear to support Hanna's rather than McKean's position. But this is beside the point. What is significant is the fact that they both share a similar vision of culture. To the extent that they stress the necessity of boundary maintenance to prevent the risk of cultural commercialization, they are mainly concerned by what can be marketed and staged for tourists. Accordingly, in most discussions concerning Bali's cultural survival, 'culture' is not understood in its broad anthropological sense, but narrowed down to those aspects subject to aesthetic appreciation, namely artistic expressions. And this indeed is precisely what the Balinese authorities have in mind when they talk of cultural renaissance, that is, what they call cultural arts (*seni budaya*), in accordance with the slogan devised by the Directorate General of Tourism: 'Tourism preserves the nation's cultural arts.'

This is the price the Balinese have to pay in order for their culture to become a tourist attraction: what they offer must be comparable to and distinctive from what is being offered by other destinations which are competing with the island of Bali for tourist money. In this respect, the disjunction of Balinese culture between heritage and capital should be understood as much more than just a rhetorical artefact – as the evidence of an irreducible tension between two conceptions of culture. Indeed, the eagerness of the Balinese to preserve their cultural heritage is not only an admission of their intent to profit from their tourist capital, but above all an attempt to root their identity in their filiation, to recover the thread of a singular history handed down from their ancestors: in short to rescue their culture from a *typology* in order to tie it to a *genealogy*.[30]

It should be clear by now that tourism had neither polluted Balinese culture, nor brought about its renaissance, but rendered the Balinese self-conscious of their culture: thanks to tourism the Balinese realize they possess something valuable called 'culture'. And as it grew valuable in Balinese eyes, their culture became distant and concrete, turning into an object detachable from themselves, which could be represented and copied, marketed and exchanged, at will.

As a matter of fact, this cultural self-consciousness goes back to the time of the Netherlands Indies, with the opening up of the Balinese social space. As we have seen, if culture has become Bali's defining feature, it is to a large extent due to the orientalists', anthropologists, artists and other distinguished visitors from the past. This prestigious cultural image in turn led the Indonesian government to choose Bali as the prime tourist destination of Indonesia when it decided to develop international tourism in order to acquire badly needed foreign currency. The result was that culture became the interface between Bali and the outside world: Balinese culture is simultaneously the trade mark of Bali as a *tourist destination* – what the Balinese display as a label which distinguishes the product 'Bali' from other products sold on the tourist market – and the marker of Balinese *identity* – what the Balinese exhibit as the distinctive emblem of their Balineseness (*Kebalian*).[31]

The problem is that the Balinese are now prisoners of a cultural image promoted by the marketers of Bali as a tourist paradise. In as much as they are expected to display evidence of their Balineseness, the Balinese run the risk of becoming signs of themselves. For all their attempts to affirm their identity, they are for ever reacting to an injunction which they cannot elude, and so much so that they come to ratify the touristic vision of themselves even when they pretend to be beyond its grip. Such is the challenge of tourism for the Balinese, a challenge which is not unlike a paradoxical injunction.[32]

I shall conclude with a revealing anecdote. A few years ago, the *Bali Post* – the leading daily newspaper in Bali – published an article entitled 'The Balinese are losing their Balineseness'. The author declared that, carried away by the admiration they saw in the tourist gaze, the Balinese turned a blind eye to the painful fact that the authenticity of their cultural identity was seriously impaired. This accusation did not go unnoticed on the island. A poll was conducted among the readers of the newspaper, from which it emerged that while 40 per cent of the answers imputed to tourism a demise of Balineseness, the remaining 60 per cent thought on the contrary that the growing numbers of tourists coming every year to Bali was the most convincing proof to the enduring authenticity of the Balinese cultural identity.

(Translated by Michel Picard and Kunang Helmi.)

Notes

This chapter is based on observations gathered during numerous trips to Bali since 1974, and more precisely on research undertaken in the island during 1981 and 1982. The field work was accomplished under the auspices of the Lembaga Ilmu Pengetahuan Indonesia and benefited from the institutional patronage of Professor Dr I. Gusti Ngurah Bagus, Head of the Department of Anthropology at the Universitas Udayana. Besides Professor Bagus, I would like to thank my colleagues in the Unité de Recherche en Sociologie du Tourisme International of the Centre National de la Recherche Scientifique – Marie-Françoise Lanfant, Claude-Marie Bazin and Jacques de Weerdt – for helping me elaborate the theoretical framework which structured my field work. I would also like to thank Kunang Helmi and Vivienne Roberts for their assistance in conveying my French thoughts in English.

1 Hanna (1972: 1). For similar opinions, see Francillon (1990) and Turnbull (1982).

2 McKean (1973: 35). For similar opinions, see Lansing (1974: 46) and McTaggart (1980: 463–4).

3 For examples of the first opinion, see Cohen (1988: 382), Dogan (1989: 223–4), Macnaught (1982: 373–4), Travis (1984: 24), Turner and Ash (1975: 155–60) and others. For the second one, see Crandall (1987: 376), van Doorn (1989: 82), Greenwood (1977: 131), O'Grady (1981: 25–34), Pizam and Milman (1984: 12) and others.

4 Travis (1982: 257).

5 On the question of the socio-cultural impact of tourism and its implications, see Lanfant (1987) as well as Picard (1979; 1987).

6 This interpretation is not unlike that of Robert Wood, who writes of 'a billiard ball model, in which a moving object (tourism) acts upon an inert one (culture)' (1980: 565).

7 This is but an over-simplification of a highly complex and poorly documented history. For a survey of the Dutch colonial policy on Bali, see Schulte Nordholt (1986).

8 Covarrubias (1987) is still to this day the most widely read book on the island of Bali. On the creation of the image of Bali as a tourist paradise, see Vickers (1989).

9 On the prevalent view of Bali among American anthropologists in the 1930s, see the collection of articles assembled in Belo (1970).

10 The title of a famous tourist brochure published in the 1930s.

11 The title of the first book written in English on Bali, published in New York in 1930 (Powell, 1986).

12 On the master plan, see IBRD/IDA (1974) and SCETO (1971).

13 This ambivalence is manifest in the survey on economic growth and tourism recently published by a pair of well-known Balinese economists, who came to the following conclusion: 'And whether the alleged negative socio-cultural effects of tourism are outweighed by its economic benefits is a question beyond the scope of this chapter' (Jayasuriya and Nehen, 1989: 347). Interestingly enough, in 1971 the SCETO consultants had asserted that 'the actual economic benefits of the operation will go to too small a minority to compensate for the social nuisances caused by the project' (1971, vol. 1: 17). This pessimistic statement was dismissed by the World Bank experts who appraised and revised the master plan in 1974: 'Assuming that the negative effects can be controlled, it is expected that the positive effects – in terms

of increased employment, incomes and foreign exchange earnings – will result in an overall impact which, on balance, is desirable' (IBRD/IDA, 1974: 25). What is significant here is not so much the fact that the World Bank experts disagreed with the SCETO consultants, but rather the basic agreement that they both share with the Balinese economists, that the assessment of the impact of tourism on a host society involves a trade-off between economic benefits and socio-cultural costs.

14 This semantic appropriation of tourism by the Balinese authorities in reaction to what had been imposed upon them by the Indonesian government was effected by resorting to an Indonesian frame of reference, first of all by means of an Indonesian – as opposed to a Balinese – terminology. Indeed, there are no words in Balinese for 'culture' or for 'tourism', whereas these words have entered Indonesian via Sanskrit.

15 See Seminar Pariwisata Budaya (1971).

16 Far more anyway than what is actually the case. As the authors of the master plan had rightly asserted, for the majority of tourists, who barely venture out of their beach resort, Bali is basically a tropical destination whose cultural image confers some extra glamour to their holiday, compared with, say, Hawaii or the Maldives. Thus the Balinese claim that tourists are really eager to discover the cultural wonders of their island is more an expression of wishful thinking – besides being an ideological stance of the utmost importance – than a statement of factual evidence.

17 Even, of course, if it is also that. Strictly speaking, there is no solution to a dilemma, as each of its terms leads to the same result, which appears at once undesirable and inescapable. The choice being impossible, the perception of a problem as a dilemma entails various escapist strategies, such as attempts to label the situation in order to symbolically control it. In this respect, the discourse of cultural tourism works as a 'magic' formula, by qualifying as Balinese a tourist policy largely controlled from outside the island. On this, see Picard (1990b).

18 For a circumstantial appraisal of these reports, see Francillon (1979).

19 The English translation cannot but imperfectly render the idea conveyed by the Indonesian terminology. The term *pembinaan* implies an intention, a concerted effort to shape, to build up and to promote a quality, which is not taken for granted but should be developed in a certain direction. On the contrary, the word *pengembangan* brings forth the idea of an opening up, or an organic growth analogous to a natural evolution, like a blossoming flower.

20 Proyek Sasana Budaya Jakarta (1979: 6).

21 The main seminar on tourism held in Bali during the 1980s is a case in point. Whereas the previous ones dealt with 'the promotion of culture and the development of tourism', the seminar organized by the provincial government in 1987 focused specifically on 'the promotion and development of tourism'. And the one and only paper dealing with culture, given by the Head of the Regional Service of Culture, was mostly devoted to specify what the Balinese culture should be in order to contribute more effectively to the development of tourism. See Pemerintah Daerah (1987).

22 One should find already a clue of what happened in the vocabulary used by the Balinese authorities. Even though the doctrine of 'cultural tourism' was phrased in the national language, when speaking of 'cultural pollution' the Balinese frequently resorted to a vernacular terminology, whereas the slogan 'cultural renaissance' is generally voiced in English. This double switch of language, first from Balinese to Indonesian – with the use of Balinese terms to express key cultural

concepts – and then the changeover to English, is a sign of a revealing shift of identity, pointing to the fact that Bali has become more and more integrated within the Indonesian state as well as within the international tourist market.

23 Originating in the work of Fredrik Barth, the notion of 'boundary maintenance' was later to be taken up in numerous studies dealing with the impact of tourism on indigenous cultures. In these studies, the capacity of a local population to maintain a duality of meanings – that is, a cultural performance will continue to have a signification for the native people independent of the presence of tourists, and it would take place even in the absence of a foreign audience – has been elected as a criterion permitting their authors to assess the integrity of the culture under scrutiny.

24 Noronha (1979: 201–2).

25 Maurer (1979: 97).

26 Maurer and Ziegler (1988: 81).

27 Proyek Pemeliharaan dan Pengembangan Kebudayaan Daerah (1971).

28 See Picard (1990a) for a discussion of the problems raised by this seminar and the way they were handled.

29 Pandji (1985: 480–1).

30 On this question, see Lanfant and Graburn (1992).

31 'Balinese culture' is also the emblem which differentiates the province of Bali from the other provinces composing the Republic of Indonesia. So much so that, strictly speaking, the touristification of Bali cannot be considered apart from its Indonesianization. On this, see Picard (1993).

32 The Balinese are not the only people to face such a challenge. Witness the studies implying that touristified peoples are beginning to question their own identity while tourists demand that they should present an authentic image of themselves. On this, see Bruner (1991), Errington and Gewertz (1989), MacCannell (1984) and others.

References

Belo, J. (ed.) (1970) *Traditional Balinese Culture*. New York: Columbia University Press.

Bruner, E.M. (1991) 'Transformation of self in tourism', *Annals of Tourism Research*, 18(2): 238–50.

Cohen, E. (1988) 'Authenticity and commoditization in tourism', *Annals of Tourism Research*, 15(3): 371–86.

Covarrubias, M. (1987) *Island of Bali* (1937). Singapore: Oxford University Press.

Crandall, L. (1987) 'The social impact of tourism on developing regions and its measurement', in J.R.B. Ritchie and C.R. Goeldner (eds), *Travel, Tourism and Hospitality Research: a Handbook for Managers and Researchers*. New York: Wiley. pp. 373–83.

Dogan, H.Z. (1989) 'Forms of adjustment: sociocultural impacts of tourism', *Annals of Tourism Research*, 16(2): 216–36.

Errington, F. and Gewertz, D. (1989) 'Tourism and anthropology in a post-modern world', *Oceania*, 60(1): 37–54.

Francillon, G. (1979) *Bali: Tourism, Culture, Environment* (1975). Paris: UNESCO (1975).

Francillon, G. (1990) 'The dilemma of tourism in Bali', in W. Beller, P. d'Ayala and P. Hein (eds), *Sustainable Development and Environmental Management of Small Islands*. Paris: UNESCO, MAB Series. pp. 267–72.

Greenwood, D.J. (1977) 'Culture by the pound: an anthropological perspective on tourism as cultural commoditization', in V.L. Smith (ed.), *Hosts and Guests*. Philadelphia: University of Pennsylvania Press. pp. 129–38.

Hanna, W.A. (1972) 'Bali in the seventies. Part I: Cultural tourism', *American Universities Field Staff Reports*. Southeast Asia Series, 20(2): 1–7.

IBRD/IDA (1974) *Bali Tourism Project: Appraisal Report*. Washington: Tourism Projects Department.

Jafari, J. (1984) 'Unbounded ethnicity: the tourist network and its satellites', *Revue de Tourisme*, 3: 4–21.

Jayasuriya, S. and Nehen, K. (1989) 'Bali: economic growth and tourism', in H. Hill (ed.), *Unity and Diversity: Regional Economic Development in Indonesia since 1970*. Singapore: Oxford University Press. pp. 330–48.

Lanfant, M.-F. (1987) 'Présentation de la table ronde internationale sur "l'impact social et culturel du tourisme international" en question: réponses inter-disciplinaires', *Problems of Tourism*, 19(2): 3–20.

Lanfant, M.-F. and Graburn, N.H.H. (1992) 'International tourism reconsidered: the principle of the alternative', in V.L. Smith and W.R. Eadington (eds), *Tourism Alternatives: Potentials and Problems in the Development of Tourism*. Philadelphia: University of Pennsylvania Press. pp. 88–112.

Lansing, J.S. (1974) *Evil in the Morning of the World: Phenomenological Approaches to a Balinese Community*. Ann Arbor: The University of Michigan Center for South and Southeast Asian Studies.

MacCannell, D. (1984) 'Reconstructed ethnicity: tourism and cultural identity in Third World communities', *Annals of Tourism Research*, 11(3): 388–9.

Macnaught, T.J. (1982) 'Mass tourism and the dilemmas of modernization in Pacific island communities', *Annals of Tourism Research*, 9(3): 359–81.

Maurer, J.L. (1979) *Tourism and Development in a Socio-Cultural Perspective: Indonesia as a Case Study*. Geneva: Institut Universitaire d'Etudes du Développement.

Maurer, J.L. and Ziegler, A. (1988) 'Tourism and Indonesian cultural minorities', in P. Rossel (ed.), *Tourism: Manufacturing the Exotic*. Copenhagen: International Workgroup for Indigenous Affairs. pp. 64–92.

McKean, P.F. (1973) 'Cultural involution: tourists, Balinese, and the process of modernization in an anthropological perspective'. PhD dissertation, Brown University.

McTaggart, W.D. (1980) 'Tourism and tradition in Bali', *World Development*, 8: 457–66.

Noronha, R. (1979) 'Paradise reviewed: tourism in Bali', in E. deKadt (ed.), *Tourism: Passport to Development?* New York: Oxford University Press. pp. 177–204.

O'Grady, R. (1981) *Third World Stopover: the Tourism Debate*. Geneva: World Council of Churches.

Pandji, G.B.N. (1985) 'Seni Wali di Bali dan perkembangannya' (Sacred art in Bali and its development), in *Laporan Pertemuan Ilmiah Kebudayaan Bali*. Denpasar: Proyek Penelitian dan Pengkajian Kebudayaan Bali. pp. 469–82.

Pemerintah Daerah (1987) *Laporan Seminar Pembinaan dan Pengembangan Pariwisata Menuju Tahun 2000 di Propinsi Bali* (Seminar on the Promotion and

66   *International Tourism*

Development of Tourism towards the Year 2000 in the Province of Bali). Denpasar: Pemerintah Daerah Tingkat I Bali.

Picard, M. (1979) *Sociétés et tourisme: réflexions pour la recherche et l'action*. Paris: UNESCO, Etablissements humains et environnement socio-culturel.

Picard, M. (1987) 'Du "tourisme culturel" à la "culture touristique"', *Problems of Tourism*, 10(2): 38–52.

Picard, M. (1990a) '"Cultural tourism" in Bali: cultural performances as tourist attraction', *Indonesia*, 49: 37–74.

Picard, M. (1990b) 'Kebalian Orang Bali: tourism and the uses of "Balinese culture" in new order Indonesia', *Review of Indonesian and Malaysian Affairs*, 24: 1–38.

Picard, M. (1993) '"Cultural tourism" in Bali: national integration and regional differentiation', in M. Hitchcock, V.T. King and M.J.G. Parnwell (eds), *Tourism in South-East Asia*. London: Routledge. pp. 71–98.

Pizam, A. and Milman, A. (1984) 'The social impacts of tourism', *Industry and Environment*, 7(1): 11–14.

Powell, H. (1986) *The Last Paradise* (1930). Singapore: Oxford University Press.

Proyek Pemeliharaan dan Pengembangan Kebudayaan Daerah (1971) *Seminar Seni Sacral dan Provan Bidang Tari* (Seminar on Sacred and Profane Dance). Denpasar.

Proyek Sasana Budaya Jakarta (1979) *Naskah Kerjasama Ditjen Kebudayaan dan Ditjen Pariwisata* (Memorandum of Cooperation between the Directorate General of Culture and the Directorate General of Tourism). Jakarta: Direktorat Jenderal Kebudayaan.

SCETO (1971) *Bali Tourism Study: Report to the Government of Indonesia*. Paris: UNDP/IBRD.

Schulte Nordholt, H. (1986) *Bali: Colonial Conceptions and Political Change, 1700–1940. From Shifting Hierarchies to 'Fixed Order'*. Rotterdam: Comparative Asian Studies Programme, Erasmus University.

Seminar Pariwisata Budaya (1971) *Hasil Keputusan Seminar Pariwisata Budaya Daerah Bali* (Seminar on Cultural Tourism in Bali). Denpasar.

Travis, A.S. (1982) 'Managing the environmental and cultural impacts of tourism and leisure development', *Tourism Management*, 3(4): 256–62.

Travis, A.S. (1984) 'Social and cultural aspects of tourism', *Industry and Environment*, 7(1): 22–4.

Turnbull, C. (1982) 'Bali's new gods', *Natural History*, 1: 26–32.

Turner, L. and Ash, J. (1975) *The Golden Hordes: International Tourism and the Pleasure Periphery*. London: Constable.

van Doorn, J.W.M. (1989) 'A critical assessment of socio-cultural impact studies of tourism in the Third World', in T.V. Singh, H.L. Theuns and F.M. Go (eds), *Towards Appropriate Tourism: the Case of Developing Countries*. Frankfurt: Peta Lang. pp. 71–91.

Vickers, A. (1989) *Bali: a Paradise Created*. Berkeley: Periplus.

Wood, R.E. (1980) 'International tourism and cultural change in Southeast Asia', *Economic Development and Cultural Change*, 28(3): 561–81.

3

Textiles, Memory and the Souvenir Industry in the Andes

Anath Ariel de Vidas

Translating the original French title of this essay into English deprives it of its pun (Ariel de Vidas, 1989). *Mémoire* is the human faculty to conserve past states of consciousness and those things associated with them. A *souvenir*, in the context of tourism, as in English, is something kept as a reminder of a place or event. In French, however, the two are synonymous; and the original title suggested a reciprocal movement between collective memory (linked to local cultural identity) embodied in the Andean textile tradition, and the contemporary commercialization of Andean textiles for tourism.

Case studies of traditional crafts destined for tourist and export markets commonly either bewail their simplification and the loss of their symbolic and functional value, or stress the subjection of indigenous groups to the external exigencies of the commercialization process. According to these views, tourism is frequently an agent of the degeneration of traditional crafts, and by extension of the cultural groups which make them. There is a reductive and Manichaean vision of the dichotomy between tradition and modernity. This chapter proposes, in contrast, that the present must be read in historical depth; and it explores the adaptation of a specific craft (Andean textile production) to the imperatives which issue from society outside its producer groups. There is an active and creative participation on the part of indigenous groups in the new opportunities introduced by tourism. This complementary dynamic of tradition and modernity, while it allows for externally imposed change, also permits the preservation of internal values, which persist not only in spite of but sometimes also because of the modernization process. Handicrafts can survive only when they are economically viable. Sold to tourists, they can sometimes serve to support social identity.

The concept of 'handicraft' (in Spanish: *artesanía*) is problematic; and there has been extensive discussion concerning its use especially in relation to tourism (Novelo, 1976; Graburn, 1976; van den Berghe, 1980; García Canclini, 1981; Meier, 1982; Lauer, 1982; Pietri-Lévy, 1989). In the context of this chapter, 'handicraft' is taken to refer to a specific form of production and employment which creates as its product an object which represents a social group. This object provides a material vehicle both for a certain symbolism, and for processes of domination and manipulation. In the modern world these objects are integrated into circuits of production, exchange and consumption which spread far beyond their indigenous milieu. In attempting to consider Andean handicraft textile production for tourism, therefore, this chapter has to address a multiplicity of its aspects: iconographic, economic, historical, technical, political, social and above all cultural.

The rise of contemporary handicraft production in the Andes is mainly due to the expansion of international tourism, in quest of art which is 'popular', 'native', 'rural', 'primitive', 'typical', and 'folk'. What does this search for the other and for elsewhere represent? What is its impact upon the craftsmen whose income depends upon the 'authenticity' of their products? What is it that is commercialized here? This chapter follows the contemporary evolution of a specific craft which has a particular place in the cultural patrimony of Andean societies, which relates it intimately to local identity. In doing so it discloses the relationships between indigenous groups and global society, and reveals tourism not merely as a disruptive new factor but also as one which makes for continuity within traditional society. We reject the idea of a 'golden age' of Andean societies which has degenerated because of tourist access, and propose instead that tourism, through its interest in textile craft, has become a factor in the revalorization of social identity (Cohen, 1988a; 1988b; Graburn, 1976; MacCannell, 1984).

Andean textile production in historical perspective

The first evidence of textiles in Andean societies dates back to the third millennium before our era. They have always been related inextricably to the ritual, symbolic and social aspects of everyday life. The complexity and high quality of pre-Columbian textiles suggest the existence of specialists in production, and a real textile industry which already coordinated economic resources in a division of labour (Gayton, 1978). Besides the everyday use of textiles for clothing, sacks or blankets, they also provided a pictorial form for myths and dogmas, and served as totemic, heraldic or political symbols and as markers of social position and ethnic identity. Murra (1975: 157) speaks of a veritable 'textile obsession' among the Incas, who not only introduced new textile forms but met their own needs through the imposition of a textile tribute on conquered peoples.

The range of textile uses in the Andes was vast, and even included bridges made of fibres which were suspended over ravines and which ensured communication throughout the pre-Columbian empires. Through the *quipus* (a means of recording in textiles, which provided an instrument for bookkeeping as well as a reminder of history and kinship) the empires were managed. Through the differentiation of garments portraying the relationship to Viraocha, the creator god, Andean textiles revealed the ethnic identity of the wearer, and these links are explicit in their *huacas* (mummified ancestors wrapped in fabrics).

This link between textiles and identity was reinforced by the order which enjoined each conquered nation to keep its distinctive cloth. Social status was marked by the *cumbi* and the *tocapus* – pictographic cloths denoting kinship and affinity. Daily sacrifices were made of ceremonial bundles of cloths (*qu'epis*) linked to memory, fertility and reproduction. For these societies without writing, textiles became the mediator between the past and the future, the world of the living and of the dead.

After the Spanish conquest in the sixteenth century the conquered ethnic groups (henceforth called 'Indians') were compelled to work in textile factories (*obrajes*) into which the pedal loom was introduced. These manufactures, which progressively integrated Andean textile production into the mercantile economy, were equal in importance to mining in the colonial economy. The system of textile tribute was continued by the new rulers. Once again, the relationship of self to other was defined through textiles.

The Spanish invasion destructured the old order not only through changes in techniques (the old belt loom fell into disuse as early as the sixteenth century), but also by introducing new motifs. New tapestries were made by the Indians for the Spanish, influenced by occidental fashion (Gisbert et al., 1987: 155).

The Andean populations always wove in response to two needs: the domestic and the external. Weaving for domestic needs persists today, in spite of modifications in its symbolic and technical character. Textiles are also produced for external demand, although in other forms particularly suited to the tourist market. The adaptation, adjustment and reintegration of textile production to the market economy is not a recent phenomenon in the Andes; neither is the appropriation of textile production by a dominant force. These are part of a continuous process which has varied according to its historical context. Tourism is only the contemporary form of ethnic domination and manipulation, and the influence which these exert upon indigenous identities, which already have a history of nearly 500 years.

The nineteenth century marked a transition in the textile relationships between indigenous communities and the dominant political power. The Indian became the purveyor of a raw material, alpaca wool, which was successfully integrated into the world market for natural fibres. This had become the basis of the economy of the Andean region by the beginning of the twentieth century. Its insertion into the international wool market, the monopolization of trade, and the absence of a significant internal market, however, diminished its benefits to the wool-producing peasants. Capitalistic penetration of all aspects of the national economies, including the various agrarian reforms, resulted in the impoverishment of peasant or Indian communities, massive emigration to urban centres and the need to find new sources of income as alternatives to agriculture. In recent decades tourism-oriented handicraft production has emerged as one such source.

Tourism and ethnic identity in the Andes

The notion of ethnicity, from the tourist's point of view, nourishes the Western quest for exoticism – for the other and the elsewhere. Unlike those destinations with tourist beaches, a visit to the Andean countries is not characterized by the 'four Ss' (sun, sea, sand and sex), and their landscapes are only promoted in a secondary way in their tourist literature. It is the indigenous populations and their cultures which supply the principal attractions for a trip to this area. In the words of a tourist brochure, Peru is 'a magical and mystical name that evokes the conquest, gold and opulence'. It is not the present that is offered as merchandise but the past; and if an 'Indian market' is presented it is not as a symbol of life and activity, but in order to underline its permanency and the immutability of its past (Fohr, 1981). The Indian is perceived as a 'prolonged Inca', or as a 'living extension of the ruins' (van den Berghe, 1980: 388). This is van den Berghe's 'cultural tourism' (p. 378); and, through this mediated image, handicraft production is offered to tourists by a group of 'noble savages', thereby acquiring its authentic value. The manual elaboration of the object by native peoples sets the seal of authenticity and originality upon the handicraft, and imparts to it a value comparable to the occidental art object, although at a much more accessible price.

The notion of ethnicity is nourished by middlemen and other agents in the name of different economic interests in the Andean multi-ethnic countries. One of these is the increasing foreign currency income from tourism purchases and the export of handicrafts. According to a study done in 1980 by SELA (Latin American Economic System) the annual value of handicraft imports from the Third World to developed countries had reached $1 billion, a tenth of which was accounted for by Latin American handicraft production (SELA, 1981). Promoting handicraft production is said to present a solution to rural employment problems in an area where land is scarce, without adding to urban over-population; to preserve domestic production without large investments; and to provide complementary income sources for agricultural families (Novelo, 1976).

The success of this kind of production is said to depend upon its 'ethnic' value, providing a warranty for the persisting expression of the artistic and technical skills of indigenous groups. The sublimation of the 'noble savage' places a bucolic, mystified and folkloric ethnic stamp upon commercial handicrafts. While representing the country's *folk* art, however, these are also seen as manifestations of *national* identity. In requiring the production of specific handicraft objects, or their modification with a view to their commercialization, the state thus promotes its own notion of indigenous culture, which emphasizes a pre-colonial past embodied in the motifs of these 'neo-pre-Hispanic crafts' rather than in contemporary poverty. The Indian is perceived as the representative of an immutable civilization that is untouched by the centuries of colonial and even pre-Hispanic domination.

Although this 'mercantile ethnicity' probably does have some influence on the craftsmen's feelings of social or cultural belonging, the textile producers themselves (who are involved willy-nilly in this looking-glass game) must be motivated to preserve (at least superficially) their 'ethnic' distinctiveness, as this imparts mercantile value to their handicraft production.

The ways in which ethnicity features in this specific inter-cultural encounter will vary, depending upon whether the indigenous population are in contact with the tourist market; whether the artisan is trapped by the cornering of the market for raw materials by middlemen; whether the artisan must accept the price fixed by the middleman for his work, or can accumulate and capitalize on his own production; and whether the craftsman is able to produce according to his own will and personal taste.

The exposition of the four case studies which follows does not pretend to provide a comprehensive analysis of the different forms which the commercial exploitation of textiles takes in the Andes. It reflects only some different Andean producers' strategies, related to the revitalization of ethnic identity, within the commercialization process. The active participation of producers enmeshed in this process is often overlooked by those who condemn the maleficent effects of tourism. They appear to consider indigenous societies as monolithic and one-dimensional. The case studies which follow, however, illustrate the complexity of the phenomenon. They hold in common the continuity of Andean textile production; adaptation to the imperatives of the market; and the preservation of a certain ethnic image.

The integration into the mercantile economy induced by tourism, often bewailed as the cause of a loss of tradition, can generate (under certain circumstances) a situation in which increased sales depend upon the investment of more 'Indianity', more 'authenticity', in the folk-art product, and perhaps by extension therefore more of oneself. The different meanings given to the ethnic image actuated by tourism-oriented handicraft production are hence in constant interplay, and exert a strong influence upon each other. The parameters within which the handicraft production of textiles is located go far beyond its mercantile value within a capitalist system, and relate social, cultural and ideological aspects of both interacting societies.

Otavalo: indigenous entrepreneurs

Perhaps the most well-known example of the commercialization of Andean textiles for the tourism market is that of the Otavaleno Indians of northern Ecuador. Otavalo is a market town (population 20,000) situated 111 km from the capital, Quito. It is surrounded by 75 Otavaleno communities whose 40,000 inhabitants combine agricultural work with commercial textile production. The Otavalo market, a 'must' in the circuit of every tourist to Ecuador, attracts each Saturday hundreds of foreign and Ecuadorian visitors, as well as other Indians. They come to buy ponchos, 'pre-Hispanic' woven belts, tapestries, blankets and other woollen objects. In addition to this market local textiles are marketed nationally and internationally, and several hundred Otavalenos are estimated to make a living from the promotion of their textiles in North and South America and in Europe.

Through weaving and the sale of textiles for tourism and for export, the Otavaleno people have integrated into a market economy while managing to preserve a degree of ethnic distinctiveness. Quechua is still their spoken language, and most of them still wear traditional dress. Above all, the men are characterized by their long braids. The relative prosperity of the Otavalenos, as a consequence of the commercialization of their textiles, has allowed them to invest in durable consumer goods, such as cars, and also capital goods such as trucks, buildings and especially land. It was the need to acquire land, giving a sense of belonging to the locality, which primarily drove their integration into the monetary economy. This has not resulted in a process of proletarianization, however, nor has it led to emigration from the community. This can be explained by the specific historical process which permitted the traditional production of textiles to be oriented towards a new objective.

The textile tradition in Otavalo dates back to pre-Hispanic times (the Cara civilization) and survived both the Inca and colonial periods. What began as the imposition of tribute in textiles, or work in the *obrajes*, thus eventually became a source of economic independence. Over the past 40 years, although dwindling under demographic and ecological pressures, the Otavalenos have taken advantage of tourism and introduced new products, materials, tools, modes of commercialization and designs. The latter include 'Inca' and 'Aztec' as well as occidental motifs. This continuous adaptation to the market has enabled them to turn their specific craft into an 'ethno-economic niche'. On the one hand they are not in direct competition with non-Indians: and on the other hand Otavaleno identity has been revalorized by external regard and economic success.

The community has undergone economic, social and cultural transformation, even so. The development of the textile sector has put an end to communal segmentation. Through the weekly market local communities have gained a sense of regional identity, which is reflected in the relative homogenization of traditional dress.

Techniques and the division of labour within the family are similar throughout the region. What does vary is the degree of involvement in commercial production, which is affected by access to both raw materials and markets. These factors affect the type of production which is undertaken, and hence the kind of customer (native or tourist) who is served, which in turn impact upon the producer's level of prosperity. A vicious circle is set up which links the type of textiles produced to a socio-economic hierarchy: and these differences are reflected most clearly in access to land.

The quantity and quality of land possessed by each family influences its place in the regional textile economy, and vice versa. Domestic units are no longer self-sufficient, and some Indians will work as salaried employees in the workshops of others, either in their own or neighbouring communities. The relative wealth gained from textile production, which facilitates the purchase of land, thus generates stratification both within and between communities. The Indian producer stays within his own environment, however, even if he works outside his own locality, which permits the continuation of his way of life and prevents the cultural alienation associated with displacement from the community and traditional occupation.

Young Otavalenos working as waged weavers prefer to invest their income in education, as well as in the purchase of land or looms. Those who are already well-off continue to participate actively in community life and local festivities. They retain their traditional dress and the Quechua language (even where they are bilingual). These choices have a favourable effect upon business with the tourists, who delight in buying their textiles from 'authentic' Indians. This strategy does imply certain consequences, however, in terms of the confirmation of their identity as members of a stigmatized social group within the framework of national society. The creation of this successful ethno-economic niche does help to maintain the ethnic dichotomy within Ecuadorian society, although it modifies the superimposition of an economic upon a social status.

This experience develops a political consciousness and a feeling of ethnic identity which probably could not have been sustained under other conditions. Otavalenos have participated actively in human rights events in Ecuador, in solidarity with other much more disadvantaged groups such as the Amazonian Indians, who currently suffer from brutal land expropriation due to oil exploitation. On these occasions music, dance, poetry, theatre and (above all) textiles are used to sensitize audiences to ethnic particularities. A leaflet distributed at one of these events read:

> For our own cultural development! For our identity! For our liberty to create!

> Andean artisans united for the reinforcement and integration of our race and culture!

In the context of a society characterized by ethnic hierarchy, dress and language are particularly significant, mainly because of the conscious choice to maintain them. The development of a new Otavaleno 'traditional' female blouse (actually a mixture of different local styles), for example, at first seems to be just a consequence of the new economic situation. On further consideration, however, it signifies a choice made at the expense of occidental dress and a will to preserve regional cultural specificity and ethnic identity. The Otavalenos still preserve endogamy, and social and work relations are mainly established within the group (Walter, 1981: 334). They maintain social distance across the ethnic dichotomy in a stratified society, but take advantage of this by offering to the market their traditional textile production.

The Otavalo example illustrates the revalorization of ethnicity through the evolution of a local textile tradition, and more precisely, through its transformation into an object for consumption by tourists. It compares in interesting and important respects with the following contrasting cases.

Taquile: communal solidarity

Taquile is an island situated 45 km from Puno, in Lake Titicaca in southern Peru, which in the late 1970s became integrated as a tourist sight into the Cuzco–Puno–La Paz circuit. Here 1,200 Quechua-speaking Taquilenos live in a traditional Andean social organization, the majority wearing a local dress. Agriculture constitutes the principal economic activity of the community, with crops redistributed between families as a result of various kinds of exchange, mutual assistance and communal obligation. Local festivities related to the agricultural cycle, charged with symbols, serve as an opportunity to display one's textile production (Zorn, 1983: 31).

This latter is the most important economic activity after agriculture, and Taquilenos make textiles from a very early age. The Taquilenos illustrate a particular case of a traditional community which benefits materially from tourism while selling its 'Indianity'.

The community has organized itself into various committees for 'tourism development'. These attend to the daily arrival of tourists in communally owned boats specially built for the purpose. The tourists visit the island to see its Inca and pre-Inca ruins, are lodged in Taquileno homes, and are invited to buy textiles in the communal cooperative store, which is managed by an elected committee. To this store the Taquilenos bring their textiles each week. These are evaluated by the committee, who assess their quality and fix the price. No bargaining is allowed. The benefits are distributed among the producers, although 2 per cent of the income is retained for the communal fund. Quality control promotes the use of wool instead of synthetic fibres, and the use of natural dyes. The aesthetic dimension of this is that the natural character of goods leads to better sales in the tourist market. Although artificial dyes would shorten the production process, much greater collective investment would be required.

The product consists of knitwear, woven vests (*chalekos*) and caps (*chullos*) made by men, and woven belts decorated with traditional motifs (*chumpi*) made by women. These belts designed for sale to tourists no longer carry their original messages (ideograms representing marriage, death, drought and other events) and are now purely decorative, although the original techniques and iconography are preserved (Braunsberger, 1983: 72).

The new demand for textiles created by tourism reinforces traditional ideals while also meeting the need for money. Custom frowns upon the wearing of old dress at festivals. This traditional ideal is reinforced, in that now these clothes can subsequently be sold on to tourists (Zorn, 1983: 165). The Taquilenos consider textile production as a means of earning money, and the exchange value of fabrics is calculated in capitalistic terms; but awareness of their use value persists as well. These two systems of valuation coexist, fundamentally opposed but mutually implicated.

The mobilization of Taquilenos for communal activity is not new. In the 1930s they pooled their funds to buy land on the island and to build boats. The monopoly which they have acquired over boat travel between Puno and Taquile is based upon this tradition, but now extends it into the allocation of accommodation, rotated among all the island's inhabitants.

The Taquilenos also benefit from their geographical location. The island is presented by tourist guides as an 'authentic and uncontaminated' place. Isolation also permits both independence and better control of visitors. The visibility of folkloric practices and the textile tradition explain the growing number of visitors (in the early 1980s an average of 750 per month: Zorn, 1983: 146) and this flow stimulates the locals to wear traditional dress for the promotion of textile sales. Tourism thus reinforces local ethnic characteristics through the wearing of local costume, the development of communal work practices and the endowing of local culture with monetary value.

The kind of tourism in Taquile is selective. There is no electricity, and no running or drinkable water on the island. Accommodation is rudimentary, and the boat journey from Puno lasts four hours. To reach the village it is necessary to walk for about 45 minutes to a height of over 4,000 metres. Thus only tourists with a certain amount of time and physical stamina, and who are not put off by the inconvenience of the rustic setting in which they stay, will make the trip. Most of these will be 'free independent travellers' or 'alternative tourists' (Crick, 1989: 313; Cohen, 1987). Consequently the modernization, acculturation and loss of tradition often associated with the tourist 'invasion' are much moderated in Taquile.

Even so there have been changes, specifically the development of textile production for the tourist market, and of other activities such as accommodation, transport and the provision of meals for tourists, and the general spread of monetary relations.

A new group has emerged which benefits more than others from these new opportunities, consisting especially of those who emigrated from the island, and who have returned to take advantage of the new situation. The income from tourism is reinvested in fertilizer and other improvements to agricultural production.

The case of Taquile is an example of indigenous economic control of textile production and its commercialization. The interaction between traditional and capitalist economies has been realized in a manner which appears to be advantageous to the Taquilenos. This can probably be explained by the fact of the direct contact between producers and consumers, eliminating middlemen. As in Otavalo, the structures of traditional communal social organization, the wearing of traditional dress, the Quechua language and original textile production have themselves become commercial attractions which satisfy the tourist's search for 'authenticity'.

Salasaca: tradition without valorization

Our third and strongly contrasting example of the commercialization of traditional Andean textiles is the case of Salasaca in central Ecuador. This village of 5,000 inhabitants has also managed to preserve its internal cohesion and cultural patrimony, expressed through the dominant Quechua language (the men are bilingual), traditional dress and local festivities and rituals. Contact with the national society began in 1934 when a road was built through the community's territory, provoking clashes with the army. In 1944 this road was surfaced, facilitating the passage of tourists both to the spa at Baños and the Amazonian region. Evangelists, anthropologists and non-governmental organizations arrived together as part of the same process.

The most important economic activity in Salasaca is agriculture, followed by the weaving on pre-Hispanic style looms of ponchos, blankets and belts for their domestic needs. They also embroider zoomorphic and anthropomorphic figures and symbols on to ceremonial clothes, although the significance of these is not made explicit (Hoffmeyer, 1985: 342). Experts who came to train indigenous artisans, and to commercialize their textile production for the tourist market, adapted these designs to tapestry weaving techniques, and to the pedal loom.

The introduction and development of this new activity not only provided economic compensation in the face of a crisis in agriculture, but also introduced a new element of competition into local stratification. The eight families who initially owned the greater part of the land are those who have benefited most from commercial textile weaving. This social group employs about 50 Salasacan weavers, and has facilities to sell their production through craft shops in the town to the tourist market, and also export agencies. The producers who live close to the road (where the tourists stop) are more prosperous because they can sell directly to the tourists without the intervention of middlemen.

The competition between textile producers in Salasaca and the difficulties which they experienced in selling their wares led to the involvement of Otavalenos, who as middlemen became the most important retailers of Salasacan textiles. The excessive growth of producers and hence of competition has reduced this lucrative activity to little more than a subsistence wage for most Salasacans. Only a prosperous minority has managed to benefit from commercial weaving by looking constantly for new markets and introducing new designs (Pita and Meier, 1985: 170–1).

One might be tempted to interpret the adaptation of Salasaca iconography and its incorporation into tapestries destined for the tourist market as evidence of the reinforcement of ethnic identity through the commercialization of textile production. There is, however, a dichotomization of textile production into two different types of weaving activities, one destined for the internal audience, the other for an external one. The traditional figures relegated to the intimacy of community rituals are revalorized and commercialized in the course of production intended for external consumption; but this new elaboration is not accompanied by any valorizing discourse. Salasacan tapestries are all made to order on the basis of motifs required by the client, on a production line basis and using designs taken out of context (even if these did originally appear in local ceremonial clothing). This, taken together with the dominant role of commercial intermediaries and the relative lack of economic success of the enterprise, might account for the lack of any movement towards the internal revalorization of indigenous textiles in this context.

Jalq'a: the recovery of an extinct craft tradition

The intervention of outsiders does not always signify the absence of an internal cultural response. A Bolivian example illustrates the way in which tourism and the interest generated in Andean textiles have rejuvenated an almost extinct craft. Jalq'a is an Indian community located in the Sucre region. The villagers lost all contact with their weaving tradition, and all the community's textiles were gradually sold to collectors. Not a single item remained as a model which might have served to perpetuate the tradition; lost too was the knowledge of techniques, the use of natural dyes, the traditional motifs and the handling of wool. A group of Bolivian anthropologists (ASUR) took the initiative to revive the weaving tradition in the community. They researched museums and private collections, travel accounts and illustrations, for textiles originating here. This recovered evidence stirred memories among the oldest women, and the forgotten textile tradition was reborn.

A community cooperative was set up for the purchase of wool, the construction and restoration of looms, and the finishing of textiles to be sold. The ASUR group, together with the International Labour Office, supported the project, training the villagers in management and accounting. The community now controls the enterprise entirely, and 250 families are currently committed to this activity. A cooperative shop has opened in the city of Sucre, through which the product is sold to tourists and to the export trade. Thus local memory and identity were recovered through textiles, thanks to an external initiative which combined commercial exploitation, tradition and modernity.

Textiles, tourism and identity

The modes of integration of traditional textile production into a new economic context are very varied. (The original thesis on which this chapter has been based reviewed several other relevant case studies.) The strategies adopted by different groups can be explained by the different historical, ecological and economic conditions within which they face modernization; the degree of their isolation or contact with global society; their access to raw materials; their proximity to regional urban and tourist centres; and the needs and mode of life of each group. The resulting product varies, ranging across Graburn's scheme of classification from the 'ethno-kitsch' to the 'artistic' (1984: 396). Processes of commercialization also extend across Cohen's (1988b) proposed categorization. Within this range of variation several generalizations are possible.

Tourism exerts a double influence on ethnic craft: it is a factor for change, but also implies a certain cultural crystallization. It can be considered as a new form of ethnic domination. It is frequently assumed that the growth in production of ethnic crafts depends upon economic need. It should not be forgotten, however, that this process rests upon pre-existent structures of production. The South American countries with the largest Indian populations and the most important craft industries are the Andean countries, in which pre-Columbian civilizations were most developed. Here ethnic crafts are part of a long tradition. Economic necessity has simply stimulated changes in the destination of this production throughout history. In that process tradition can be lost; but it can also be conserved or acquire new forms.

In the cases which we have reported, revitalized ethnic crafts often reinforced feelings of ethnic identity. The objects produced, the techniques of production and the motifs are drawn from the producer's culture. The position of the family unit is consolidated within the community, and although producing articles for external consumption the artisan is not dislocated from his social, economic or cultural environment. Moreover, the commercial value of the object depends upon its bearing the seal of ethnic identity.

Outlets for the sale of Andean textiles – the cooperatives and other associations which manage them – are now more numerous than those for any other kind of Andean craft production. Taking into account the symbolic importance which textiles have always had in the region, this is not a coincidence. They bear witness to the continuity of a historical pattern, in which textiles have been produced to serve external demand, but while confining the producers within their traditional structures have at the same time revalorized their cultural patrimony, of which their ethnic identity is one part.

Tourism is not, of course, the only factor which makes for change in traditional societies; and neither is its quest for exoticism the only factor making for cultural revitalization. The consumption of folklore, which reinforces a cultural patrimony (such as dance, music carnivals or ethnic crafts), nevertheless can become the means through which culture is preserved, provided that its basis is dynamic and not static.

Within this process ethnic divisions have their part to play. The economic situation confronts the producers with a choice as to their way of life. Either they may integrate into a capitalistic, urban, industrial class system, which does not necessarily hold out any prospect of the amelioration of the producer's life, or they may retrench a 'traditional' way of life. In this situation ethnicity can become a defence mechanism. According to Raveau it offers a feeling of collective belonging to a mythical or historical past which might be projected into a possible communal or utopian future

(1976: 475). Andean textiles embody and represent these kinds of feelings.

The persistence of the Andean textile tradition can be traced across a diversity of countries. Its continuing vigour is reflected in the introduction of heteroclite motifs, drawn from archaeological discoveries and occidental designs (the neo-pre-Hispanic style). These innovations pose the problems of 'authenticity' and the 'loss of tradition'. They cannot be considered simply as adulterations of the textile tradition, however; on the contrary, they express its vitality and capacity to integrate changes in response to different environmental influences. As Ribalta has observed, renovation and tradition are the proper basis for the elaboration of a craft (1981: 11). The survival of an indigenous craft tradition demonstrates the energy and resilience of ethnic groups facing global society. Handicrafts reflect a historical process: and if a craft object originally reflected in its symbolism a religious, political or social context, nowadays its 'authentic' values lies in its relation to the occidental consumer. Wolf has made the point that the global process which starts with occidental expansion also constitutes a part of the history of 'discovered' peoples (1982: 385). The handicrafts of the groups which we have been studying, with their 'non-traditional' motifs and techniques, can only be understood through their multiple intra- and inter-cultural relations.

Tourism is currently the major factor making for the growth of Andean textile production. It implies a multiform process of interconnection between cultural, economic and ideological values on the part of both of the interacting societies. The textile tradition sold to tourists, although metamorphosed, nevertheless displays the essential and continuing character of Andean societies, and has undergone changes in parallel with them. Instead of dwelling on the dialectic of the maleficent or beneficent effects of tourism on visited societies it will be more pertinent to focus upon their social, economic and cultural reorganization in response to that access. For between collective memory encapsulated in textiles, and the souvenir industry, the social fabric of the Andes unravels and reweaves itself continually.

(Translated by John Allcock.)

Note

The author wishes to thank Thérèse Bouysse-Cassagne, Sophie Desrosiers, Antoinette Milinie-Fioravanti and Marielle Pépin-Lehalleur for their helpful comments on earlier drafts of this chapter.

References

Ariel de Vidas, A. (1989) 'L'artisanat textile andin. L'exploitation commerciale – tradition et modernité'. Unpublished master's thesis, University of Paris X, Nanterre.

Braunsberger, de S.G. (1983) 'Una manta de Taquile – interpretación de sus signos', *Boletín de Lima*, no. 29: 53–73.

Cohen, E. (1987) 'Alternative tourism: a critique', *Annals of Recreation Research*, 12(2): 13–18.

Cohen, E. (1988a) 'Authenticity and commoditization of tourism', *Annals of Tourism Research*, 15(3): 371–85.

Cohen, E. (1988b) 'The Commercialization of ethnic crafts', in *Craft Reports from all around the World*. Copenhagen: World Crafts Council. pp. 94–104. Reprinted in *Journal of Design History*, (1989) 2(3): 161–8.

Crick, M. (1989) 'Representations of international tourism in the social sciences: sun, sex, sights, savings, and servility', *Annual Review of Anthropology*, 18: 307–44.

Fohr, D. (1981) 'Mythes et réalités de l'Amérique Latine à travers le dépliant publicitaire touristique – étude d'une vision'. Unpublished PhD thesis, University of Paris III.

García Canclini, N. (1981) *Las culturas populares en el capitalismo*. La Habana: Casa de las Americas.

Gayton, A. (1978) 'Significado cultural de los textiles peruanos: producción, función y estética', in R. Ravines (ed.), *Tecnología Andina*. Lima: IEP.

Gisbert, T., Arze, S. and Cajias, M. (eds) (1987) *Arte textil y mundo andino*. La Paz: Gisbert y Cia.

Graburn, N. (1976) *Ethnic and Tourist Arts: Cultural Expressions from the Fourth World*. Berkeley: University of California Press.

Graburn, N. (1984) 'The evolution of tourist arts', *Annals of Tourism Research*, 11(3): 393–419.

Hoffmeyer, H. (1985) 'Diseños Salasacas', *Cultura*, VII(21): 339–55.

Lauer, M. (1982) *Crítica de la artesanía – plástica y sociedad en los Andes peruanos*. Lima: Desco.

MacCannell, D. (1984) 'Reconstructed ethnicity: tourism and cultural identity in Third World communities', *Annals of Tourism Research*, 11(3): 375–91.

Meier, P. (1982) 'El artesano tradicional y su papel en la sociedad contemporánea', *Artesanía de Américas*, 12: 3–21.

Murra, J. (1975) 'La función del tejido en varios contextos sociales y políticos', in *Formaciones económicas y políticas del mundo andino*. Lima: IEP.

Novelo, V. (1976) *Artesanías y capitalismo en México*. Mexico: SEP-INAH.

Pietri-Lévy, A.-L. (1989) 'Artisanat Latino-Americain: quand l'art populaire devient une marchandise.' Unpublished state thesis, University of Toulouse II.

Pita, E. and Meier, P.C. (1985) *Artesanía y modernización en el Ecuador*. Quito: CONADE-Banco Central del Ecuador.

Poirier, J. and Raveau, F. (eds) (1976) L'autre et l'ailleurs: hommage à Roger Bastide. Paris: Berger-Levrault.

Raveau, F. (1976) 'Ethnicité et mécanisme de défense', in *L'Autre et ailleurs: hommage à Roger Bastide*. Paris: Berger-Levrault. pp. 475–9.

Ribalta, M. (ed.) (1981) *Folk Art of America*. New York: H.N. Abrams.

SELA (1981) 'La artesanía, arma de doble filo', *América Indígena*, XLI(2): 191–2.

van den Berghe, P. (1980) 'Tourism as ethnic relations: a case study of Cuzco, Peru', *Ethnic and Racial Studies*, 3(4): 375–92.

Walter, L. (1981) 'Otavaleno development, ethnicity and national integration', *América Indígena*, XLI(2): 319–37.

Wolf, E.R. (1982) *Europe and the People without History*. Berkeley: University of California Press.

Zorn, E. (1983) 'Traditions versus tourism in Taquile, Peru: changes in the economics of Andean textile production and exchange due to market sale'. Unpublished master's thesis, University of Texas, Austin.

4

Frontier Minorities, Tourism and the State in Indian Himalaya and Northern Thailand

Jean Michaud

Frontier political dynamics and ethnic minorities

The borders of the states of South and South East Asia have been clearly influenced by the effects of the inter-Asian historical process and also of the period of European colonial encroachment. The British withdrawal from imperial India in 1947 and the consequent partition of territories was largely based on a compromise, recognizing the rights of certain groups to autonomous rule in accordance with historical territorial occupation and religious affiliation, in the main to Hinduism, Islam and Buddhism. This contemporary settlement thus took into account a pre-existing pattern that had achieved its form under the influence of events acted out over millennia in the Indus and Ganges Valleys, the Persian Empire, the Deccan Ranges, the Tibetan Plateau and, further to the north, the growth of the Chinese Empire. With such a heritage, political centralization is an ancient reality in South Asia, although state policies for ethnic minorities, if they existed at all, were generally *laissez-faire*, unless some intervention seemed urgently called for by events.

In continental South East Asia, the existing political divisions show how Malaysia, including the islands of Singapore at that time, and Burma, vassals of the British crown, in large measure agreed to recognize as their borders those fixed by the colonial occupiers for their empire. The same can be seen in the former French Indo-China in what are today Laos, Cambodia and Vietnam. Finally, almost by default it could be said, but also due in part to geostrategic considerations among the European powers, and certainly because of the able diplomacy exercised by Siamese monarchs, Thailand's traditional borders were largely left intact by Europeans as they never colonized the kingdom (Wyatt, 1984). Here also the regional political pattern had long been influenced by historical processes, well before the sixteenth century and the arrival of Western settlers. In successive stages that had begun under the early kingdoms and empires, these had vied with each other for control over the resources of the peninsula down through many centuries. The outcomes of their convoluted and continual struggles had inevitably had a strong influence on the cultural settlement patterns of the regions, clearing several core areas for specific cultural identities in locations that in several cases have not changed significantly since. The minorities who lived in the mountains or in archipelagos and thus were largely isolated from these circumstances were often able to evolve at their own pace (Bruneau, 1981).

Thus in South Asia as in South East Asia the high plateaux, the mountain ranges and the archipelagos have over centuries provided space for hunter-gatherers and shifting cultivators who as a result have been able to lead relatively independent and largely self-sufficient lives, and thus remain culturally distinct from what have become the national majorities (see Wijeyewardene, 1990). Therefore, two distinct patterns exist within both regions, each super-imposed on the other. One is the so-called modern nation-state exerting political control over a territory with fixed and delineated frontiers, inherited from colonial days but also from the centuries of regional strife between competing kingdoms and empires. The other, an equally ancient pattern, though more diffused, is based on centuries-long customary rights and long-forged self-representations of cultural identity, on the grounds of which the minorities claim the right to recognized privileges. Still, modern frontier lines have generally been fixed using somewhat abstract criteria, such as a watershed, which inevitably is at a high altitude, a cease-fire line, or even an unsurveyed line drawn on a map -- all lines in territory that is preferably remote from the national capitals and the resource and population concentrations of the nations concerned. The point at issue here is that whatever the initial conditions that led to their being drawn in this manner, such border lines all too frequently slice through mountainous regions where ethnic minorities have long traditions of living, trading and moving around, without any attempt being made by the rulers to take into account these social activities among the affected ethnic minorities since their societies are judged marginal to the national interests.

Among these peripheral groups henceforth legally inhabiting national territory -- though as in Thailand without necessarily being granted full citizenship -- a key factor that influences the pace of transition from living according to customary law to being incorporated into modern legality is the degree of difference between the ethnic identity and the national identity as defined by the powers-that-be in the capital. Generally speaking the national identity is derived from the ethnic group that is the largest in number, the most powerful, the wealthiest, or some combination of the three. It is equally inevitable that such a group should inhabit and exert control over the most fertile regions within their territorial boundaries – the river basins and the coastlines. As a self-evident corollary, ethnic minorities with their differing cultures tend to be concentrated in the highlands and other less fertile zones of the interior, remote from the valleys and littorals. Since their production capacity and opportunities for trade are restricted by these same factors, they also have less economic clout than the majority populace. Their political organization may also be diffuse owing not only to the nature of the terrain but also to their isolation in small groups as a result of their historical evolution over centuries, in which small communities have gone their own largely self-sufficient ways.

Ladakh and northern Thailand: state strategies

The two highland groups considered here fall within the above categories. The Ladakhi in north-west India live along the Himalayan frontier lines fixed by the cease-fire that concluded the first hostilities between India and Pakistan in 1947–8, and by the war between India and China over Aksai Chin in 1962 (Lamb, 1991).[1] The highlanders of many ethnicities of northern Thailand belong to populations that straddle the borders of China – where the vast majority of highlanders still live – Burma, Laos and Vietnam.[2] Many are still arriving in Thailand, mainly as swiddeners in search of new land or as refugees (Lim, 1984).

Despite their many differences, common themes in both contexts have led to similar strategies of development by the two states. In both cases, ethnic groups who until late into this century could move around their relative mountain ranges without let or hindrance now find their lives bounded and circumscribed by the imposition of international frontiers and confronted by states concerned to impose limitations on their movements. Politically and economically the two regions are peripheral tributaries of their regional capitals, which control them administratively and on behalf of the central powers in Delhi and Bangkok. As regions lacking easily reachable resources to be tapped and traditionally occupied by subsistence agriculturalists, these border areas, from the state's viewpoint, must above all be kept populated. This policy has two aspects. First, the authorities' aim is to prevent a troublesome and costly migration of the groups to more densely populated regions or to the outskirts of the towns where they would place additional strains on already inadequate infrastructures. Secondly, the state wishes to use these groups to serve important national interests: to maintain a population base in a contested border region in Ladakh's case, and to affirm control over frontier regions considered to be too permeable in that of Thailand. In military minds – decisive actors in both countries – the challenge of tackling the complex tangle of interrelated problems posed by the control of these border lands is distilled into several unshakeable convictions embodied in no-nonsense, straightforward propositions that define the briefs of development projects: the purpose is to maintain if not increase the present population levels in these sensitive regions, preferably in sedentary, reliable settlements of a populace sharing a sense of national identity (Evans, 1986). To achieve this, an efficient strategy should either encourage and facilitate some controlled internal migration from the lowlands into the highlands, assimilate the highlands indigenous minority groups and leave them in place, or ideally foster both. The peasants, being thus 'planted' in the frontier lands, have been called the state's territorial occupation spearhead ('la paysannerie comme fer de lance territorial de l'État') by de Koninck (1986; 1993), and this process of 'internal colonialism' was labelled and denounced as a form of exploitation by Hechter (1975).

All local development programmes, whether the government's own or those from outside authorized by it to work in the region, incorporate these objectives from the outset and actively promote them. Programmes are initiated by the state which in fact accelerate the sedentarization of nomadic groups; obligate subsistence farmers to shift to cash cropping (Mongkhol, 1981 for example); introduce obligatory education in the national language (in India, Hindi/ Urdu); induce the monetarization of the local economy; lead to political proportional representation; and thus finally achieve economic, political and cultural subjugation, which is then carried further by the widespread introduction of the mass media that in all its forms promotes the values of the capital city.

Of particular interest for our analysis is the growth of a modern tourist industry in both regions. This has resulted, as the attempt is made here to demonstrate, in the central powers, whether as a result of deliberate foresight or not, being offered an additional opportunity to extend their hold further into these previously isolated communities by means of increasing the minorities' dependency on the national economy, in turn precipitating fuller and irreversible integration with the national identity.

Local conditions for tourism

When a government finds itself in a position to introduce tourist development activities, a scenario such as described above is generally already in operation under the rubric of a master plan for all future economic development within the region. In both cases under consideration here, to introduce this new element into the ongoing operations, the additional administrative and infrastructural outlays were minimal when compared with the investments required in other developmental fields. Of course, though, some financial and other extra inputs were inevitable.

There was, for instance, the crucial matter of easy accessibility. Providing adequate transportation facilities for residents, civil servants and local merchants is one thing; upgrading them to provide facilities considered suitable by foreign tourists is quite another. Ladakh had to wait for 25 years after Indian independence before Delhi and the army were confident that opening it up to unrestricted transit by civilians would not have any adverse effects on national security. From 1974, the military finally permitted private bus companies to begin a regular service between Srinagar and Ladakh. Vigorous lobbying on the part of long-established Kashmiri merchants, old hands at the tourist game, played an important part in securing this relaxation of control, and contributed to finding new common grounds for the old rivalries between, roughly speaking, Muslim Kashmiri and Buddhist Ladakhi, until then confined to regular trade competition on well-defined territories. The army was in any case able to rely on the basic state of the infrastructure, geographical factors and the harsh climate to regulate the inflow of visitors. The sole mountain highway leading to Ladakh traverses many precipices, is subject to frequent landslides, and is closed by inclement weather from October to May when the high passes are blocked by snow. Additionally, daily troop and military supply convoys are accorded top movement priority at all times when the route is open. The inauguration of airline passenger flights in 1979 made a modest increase in numbers possible but the tourist flow has remained stable since.[3]

As for the north of Thailand, the situation is less complex. The whole region has always been open to outsiders except at certain specific limited times and places. This has been due, for example, to intensive smuggling activities across the borders with Burma and Laos or armed insurgencies or intrusions (often linked to the former) at a very local level which has resulted in *ad hoc* closures of certain areas by the security forces until they have dealt with these localized outbreaks. Even now, such contingencies occasionally crop up but the rest of the north remains unaffected. For the sake of state control and market accessibility, new roads are still being bulldozed up to previously isolated highland villages, but as most of the highland population is without pick-up trucks, these roads supplement the more direct though often steep tracks which still remain in use.

Such limitations as these, in general of a largely political nature, which discourage investment in the usual type of holiday resort, do provide ideal circumstances for the promotion of trekking tourism, probably the most important sort of tourism visiting the highlanders of northern Thailand and Ladakh.[4] This type of tourist wants to be in contact with the locals and enjoys sharing their means of transport – at least for the 'adventure' stage of their itinerary – so they are willing to put up with the existing state of facilities. There is no road, so the only way is on foot? No trekker worth his salt is going to let that deter him. What's more, a certain 'risk' adds to the flavour of the exploit. In fact, for the trekking tourist an arduous journey through difficult terrain with political or bureaucratic obstacles to be circumvented *en route* adds to rather than detracts from the satisfaction to be derived from his discoveries, as well as serving as a guarantee of the 'authenticity' of the ethnic minorities he has tracked down.[5]

In the field

Both northern Thailand and Ladakh were early on included on the tourist promoters' lists of exotic destinations, actually both from the early 1970s. The emphasis was on their ethnic and environmental qualities, though the choice of language used to extol these was naturally somewhat different.[6] Tourist publications underline some distinctive characteristics of each region in their literature. For example, in the case of northern Thailand, what is stressed is the labyrinth of mountains of medium elevation, mantled in wild tropical forests, in whose depths dwell hospitable and colourfully costumed tribal groups of various origins, and where mystery casts its shade across a clandestine harvest of opium in a location with an evocative name, the golden triangle. As for Ladakh, it is sold as an ancient caravan trail, a high desert valley enclosed by the natural barriers of the Himalayas to the south-west and the Karakoram ranges to the north-east. The population, largely of Tibetan culture, provides a unique opportunity to discover the mysterious world of Tibetan lamaism uncorrupted by Chinese influence.

In highland northern Thailand, a visiting relative or friend is normally put up in the house of somebody belonging to the same lineage or clan, or with close friendly relations to it. Traditionally, no commercial form of hospitality exists. When a group of trekkers arrives – generally around 10 people for one night only – their reception and accommodation cannot be fitted into the traditional pattern. Space is needed to allow room not only for sleeping but for dining and relaxing together, as well as facilities for ablutions and for laundering clothes, and often latrines. All of this will require the construction of one or several adapted buildings by the families willing to host tourists regularly. The guide will bring most of the food with him and cook it in ways his clients are familiar with. Basic commodities such as tea, rice and firewood are generally supplied free by the hosts. The only real revenue the villagers will realize is from the accommodation charges[7] and the opportunity to sell everyday utensils and other objects that are now promoted to the rank of handicrafts, whether these are made in the village itself or bought in Chiang Mai to be resold for a small profit.[8] As for employment, people in the village – not necessarily highlanders – may occasionally be hired as porters or as short-term guides. To supervise communication between the villagers and the visitors is the task of the guide-cum-interpreter (see Cohen, 1982), the final link in the supply and demand chain, rarely a highlander himself. The communication language is Thai, and therefore trekkers and villagers cannot converse directly.

In Ladakh, the villages have been permanent settlements for centuries owing to the exigencies of geography, the climate, the caravan trade and feudalism. There are far fewer villages than in highland Thailand and, owing to the marginal nature of the eco-system – high-altitude desert – they are located in the few places that permit agriculture, that is, along water courses and in valley bottoms. The tracks leading to them have long been in use for transporting merchandise, and these are the routes the trekkers will follow. In Ladakh, the tourist agency will draw up an itinerary rather than a specific set of villages. In fact, what with the military restrictions and the difficulty of the terrain, supply is a problem and the agency rarely has any alternative routes to choose from. In these valleys, growing crops in a rocky soil that has been laboriously irrigated results in low yields, and any small surpluses have traditionally been bartered for other basic necessities. Here also, the agency ensures that the guide brings in all the food for the party and cooks it for them himself. Wood for cooking fires is not easily available because of the lack of trees, so he will also carry in a gas stove and some extra fuel. The absence of vegetation also poses problems in constructing accommodation for the groups of tourists (the local style is to build with dried mud bricks with a wooden frame structure). Thus it often happens that visitors take shelter for the night in a stable or a field hut. Alternatively, trekkers can sleep in the open air – it scarcely ever rains so it is only necessary to be well covered against the night's chill – and bathe in the river if they feel like it. Given this, agencies can even operate tours without having any dealings at all with the villagers. The only way the village can then hope to derive any money from the passing visitors is by selling them such things as dried fruit or handicrafts, which again may be made in the village or bought from the nearby market town, Leh, for later resale to tourists. There are no opportunities for hired labour as porters or guides since the tracks are few and easy to follow, and ponies and donkeys are used for porterage.

In the case of Ladakh to a certain extent, but more so in the case of Thailand, the direct economic cost for the villagers is the time they spend waiting for the arrival of the visitors and, when they have arrived, for attending to their requests for water, tea, fruits or alcohol. In the context of a subsistence economy, the time thus spent instead of working in the fields may represent a large cost. Also, if it has been necessary to construct accommodation, these buildings must be maintained at the hosts' expense. In addition, villagers often lend extra blankets or provide supplementary food for free if the guide has lost some *en route*, or is short for whatever reason. And finally, there is the guide himself who has to be provided for, frequently meaning that he must be put up for free and given a percentage of the profits on their sales to the group. In fact, keeping the guide sweet is vital if the flow of potential customers is to be maintained.

As for the matter of indirect costs, as well as the long-term social and political consequences which affect the cultural equilibrium of the villagers, this is clearly a complex issue with ramifications far beyond the simple financial cost–benefit analysis.

Tourism: a catalyst for integration and resistance

As already emphasized, in both these cases the villagers linked to the ethnic and environmental tourist networks are located in peripheral border regions and subject to a high level of state intervention in the modern period. In general, such villages have also been involved for some years in governmental administrative programmes and/or non-governmental organizations' development projects.

From the point of view of the powers-that-be, sustaining a policy of investment in these peripheral regions (which are often seen as lacking worthwhile or easily exploitable natural resources) in order to maintain a stable population level is highly costly, so much so that for some governments in comparable situations only the mandate of national security is felt to justify it. In India and Thailand, the funds poured into state development projects in our two regions are astronomical in comparison to the tiny number of direct beneficiaries, as also to the meagre results attained in terms of productivity. Seen in the perspective thus presented, and bearing in mind its modest scope, tourism does help to defray these expenses; whatever money it injects directly into the local economy has not come from the state's own coffers. In Thailand, if they have recently been made to switch from nomadic shifting cultivation to farming in a settled location, the subsequent consequences for highlanders can be considerable. These may frequently include the impoverishment of the soil in their fields over several years, through leaching and erosion, and the necessity thereafter of using chemical fertilizers plus herbicides and pesticides (see Boulbet, 1975; Kunstadter et al., 1978). To this must be added the inability to acquire new land because none remains unoccupied or unclaimed by the state, or because of lack of capital or proof of citizenship. All of this may be further compounded by a government policy of crop substitution whereby they are forbidden to grow a traditionally profitable though illegal crop, the opium poppy, and required to plant instead new unknown species for which it is theorized there will be a demand on regional, national and international markets. Thus the villagers become the potential victims of poor planning by outsiders and subject to exterior forces over which they have no control (Kesmanee, 1989). As for Ladakh, all the development projects are naturally enough concerned with providing water and energy to the desert villages. Both are in short supply, especially the former. All kinds of water collecting techniques are being implemented as well as alternative energy experiments like methane gas, windmills of many designs and, of course, solar energy for cooking (Norberg-Hodge, 1991). In brief, everything is being done to produce more simply in the hopes of sustaining a steadily increasing populace – a completely new phenomenon regionally – which is already a goal that is pushing the limits of possibility of the local water courses and the land available that is suitable for farming. Added to this is the unfortunate combination of more mouths to feed in each family, since the tradition of entering the monkhood no longer appeals to the young men (although the Indian army provides a significant alternative for young recruits), while at the same time state schooling prevents many children from working in the fields alongside their parents. To make ends meet, families must now find the means with which to buy provisions on the open market that they once produced for themselves or could acquire by barter, such as milk, salt, sugar, barley flour, fodder for their domestic animals and so forth (Kaplanian, 1981).

Paradoxically, one of the main causes of these difficulties that force the people to struggle for survival, the geographical factor, is precisely what provides a large part of the attraction for one of the few alternative economic options open: tourism. In both our cases, owing to the low density of the populations and the absence of any large-scale industries, the opportunities for regular employment for unskilled work are too scarce to absorb the already available workers and any others who would willingly sell their labour. Thus when harvests are bad, and the villagers are hard pressed to get by, they are by necessity very receptive to any employment opportunities that demand little capital and almost no training in new skills. The advent of tourism offers such a break. If tourism brings only minimal financial returns to the villagers, as we have suggested, nevertheless what it does bring in helps to sustain the existing village scene. To take part in this new business seems sensible. To refuse to get involved when there are no visible alternatives would be an unaffordable luxury for many.

But above all, tourism may have effects, in ways that are not readily quantifiable, which are extremely influential in the long run. Having come this far, it should now be permissible to take as axiomatic the proposition that tourism is a force that contributes to the sedentarization of populations new to this way of life in fixed settlements and which, moreover, helps accelerate the monetarization of the village economy. Furthermore, as has been ably demonstrated by Nuñez (1963), Greenwood (1989) and Wood (1984), the promotion of ethnic tourism provides states with an unanticipated opportunity to intervene in the processes that direct cultural change by means of posing as the arbiter of the promotional image that is presented to foreign tourists of their very own national minorities. At the local level, the combined effects of the above-mentioned forces set in motion a chain of events with distinct social and political consequences, and it is in that field that we propose to see the specific consequences of tourism as an economic activity.

In both lineage societies (Thailand's highland groups) and feudal ones (Ladakh), by customary usage most political power is the acknowledged monopoly of the village male elders. In this tradition, younger men can only hope to achieve a leader's role as they get older, till which time they must exercise great patience. Tourism inevitably disturbs this equilibrium. The entrepreneurial possibilities which it offers to the villagers most strongly attract those who have no immediate access to the family patrimony, those most ambitious to become wealthy, and those who are keenest to get a grip on the local reins of power as soon as possible. The elders, on the contrary, tend to want to cling on to their present position of control, and most often seem unaware of any possible medium- and long-term consequences of the social changes that are now under way. After some time at this pace, it has been observed in Ladakh (Michaud, 1991) and in a small number of comparable situations (Altman, 1988 in aboriginal Australia; Fisher, 1990 in Nepal; Din, 1988 in Malaysia; Michaud et al., forthcoming in Melanesia) that some of the village youths have come to innovate in allying themselves economically with outsiders. Villagers from the first school-educated generation could learn rudiments of English and the basics of entrepreneurship, and came to have regular direct dealings with the intermediary levels of the tourist industry, the guides, merchants and agents. Helped by the modernization effort promoted by the state apparatus, they could begin to use the lever of economic power they had just discovered to force the hand of the village elders and to introduce a new economic system to the village, one which was but recently alien to their circumstances. In other words, the economic activities that are inherent in the development of the tourist industry foster the growth of competition over money and power, while the network of new contacts combined with business success inevitably brings a new-fangled style of politics in its train.[9]

Also, the state's liberal expectations seem not to take into account that the appearance at the village level of new alliances and new rivalries between locals, as part of the growth of competitive capitalism, grafts itself on to ancient but still flourishing social systems different from the mainstream. The forms that the resulting synthesis can assume vary enormously. Factors like the survival of indigenous religions, cosmologies and languages are certain to become important when the time comes for political formalization and, eventually, resistance to state policies. Moreover, new cultural behaviours and desires may simply jump over national limits and join directly with foreign standards. It should be noted that in the absence of national visual media, the groups of foreign trekkers and their guides from the outside world have been the most powerful role models promoting occidental values and the consumption of industrial goods. These privileged travellers, by their manners, equipment and clothing, are being viewed as vivid heralds come to announce the advent of the modern paradise. This might well be one of the most concrete manifestations of tourism as an influential factor in the process of internationalization (Lanfant, 1980), and it is likely that the state cannot do much to control this process in the field. Specific situations involving foreign tourists witnessing repression directed towards local communities have already proven that international tourism can genuinely influence the balance of power between local communities and centralized states. The killing of local participants by the military during a burial ceremony in occupied Timor in November 1991 was witnessed, videotaped and made public by tourists present at the scene. Jakarta was significantly discomfited by this world-wide disclosure. Witnessing a similar situation in Tibet under Chinese control, Schwartz (1991) gives an account of the spontaneous alliance between foreign tourists and Tibetans to denounce internationally the brutal Chinese interventions in Lhasa in 1987–8. There also, tourist videotapes and photographs were smuggled out and did much to bring the problem to public attention. In the wake of such events, the understanding of the potential of the tourist presence as a factor in resistance to the state's aggressive assimilationist practices seems to be spreading rapidly among oppressed minorities, and some national authorities are reacting consequently in limiting tourist circulations in areas of 'disturbances'.

Concluding remarks

While references are made to a number of authors who have written peripherally about the subject, those invoked to support the main thrust of our argument – about the relationship linking tourism, state control and the ethnic minorities in border regions – are fewer. This may reflect the present state of knowledge of the social sciences in this area. Or perhaps it would be more accurate to recognize that this conjunction of factors occurs along the boundaries of such established disciplines as frontier geography, Third World political economy and the anthropology/sociology of tourism, which so far it has rarely seemed necessary to combine. Therefore, drawing general conclusions on the basis of only two case studies, considered in the short term, would most probably be premature (see Wilson, 1993 on the problems of short-term studies of tourist cases).

Nevertheless, some issues can be stressed. In both our cases, the integration and assimilation of peripheral minorities into the national identity, control over border areas, and security of the frontiers are state priorities (Bhruksasri, 1989; Patel, 1984). By means of controlling population movements, fostering fixed settlements, promoting agricultural dependency and monetizing economic exchanges, the state provokes the integration of highland minorities within the national economy, the first step on the road to acculturation along national lines. Parallel to this, as in the rest of the world, developing the tourist industry in yet untapped regions is a business strategy for private interests looking for increased profitability in a highly competitive field. When analysed with the help of field observation, as far as trekking tourism – or, in Smith's typology (1989), ethnic and environmental tourism – is concerned, the process and outcomes from the latter in terms of providing an appealing economic alternative to the decline of agricultural revenues, favouring the switch from subsistence economy to commercialization, and accelerating the linkage to the national market, may very well serve superbly the interests of the state. In our examples this is not necessarily as a main activity, or one that can do the whole job by itself, but as a convenient economic activity, as a catalyst accelerating the integration and control processes directed towards minorities by central powers. On the possibility that resistance from local communities may appear in the course of this process, sometimes even stimulated by it, no doubt exists. The durability and efficiency of this resistance by minority groups to mighty state power, though, have still to be investigated, along with the resistance to irreversible economic, religious and linguistic integration into the national identity.

Notes

I owe many thanks to Geoffrey Walton, in Chiang Mai, for translating from French and making many useful suggestions. I am indebted also to the Fonds pour la Formation de Chercheurs et l'Aide à la Recherche and to the Fondation Desjardins in Quebec, as well as to the International Development Research Council of Canada, the Social Sciences and Humanities Research Council of Canada, and the Canada-ASEAN Centre for the financial support that made possible the research on which this chapter is based.

A related article was published (Michaud, 1993) in a noticeably longer form, with an ethnographic focus. That article further develops the issue of border populations visited by tourists, and focuses on the political economy of central state versus highland minorities.

The choice of the two locations came about as a result of research carried out on Ladakh in 1987–90, where I had previously worked as a tourist guide, and on northern Thailand since 1989 when I began working on my PhD. The social complexities of these two contrasted regions cannot be compared here in any serious way. Thus the comparisons to be drawn are selective ones that should be viewed as useful analogies rather than an attempt to impose strict symmetries.

1 The Indian census gives, for 1981, a total of 301,000 inhabitants in the district

of Leh, state of Jammu and Kashmir, of which a majority are Buddhist Ladakhi of Tibetan tradition. A fraction of the settlers in Kargil district, namely in the vale of Zanskar, are also of the same cultural group.

2 The Tribal Research Institute's 1987 census gives a total tribal population of 551,000 individuals in northern Thailand (McKinnon and Vienne, 1989: Appendix I).

3 It must be said here that most data for the Ladakh research were collected in 1988 or before. Therefore, this analysis does not specifically take into account the various changes that have taken place in Ladakh and Kashmir since the beginning of the still ongoing unrest in 1989.

4 'Trekking tourism' is a fuzzy concept that always seems to be considered self-evident. In tourist promotion literature, it generally refers to a mild sort of adventurous expedition where nature and primitives are to be met. Outside these essential dimensions, a wide variety exists. A good number of social scientists have used it as a definite type of tourism, but to my knowledge, no definition has ever been given, nor has the phenomenon been analysed in itself. Using 'trekking tourism' here is a compromise that reflects the tourist industry terminology in the field.

5 The concept of authenticity – in particular the notion of 'staged authenticity' – has been at the centre of lively debate for nearly 20 years in the social science of tourism, in particular the landmark work of Dean MacCannell (1976). Malcolm Crick (1989) proposed a good summary of the views of the principal authors.

6 The use of these two epithets is not widespread in tourist literature. My choice is based on Valene Smith's (1989) typology of tourist motivations. Comprising a total of five categories, I believe the categories 'ethnic' and 'environmental' together represent adequately the blend of motivations present in trekking tourism.

7 Around $1 per person per night, for at least 12 years at the time of writing.

8 My calculations in northern Thailand show that ultimately what really remains in villagers' hands from the initial payment by trekkers to the trekking agency is meagre, around 3 per cent (Michaud, 1992).

9 To clarify the point, any other economic activity offering comparable entrepreneurial opportunities would probably have similar effects. In this sense, there is nothing unique about tourism as a generator of economic enterprise, although perhaps it is particularly suited for linking isolated populations with few other economic resources.

References

Altman, J.C. (1988) *Aborigines, Tourism, and Development: the Northern Territory Experience*. Australian National University, North Australia Research Unit.

Bhruksasri, W. (1989) 'Government policy: highland ethnic minorities', in J. McKinnon and B. Vienne (eds), *Highlanders of Thailand*. Bangkok: White Lotus–ORSTOM. pp. 5–33.

Boulbet, J. (1975) *Paysans de la forêt*. Paris: Publications de l'École française d'Extrême Orient, vol. CV.

Bruneau, M. (1981) 'La drogue en Asie du Sud-Est. Une analyse géographique du triangle d'or', *Hérodote*, 21 (April–June): 116–45.

Census of India (1981) *General Population Tables, Jammu and Kashmir*. Series 8, part II-A, p. 71.

Cohen, E. (1982) 'Jungle guides in northern Thailand', *Sociological Review*, 30: 236–66.

Crick, M. (1989) 'Representations of international tourism in the social sciences', *Annual Review of Anthropology*, 18: 307–44.

de Koninck, R. (1986) 'La paysannerie comme fer de lance territorial de l'État: le cas de la Malaysia', *Cahiers des Sciences Humaines (ORSTOM)*, 22(3–4): 355–70.

de Koninck, R. (1993) 'La paysannerie et l'État: une affaire de compromis . . . à suivre', *Réfléchir sur les sciences sociales, ESPACES TEMPS, Le Journal*, 53/54: 130–44.

Din, K. (1988) 'The concept of local involvement and its application to Malaysian island resorts'. Paper presented to the First Congress on Tourism (GAPP), London.

Evans, P.B. (ed.) (1986) *Bringing the State Back In*. Cambridge: Cambridge University Press.

Fisher, J.F. (1990) *Sherpas: Reflections on Change in Himalayan Nepal*. San Francisco: University of California Press.

Greenwood, D. (1989) 'Culture by the pound: an anthropological perspective on tourism as cultural commoditization', in V.H. Smith (ed.), *Hosts and Guests: the Anthropology of Tourism* (2nd edn). Philadelphia: University of Pennsylvania Press. pp. 171–86.

Hechter, M. (1975) *Internal Colonialism*. Berkeley: University of California Press.

Kaplanian, P. (1981) *Les Ladakhis du Cachemire, montagnards du Tibet oriental*. Paris: Hachette, L'Homme Vivant.

Kesmanee, C. (1989) 'The poisoning effects of a lovers' triangle: highlanders, opium and extension crops, a policy overdue for review', in J. McKinnon and B. Vienne (eds), *Highlanders of Thailand*. Bangkok: White Lotus–ORSTOM. pp. 61–102.

Kunstadter, P., Chapman, E.C. and Sanga, S. (eds) (1978) *Farmers in the Forest: Economic Development and Marginal Agriculture in Northern Thailand*. Honolulu: University Press of Hawaii, East–West Center.

Lamb, A. (1991) *Kashmir: a Disputed Legacy 1846–1990*. Hertingfordbury, UK: Roxford.

Lanfant, M.-F. (1980) 'Introduction: le tourisme dans le processus d'internationalisation', *Revue internationale des sciences sociales*, 32(1): 14–45.

Lim, J.-J. (1984) *Territorial Power Domains, Southeast Asia, and China: the Geo-Strategy of an Overarching Massif*. Singapore: Institute of Southeast Asian Studies, Regional Strategic Studies Programme; and Australian National University, Strategic and Defence Studies Centre.

MacCannell, D. (1976) *The Tourist: a New Theory of the Leisure Class*. New York: Schocken.

McKinnon, J. and Vienne, B. (eds) (1989) *Highlanders of Thailand*. Bangkok: White Lotus–ORSTOM.

Michaud, J. (1991) 'A social anthropology of tourism in Ladakh (India)', *Annals of Tourism Research*, 18(4): 605–21.

Michaud, J. (1992) 'Economic and political implications of tourism in highlanders' communities of northern Thailand: evaluation at the village level'. Paper presented at the Fifth Conference of the Northwest Regional Consortium for Southeast Asian Studies, jointly with the Canadian Council for Southeast Asian Studies, Vancouver.

Michaud, J. (1993) 'Catalyst of economic and political change: tourism in highland minorities in Ladakh (India) and northern Thailand', *Internationales Asienforum*, 24(1–2): 21–43.

Michaud, J., Maranda, P., Lafrenière, L. and Côté, G. (forthcoming) 'Ethnological tourism in the Solomon Islands (Melanesia): an experience in applied anthropology', *Anthropologica*.

Mongkhol, C. (1981) 'Integrated agricultural development as a strategy to stabilise the Hill Tribe people in northern Thailand'. MA dissertation in rural social development, Agricultural Extension and Rural Development Centre, University of Reading, UK.

Norberg-Hodge, H. (1991) *Ancient Futures: Learning from Ladakh*. San Francisco: Sierra Club.

Nuñez, T. (1963) 'Tourism, tradition and acculturation: weekendismo in a Mexican village', *Southwestern Journal of Anthropology*, 34: 328–36.

Patel, M.L. (1984) *Planning Strategy for Tribal Development*. Tribal Studies of India Series. Delhi: Inter-India.

Schwartz, R. (1991) 'Travelers under fire: tourists in the Tibetan uprising', *Annals of Tourism Research*, 18(4): 588–604.

Smith, V. (1989) 'Introduction', in V.H. Smith (ed.), *Hosts and Guests: the Anthropology of Tourism* (2nd edn). Philadelphia: University of Pennsylvania Press. pp. 1–17.

Wijeyewardene, G. (ed.) (1990) *Ethnic Groups across National Boundaries in Mainland Southeast Asia*. Social Issues in Southeast Asia. Singapore: Institute of Southeast Asian Studies.

Wilson, D. (1993) 'Time and tides in the anthropology of tourism', in M. Hitchcock, V.T. King and J.G. Parnwell (eds), *Tourism in South-East Asia*. London and New York: Routledge.

Wood, R.E. (1984) 'Ethnic tourism, the state, and cultural change in Southeast Asia', *Annals of Tourism Research*, 11: 353–74.

Wyatt, D.K. (1984) *Thailand: a Short History*. New Haven and London: Yale University Press.

5

International Tourism and the
Appropriation of History in the Balkans

John B. Allcock

Heritage as a political concept

The area around Bradford in England was, until about 20 years
ago, heavily dependent upon the woollen textile industry.
Advancing technology and foreign competition have destroyed
what had been the economic bedrock of the region since the 1850s.
In the search for other economic opportunities Bradford turned to
tourism.[1] The 'jewel in the crown' of the tourist industry locally is
the village of Haworth. This otherwise undistinguished former
sheep-raising and weaving community is now famous as the home
of the Brontë sisters, Anne, Charlotte and Emily, who lived in the
village during the first half of the nineteenth century.

The parsonage where the family lived, and the moorland area
which surrounds it and which provided the setting for much of
what they wrote, has become a literary shrine, which receives
annually around 158,000 visitors.[2] An anecdote about Haworth,
told to me by one of my students who lives there, will serve well to
identify the focus of my chapter.

A local character, well known in the community as a raconteur,
took to regaling visitors to the pubs in Haworth with stories about
the Brontë family. These were often scurrilous and typically
apocryphal. He could be relied upon to gather a good audience,
however, and believing that he could benefit from his skills as a
performer he asked the publicans to serve him with free beer in
recognition of the custom which he claimed to attract. He was
banned from every hostelry in the village!

The point of this story will be readily grasped. Tourism has
become a powerful interest which has the capacity to sanction
effectively versions of the reality upon which it feeds. The Haworth
parsonage presents an element of what has come to be known as
our 'heritage'. However, 'heritage' is not just that which has come
down to us from the past: it is one version of that past, which

potentially competes with other possible versions, but which has come to be sponsored as appropriate and acceptable.[3] Typically the ruling considerations which shape the construction of the past as 'heritage' in this way have to do with the perceived demands of the tourist industry.

I am happy to join that 'company which no man can number' of those who have paraphrased Joseph Goebbels. When I hear the word 'heritage' I reach for my gun. Philistine he may have been, but Goebbels was not stupid. As Hitler's Minister for Propaganda he had a powerful awareness of the fact that culture is never politically neutral; and his response to the claim that something might be evaluated as no more than culturally relevant was to insist that to speak of culture is to speak of politics.

The central tenet of my chapter is that to speak of heritage is to speak of politics. To designate any object, practice or idea as a component of heritage (or equally to *exclude* any item from this designation) is to participate in the social construction of a reality which is *contested*. It is to prefer one symbolic universe over others. It is to seek to reproduce some element of contemporary structure by interpellating the recipients of this discourse as very particular kinds of subjects. The discourse of heritage is an inherently political discourse, which by ordering the past orders also the present.

A primary focus of this volume is the role of tourism in processes of identity construction. Many of the chapters collected here illustrate vividly the ways in which identity emerges as a negotiated product of the development of tourism. The material which I present here underlines the need for social scientists to sensitize themselves to the dimension of power in that negotiation process. I would go so far as to say that the 'appeal to identity' which is made before the tribune of tourism typically takes place within an asymmetrical contest for control.[4]

Among the most important of the resources which can be deployed in that contest is control over the past, which in validating some appeals to identity and invalidating others establishes and legitimates social relationships over a far wider area than the field of tourism itself. In this chapter I set out to explore the ways in which the discourse and practice of heritage function in relation to attempts to create and consolidate identities, and the significance of the type of exercise in identity construction within wider political processes. I propose to do this by presenting for discussion two examples of the political appropriation of history by means of the designation of tourist sites or objects of interest as 'heritage', drawn from my own research experience in Yugoslavia.[5]

Case study 1: when is a church not a church?

Standing on a wooded hillside overlooking the old Macedonian city of Ohrid is the ruin of a building. For the benefit of tourists this site is signed as a church, dedicated to St Pantelejmon. It is perhaps puzzling, therefore, when the visitor approaches this structure, that it bears all the outward signs of its having been a mosque. The cubic form lacks the apses, transepts and other architectural features which are typical of Orthodox churches. The size of the windows is entirely out of keeping with local Christian traditions. The sense of incongruity is sustained when one inspects the interior, which clearly possesses the characteristic niche (*mihrab*) and pulpit (*minbar*) found in any mosque.

Only on closer enquiry does it become apparent why this place is offered to the tourist as a specifically Christian monument and not as an Islamic one. Excavation in the grounds surrounding the building displays the outline of an earlier edifice, over which a later one has been raised. The few courses of stone which remain do indeed enable one to pick out the characteristic shape of an early Orthodox church. Inside the walls a section of the floor has also been excavated in order to display the base of a pillar, upon which it is possible to make out a fragment of painted fresco.[6] Next to this lies a stone slab, usually decorated with flowers and marked by a photographic copy of a portion of fresco from another church. It is a portrait of St Clement of Ohrid. The site is marked as his grave, and in spite of the extremely rudimentary nature of the remains of the tenth-century church, this is why we have come to the place.[7]

It would be possible to tell another story about the church of St Pantelejmon. It was, indeed, also a mosque. The region fell under the rule of the Ottoman Empire at the end of the fourteenth century. The exact fate of the original Christian place of worship is unknown, although it is known that on the site of this church a mosque was erected around the middle of the fifteenth century, which came to be known by its Islamic name of the Imaret-džamija. Why are we now directed as tourists to a Christian and not to an Islamic site? I have asked this question in Ohrid, and received the following answer.

St Clement was, of course, not just any old saint. He holds a very high place in Orthodox tradition generally as one of the missionaries originally associated with the conversion of the Slavs. His name is especially revered in Macedonia as one of the founders of the Ohrid school of church literature, and hence as a central figure in the process of substantiating a claim to the historical continuity of a distinctive Macedonian Slav culture of great antiquity. The original building is said to have played a significant part in this cultural tradition, as it is believed to have been the site not only of a church but also of a prominent centre of monastic learning. In view of the importance of these associations it is therefore not surprising that it is the connection with St Clement which marks the site as worthy of attention today.[8]

While this argument may be taken seriously – as it is advanced seriously – I wonder if it is the whole story. Although destroyed during the Balkan Wars (1912), when the Turks were finally ejected from this part of Europe, the mosque was a structure of considerable significance for the local Muslim community. The Imaret-džamija was visited by Sultan Bajazet II, and possibly for this reason became known as the 'imperial mosque'. It is the site of the grave of its founder, Sinan Chelebi, who along with the mosque itself established an important charitable institution (*waqf* or *vakuf*) for the care of the poor. Its elevation above the status of ordinary mosques might be suggested by its possession of two minarets.

The point at issue here is not that the tourist authorities in Ohrid should have decided to mark the site as a mosque *instead of* as a church. Had the building been complete, and even recently functioning as a place of worship, a reasonable case might have rested upon the fact. It is, however, a ruin and one which has not been in active use for religious purposes of either kind for many years. There seems to be no reason why *both* sets of associations could not have been offered to tourists in interpreting the site. The site itself does not impose a choice of interpretations: a choice has been imposed upon the site. My argument is that the choice which was made has been framed *politically*. History (or heritage) has been appropriated by politics.

In order to understand why this has come about it is necessary to look briefly at the significance of the development of tourism for Macedonia in general, and for this part of the republic in particular.

The republic of Macedonia, which was created within the Yugoslav federation in 1945, has continually been made aware of the fact that its legitimacy is contested by its neighbours. Even within Serbia the more extreme nationalists hanker for the pre-war days when it was known officially as 'South Serbia'. Many Bulgarians still do not accept the revision of the Treaty of San Stefano at the Congress of Berlin, and claim that Macedonian Slavs are really Bulgarians. The Greeks tend to be uninterested in the niceties of the differentiation of various south Slav groups, but are immensely suspicious of the possible implications of the existence of a state which usurps (as they see it) a name which is so centrally a part of Greek history. The Greek government has fought a long and hard battle against any form of international recognition of an independent republic bearing the name 'Macedonia', in the wake of the disintegration of Yugoslavia, and only with the greatest reluctance has compromised in accepting the unwieldy title 'the Former Yugoslav Republic of Macedonia'.

The fact that the republic includes a very large Albanian-speaking minority along its western border (at least one-fifth and possibly a third of the total population) means that even if the existence of a Macedonian state is not questioned by Albanians, its borders are.[9] The defence of the credentials of the Macedonian state, and its claims to be based upon the existence of a distinctive group – Macedonian Slavs, or Macedonians as they prefer to call themselves – has preoccupied the Macedonian leadership with varying degrees of intensity ever since 1945.

In pursuit of evidence of a specific Macedonian identity, language has played a large part. The energy expended upon the creation of an autocephalous Macedonian Church within the Orthodox communion (in 1967), even at the cost of causing great offence to other Orthodox communities, shows that language has been closely followed in importance by religion. In this endeavour Ohrid has a pre-eminent place: its undoubted former importance as a centre of ecclesiastical art and learning is interpreted as evidence of the fact that, before it was submerged by the Ottoman advance, Macedonia was not a mere cultural appendage of some other power, but was an influential power in its own right. The association of Ohrid with the great St Clement is seen as carrying weight in this argument.

If it is vital that the cult of St Clement is promoted officially as a central component of the heritage of Macedonians, then it is equally important that the indigenous history of Islam is marginalized. The proverbial '500 years of Turkish night' are dismissed as a mere interlude in the story of Macedonian civilization which has contributed nothing either memorable or valuable to it.

Possibly of greater significance here, however, is the fact that the vast majority of Albanians living in Macedonia are Muslims. Although the Imaret-džamija is a Turkish construction and has no specifically Albanian associations, it is symbolically important that the greater significance and antiquity of the *Christian* heritage in the region is affirmed. The presentation of the site in question as 'the Church of St Pantelejmon', and not as a mosque, is therefore a heavily politicized action, which simultaneously affirms the uniqueness and continuity of the Macedonian Slav heritage, while laying down an important territorial marker in relation to the perceived threat from Albania.[10]

Case study 2: the politics of the folk fiddle

As elsewhere in the world, folklore is a very visible element among the array of presentations offered to tourists throughout the Balkans. The music, dancing and colourful costumes which have been handed down from the rural past of these societies are everywhere on display, both at performances arranged for the benefit of tourists and as souvenirs for sale. Initially this may seem to be unexceptionable, or indeed a beneficial consequence of the growth of international tourism. After all, to give pride of place to the products of specifically *peasant* communities would seem to escape the frequent accusation that tourism tends to reinforce the privileged position of elite cultures. Possibly it is true that the reproduction of these artefacts and practices preserves aspects of indigenous culture which might have been swept away by the advancing tide of urban and industrial life.[11] Nevertheless, I want to argue that the *specific forms* in which folklore is offered to tourists in Yugoslavia are highly politicized, and illustrate another dimension of the process by which the incorporation of heritage for tourism involves the political appropriation of history.

There are two levels at which traditional peasant culture in the Balkans might be characterized: the region and the locality. In spite of the fact that the Balkan peninsula is the home to a wide diversity of linguistic groups, separated by historical experience and religious allegiance, anthropologists readily recognize the overarching cultural unity of the region as a whole.[12] Much of the diversity which has been documented has to do with broad differences of ecology and economy, so that elements of the way of life of pastoralists, for example, recur throughout the area, and set off those who live this way of life from those who live principally by tilling the soil. Nevertheless, within these general unifying patterns there is immense difference of detail, and these peculiarities can be associated often with very specific localities.

Two illustrations from the realm of folklore will make the point. Bagpipe music is typical of pastoral peoples across the entire Balkan region, and there are many similarities between both the instruments and the musical forms which are used. The female costume traditionally associated with the Konavlje area around Dubrovnik is really quite distinctive, and stands apart as much from any other Croatian costume as it does from the costume of more distant regions.

The presentation of folklore to tourists, however, typically is not framed by reference either to the region or to the locality. It is presented as *national* folklore. The use of this term is chronically problematic in this region, as indeed it is among all Slav peoples. The Serbo-Croat word *narodni* (and its close relatives) is translated both as 'national' in the sense in which it would be used in English or French, and as 'folk' rather along the lines in which the Germans use the term *Volks-*. When we examine the use *in context* of this idea, however, it is interesting to observe the ways in which the terms *narodna nosňja* (folk/national costume) or *narodna muzika* (folk/national music) or *narodni ples* (folk/national dance) have come to be used. Whereas each of these alternative designations could be said to have linguistic warrant, in tourist discourse the term 'national' is almost inevitably preferred over the possible alternative 'folk'.

This suggests that these things have acquired quite clearly *political* significances, in that they are being presented as costume, music or dance proper to a particular *state*. In this way, folklore has come to be used as the identifying badge of particular political communities which are only tenuously and partially rooted in peasant society. The process of politicization of folk culture in Yugoslavia has gone through two distinct phases.

In the years following the Second World War a great effort was made to create a common sense of Yugoslav citizenship, framed within a shared commitment to socialism, which would embrace all the peoples of the federation. The wartime partisan slogan *Bratstvo i jedinstvo* (brotherhood and unity) expressed this ambition. Although the expectation that it might be possible to submerge regional differences within a common socialist and Yugoslav identity had been considerably blunted by the time the boom in tourism got under way in the mid 1960s, elements of this view were still obviously visible in the presentation of folklore to tourists.

Several dance troupes were set up, most notably the federal ensemble Tanec, which constructed their programmes around selections of dance and song, appropriately costumed and accompanied, drawn from all parts of the federation. The link between this image of 'brotherhood and unity' and the unification of the population under socialism was heavily underscored by the well-known Tanec opening routine, in which intermingled among the dancers dressed in 'national' costume were others dressed in pointedly proletarian dungarees. It was a common device of presentation to have dances with acknowledged regional provenance performed by the entire company, dressed in a mixture of regional costume. Whereas great care was taken at one level to ensure the authenticity of details of costume, musicianship and so on, the whole performance was subordinated to the overall aim of conveying a sense of the overriding unity of historical culture within the state beneath a surface of kaleidoscopic diversity.[13]

As Yugoslavia underwent a steady process of confederalization after the mid 1970s, the growing prominence of republican political elites, and the moves towards republican economic autarky, came to be reflected in changes in the presentation of folklore to tourists. The pan-Yugoslav gloss on folklore was replaced by a specifically *republican* emphasis. Tourists were much more likely to be shown, for example, 'Croatian' or 'Slovene' *national* culture. Folklore in each of these phases is being subjected to an obvious politicization, in that the cultural products of a diversity of rural communities are being appropriated as the 'heritage' of states. These states are of very novel formation, and yet seek to buttress their legitimacy by entirely spurious appeals to the supposed continuity of a cultural heritage which is far older and more prestigious. This specific point could be argued with respect to any of the Yugoslav republics. I will illustrate it here by more detailed reference to Croatia.

It has been a characteristic of Croatian nationalism since the nineteenth century to refer to the 'thousand-year' history of a Croatian political community. This idea is a total nonsense unrecognized by any respectable historian outside Croatia. A full history of state formation in the region is obviously inappropriate here, but a few central points can be made concisely. Given the usual sociological cautions about any use of the term 'nation' to describe medieval political realities, it is possible to recognize a 'Croatian' state in the northern Adriatic during the tenth and eleventh centuries. This bore little relation to the modern Croatian republic, as it excluded Slavonia east of the confluence of the Sava and Bosna rivers, extended no further south along the coast than the Neretva, and lacked most of Istria. It did include the greater part of Bosnia. The death of the last Croatian king Zvonimir in 1089 saw the crown pass to the Hungarian dynasty. The precise legal nature of this arrangement remains contested by historians.[14]

The Croatian state was battered by subsequent historical changes in the Balkans over subsequent centuries, especially by the rise of a Bosnian state under Tvrtko, the expansion of the Venetian state and in the fifteenth century the Ottoman invasion. This obliterated any semblance of a Croatian state briefly after the defeat at Mohács in 1526, and Turkish suzerainty was extended briefly as far north as Vienna three years later. Turkish power north of the Sava was not finally broken until the War of the Holy League, in 1699. Large areas of what is now the republic of Croatia were incorporated by the Habsburgs into a so-called 'military frontier' from the end of the seventeenth century, which was directly answerable to Vienna rather than Budapest. Venetian power waxed and waned along the Adriatic. The existence of an independent republic of Ragusa (modern Dubrovnik) until its overthrow by the armies of Napoleon should not be overlooked. The territory which now falls within the republic of Croatia was never part of a single unified state before the creation of the kingdom of the Serbs, Croats and Slovenes at the end of the First World War.

The idea of a 'thousand-year' history has served two significant ideological purposes over the centuries. At first the insistence upon a presumed continuity with the kingdom of Zvonimir was principally significant as a legal symbol deployed during the late eighteenth and nineteenth centuries in order to defend the rights of the Croatian landed nobility *vis-à-vis* the Habsburg crown. The reference is clearly to an entitlement which is of greater antiquity than the union with Hungary. Following the unification of the Croat lands within a Yugoslav state, the entire rhetorical focus of this image of historical continuity has shifted. The Croatian nobility was finished as a political force by this time, but the same rhetoric was taken over by more modern political forces as a defence against other south Slav (and typically Serbian) attempts to control Croatian political and economic destiny. It has survived into our own day, when it has found service in the hands of a new nationalistic anti-communist elite.

The political unification of the Croatian republic presents a particularly severe problem of legitimation. Historically, ethnographically, linguistically and economically it has no continuous history. The materials from which a sense of a *common* heritage can be built are scarce indeed. Even the commonly heard emphasis on the importance of the legacy of the Habsburgs (which sets off Croats from the 'Ottoman' areas to the south and east) obscures the significant fact that 'Croatia' was divided between Austrian and Hungarian spheres of influence. Even more significant in some eyes is the fact that this abandons symbolically important parts of the notional 'Croatian lands'.[15]

Into this symbolic vacuum it has been found expedient to import folklore as a significant constituent of heritage. Notwithstanding the diversity of *local* traditions which must be subsumed within this notion of folklore as the foundation of 'national' culture, the images of a rural past of infinite antiquity and undoubted prestige undergirds the claim that the Croatian people do indeed possess a heritage which has been passed down unbroken over the centuries. In a state in which the current regime attempts to deny its own continuity even with the history of the past 40 years, this is an asset which I expect to find exploited with unremitting vigour in the future.[16]

Conclusion: history, politics and the rhetoric of heritage

At first sight the contrasts between these two illustrations may appear to be as noteworthy as the similarities. In the first case, one of two possible interpretations of a historical site (Christian or Islamic) is preferred over the other in the designation of the site as an item of Macedonian national heritage. In the second case a specious unity is attributed to a very loosely related, indeed disparate, selection of items drawn from a rural past in the attempt to weld together an image of a coherent, Croatian, national heritage. There are, nevertheless, significant points which are common to both cases.

Both illustrations are intimately linked to the problem of the legitimation of new states and the creation of a sense of national identity. By designating features of the past specifically as 'heritage', the items in question are endowed with an elevated status reminiscent of Émile Durkheim's concept of 'sacredness'. 'Heritage' does not just refer to elements of our past: it designates things towards which we have an *obligation*. That obligation holds because the item in question is regarded as peculiarly important in defining an aspired identity. The identification of heritage therefore involves an attempt to create a sense of there being a moral bond which draws together a given community (the Macedonian or the Croatian nation) around the object in question (a historic site or folklore) and sets it off in significant respects from others. Because the identities in question relate to national cohesion and thus to the legitimation of state structures, and aspects of the past are being appropriated by the state, it is appropriate to say that in this process the past is becoming politicized.

A key feature of both of these cases is the part played by tourism. I do not wish to go back here to the old 'impact' model of tourism and affirm that tourism 'causes' this type of cultural development. On the other hand, I want to go beyond the relatively weak claim that tourism simply provides some kind of occasion or opportunity for these things to take place. If so there would be no *intrinsic* connection between the events in question and tourism.

Tourism is an integral part of the process described in two respects. It provides institutionalized and prestigious *forms* through which these ideological processes can be mediated (the presentation of a site; the performance). It also provides the ready-made *rhetorics* of presentation which conjure these politicized views of the past into being. A general view of the nature of culture, as well as the nature of tourism, is implied here which it is perhaps appropriate to bring to the surface.

I look at culture as a configuration of *resources* which are available to actors in the structuration and restructuration of their world. Tourism does not stand apart from host cultures as a kind of obtrusive appendage which is tacked on in order to help them to cope with the arrival of tourist 'guests'. The forms and rhetorics of tourism stand on all fours with the other resources which are available to that community.

I am impressed by Goffman's celebrated distinction between 'front stage' and 'back stage'; but it is at least potentially misleading in one respect.[17] Couched as it is in terms of the interactive collaboration of members of a 'cast' to ensure the effective presentation of some collective self-image before an audience, it tends to suggest a kind of wisdom possessed by those who are able to retire 'back stage', and their capacity to sustain a subjective distance between the act and things as they really are. Unlike the sincere man of the old adage, they are not taken in by their own propaganda. This view fails to address the mechanisms of ideology, and at the same time falls short of an adequate conceptualization of the processes of identity construction.

There is no hard and fast distinction between front and back stage, so that ideological communications which are addressed front of stage are also effective in interpellating even the stage hands behind the scenes. The ideological process cuts across these presumptively separate spheres of communication and draws them together.[18] They are able to do so precisely because their burden or content is the identity of the actors in question.

International tourism does not remain a communicative process which operates across the boundaries of putatively different cultures, those of the 'sending' and the 'receiving' society. It has become a part of the fabric of *both*. To present our past to the tourists in the guise of our 'heritage' is simultaneously to address them as customers who are involved within the circle of commodity exchange, and to address ourselves as the subjects of ideology, whose identity is authenticated and affirmed in the very images which the tourists consume.

Notes

A preliminary version of this chapter was presented to the Colloque Tourisme International: Mémoire, Mythe, Patrimoine, in Nice, November 1992. I wish to record my thanks to colleagues for their helpful comments on that occasion.

1 For some discussion of this process, see Buckley and Witt (1985 and 1989).

2 Figure for 1991 supplied by the Tourist Information Centre, Haworth. This figure may be placed in the context of the number of enquiries handled in the same year by the Tourist Information Centre in Haworth (176,475) and the number of passengers on the neighbouring steam-driven Keighley and Worth Valley Railway (155,582). The latter is also an important tourist asset, since it featured in the film version of E. Nesbit's story *The Railway Children*.

3 I acknowledge here the importance of Robert Hewison's (1987) work in shaping my approach. His argument has been to some extent anticipated by Donald Horne (1984).

4 The notion of an 'appeal to identity' is discussed by Marie-Françoise Lanfant in Chapter 1 in this volume.

5 I know that to all intents and purposes Yugoslavia no longer exists. I propose to continue to refer to the states of what was formerly Yugoslavia by that name, even so, for two good reasons. In the first place it is tedious to keep repeating a series of more or less cumbersome euphemisms of the kind I have just used. In the second place, for the most part Yugoslavia did exist at the time during which my research was being conducted. I appeal to the well-established convention of the 'ethnographic present'.

6 In fact this fresco itself is a reconstruction. None of the original fresco painting remains. The site indicates the remains of two churches built in different periods. The earlier, tenth-century, church of St Clement was actually replaced by a later (probably fourteenth-century) building.

7 Despite this fact, St Clement is not actually buried there. Although St Pantelejmon may indeed be the place of his original burial, his remains were moved to the church of The Mother of God Prvilepta following the arrival of the Turks.

8 The information about the presentation of this site is based upon the most recent tourist guidebooks published by Biljana, Ohrid, 1986, supplemented by various items of earlier Macedonian publicity material dating back to 1967.

9 The Yugoslav census of 1991 estimated the Albanian population of Macedonia to be 21.4 per cent of the total. Albanians boycotted the census. This estimate is widely believed to be substantially inaccurate, and the true figure is probably at least 25 per cent. Albanian claims that Albanians make up 40 per cent of the republic's population are almost certainly a generous overestimate.

10 This point is spelled out in more detail in the Introduction to Allcock (1990).

11 In this respect there has been a tendency within the literature to replace the first (very negative) phase of the impact model of tourism by a rather idealized and positive model. Both versions of the impact model are equally in doubt these days.

12 The importance of elements of the cultural unity of the Balkan region is dealt with in Stahl (1986). See also Cuisenier (1979); Stoianovich (1994).

13 I bracket for the purposes of the present discussion other obvious 'inauthenticities', such as the use of modern materials in costume, or the performance of folk dance on stage to an audience seated in rows.

14 C.A. Macartney has written that, 'the original relationship [between the Croatian and Hungarian crowns] was incapable of definition by modern terms' (1937: 357).

15 The controversial status of the territory which is to be considered as the historic Croatian lands was underlined during 1993 by the open rifts within the Croatian political elite over the claims which should be pursued in connection with the partition of Bosnia-Hercegovina. The round of academic revisionism prompted

by the secession of Croatia from the Yugoslav federation has produced a new wave of academic opportunism in this area, including the entirely specious attempt to identify the characteristics of a separate Croatian language.

16 In 1991 the former Trg Žrtava Fašizma (Square of the Victims of Fascism) was renamed the Trg Hrvatskih Velikana (Square of the Great Croatians). It seems that the struggle against fascism is no longer a part of the heritage of the Croatian people!

17 See especially Erving Goffman (1969).

18 Another approach to this issue is Fred Inglis's (1990) critique of what he calls the theory of the 'ideological fix'.

References

Allcock, J.B. (1990) 'Studies in the sociology of tourism: with special reference to the role of tourism in the development of Yugoslav society'. PhD thesis, University of Bradford.

Buckley, P. and Witt, S. (1985) 'Tourism in difficult areas: case studies of Bradford, Bristol, Glasgow and Hamm', Part 1, *Tourism Management*, 6(3): 205–13.

Buckley, P. and Witt, S. (1989) 'Tourism in difficult areas', Part 2, *Tourism Management*, 10(2): 138–52.

Cuisenier, J. (ed.) (1979) *Europe as a Cultural Area*. The Hague: Mouton.

Goffman, E. (1969) 'Regions and region behaviour', in *The Presentation of Self in Everyday Life*. Harmondsworth: Penguin.

Hewison, R. (1987) *The Heritage Industry: Britain in a Climate of Decline*. London: Methuen.

Horne, D. (1984) *The Great Museum*. London: Pluto Press.

Inglis, F. (1990) *Media Theory: an Introduction*. Oxford: Basil Blackwell.

Macartney, C.A. (1937) *Hungary and her Successors*. Oxford: Oxford University Press.

Stahl, P.H. (1986) *Household, Village and Village Confederation in Southeastern Europe*. New York: Columbia University Press, East European Monographs.

Stoianovich, T. (1994) *Balkan Worlds: the First and Last Europe*. New York and London: M.E. Sharpe.

6

Industrial Heritage in the Tourism Process in France

Claude-Marie Bazin

The analysis on which this chapter is founded is the fruit of many years of research within the CNRS team called Unité de Recherche en Sociologie du Tourisme International (URESTI). It was within this framework that I was induced to link industrial archaeology and tourism, which are generally considered separately, in one and the same approach.

The impetus for centring my research work on the industrial archaeology movement came from my own personal experience: the ancient medieval forge belonging to my family had been converted into a museum. Being an academic has enabled me to comprehend the inner working of the mediations occurring within this process – mediations which otherwise would have been difficult to grasp.

Thus, by means of a dialectic between theoretical paradigm and actual field experience, I attempt to unravel the complex process of the transformation of a site that was formerly industrial capital into a site that is now tourist capital, after it had already achieved the status of cultural heritage (Bazin, 1987). During the course of my research I was led to reflect on the current extension of the term *heritage* and, in particular, to assess how the question of origin makes its appearance between the past of heritage and the present of patrimony.

Extension of the notion of heritage to include industrial civilization

Since the beginning of the 1960s, the citizens of Western societies have been encouraged to develop a passion for and to mobilize urgent support to save the vestiges of their material history associated with so-called industrial, and even proto-industrial, civilization. Thus an entire section of the past emerges which, until then, had been kept apart from 'national heritage'. The only way to avoid its disappearance, perceived to be a disaster, is to elevate all these traces and souvenirs of humanity to the status of heritage – the status which castles, cathedrals and works of art have long achieved – in order to assure their continuing existence. Once part of the national heritage, these witnesses of industrial civilization are returned to the citizens. They are then incorporated into the collective memory of the citizens, contributing towards the foundation of their identity, be it on the national, regional or local level. *Pater, heres, arche* – patrimony, heritage, archaeology: such are the terms that designate this movement of industrial heritage,

I have already indicated that this interest in the vestiges of industrial civilization was organized in other Western nations well before France (Bazin, 1987): in England since 1960, in Sweden since the end of the 1960s, in America where it really took off in 1974, in Quebec in 1976, and at differing periods in different regions of the Federal Republic of Germany, whereby the forges in Bochum achieved recognition from 1960 (ICCIH, 1981). In France, even if the first faltering attempts began in 1973, it has only been some 15 years since this interest became significant and gained ground, and only ten years since it was officially recognized as being part of the national heritage (Actes des Colloques de la Direction du Patrimoine, 1986). What was the cause of this delay? A clear answer has yet to be found: too many interpretations are proposed by historians for us to decide. Let us content ourselves by quoting the pioneer in this domain, Professor Maurice Daumas, Director of the National Conservatory of Arts and Crafts, who, shortly before his death, wrote: 'In France the conception of industrial archaeology was acquired by means of a sort of osmosis . . . One cannot report an event comparable to the destruction of Euston Station in England' (1980: 437).

However that may be, it was recognition as part of the national heritage that enabled the works of industrial society to reunite with the 'world heritage of mankind'. It was then that official discourses and declarations could develop, revealing a real change in perspective: 'One must try to liberate oneself from a certain vision of heritage in which what was regarded as popular had no place' (Querrien, 1983: 8). From then on, castles and cathedrals no longer enjoyed exclusive rights as national treasures.

Consequently, we are now witnessing a vertiginous series of extensions of the notion of heritage. We now find the following included under one and the same term, with the same respect due to the witnesses of the past and with the same function of identification expected of them: the knife (Museum of Cutlery, Thiers, France), the clog (Clog Museum, Soucht, France), and the cathedrals in Saragossa and Chartres; the stable (Eco-Museum of

Fourmies, France) and the castles of the Loire valley; an ancient wooden bridge (Mader, Austria), the House of Labourers (Hoersen Museum, Belgium), and the palace (Versailles); the virgin spaces of nature (game reserves in Kenya) and urban parks (Cultural Park in Lowell, USA); mythical figures and all the heroes throughout the ages; folklore festivals and the opera; trivial happenings which make up local history and events of historical magnitude; the last worker of an abandoned factory and the industrial magnate; the recently constructed nuclear plant and the former forge dating from the fifteenth century.

The question then arises: what has tourism to do with this story? Looking for the answer, I am conscious of the difficulty faced by constructing a theory which permits one to seize in a single explanatory logic all the scattered facts which I am assembling in my field of research. My subject of investigation has led me to study and analyse international tourism, according to the hypothesis that it is to be understood as 'total social fact' (Lanfant, 1980). This hypothesis led me to unite in one framework those multiple facts which are all too often approached separately during field work. Hence there is the possibility of establishing a *connection* between a patrimonial undertaking and a tourist undertaking.

Now, it is rather surprising to realize, after having studied the vast field of academic and official literature on the subject of national heritage, that it has rarely been linked to the development of tourism. Thus I have studied the founding texts of industrial archaeology in France, such as the seminal above-mentioned opus of Maurice Daumas (1980), first in its genre; the proceedings of the major conferences on industrial archaeology in 1972, 1975, 1981, 1984 (International Committee for the Conservation of Industrial Heritage, ICCIH); and various academic papers and doctoral theses, among which I have retained Professor Yvon Lamy's *Iron Men in Périgord* (1987) as it deals precisely with our forge. Relying on a method based on Lévi-Strauss's structural analysis, I have analysed the statutes of the Committee of Information and Liaison for Industrial Archaeology (CILAC), an association which has been the driving force of this movement in France since 1980 and which, above all, integrated it into the network of the ICCIH. I have already given an in-depth analysis of the CILAC's statutes (Bazin, 1987). In addition, I have carried out a survey of the founding texts of numerous associations active in this domain, of which more than 7,000 exist in France. These various texts are surprisingly silent about the phenomenon of tourism in so far as it participated from the beginning in constituting industrial heritage, even though it did not consciously intervene in the intentions of the pioneers of industrial archaeology. Admittedly, it is acknowledged that these sites should be visited by the 'public', a term preferred to 'tourist', but, by and large, national heritage and tourism are not approached by deliberately linking them together.

What is behind the reluctance of those academics or agents involved in the cultural institutions to clearly approach this patrimonial movement which leads to the touristification of our societies? Could it be the obligatory conversion of culture/heritage into a tourist product? Could it be that tourism is associated with the economy and national heritage with culture, that the tenacious tendency to separate economy and culture is present here? This is all the more regrettable as it blocks the possibility of including in a single theoretical framework those phenomena, national heritage and tourism, which are closely connected in the field.

Unlike academics, politicians are strongly in favour of turning heritage into a tourist asset. To attain this target, they then take into account the link between economy and culture. Thus, regarding the field of industrial archaeology, official declarations appealing to industrial heritage and tourism to collaborate are not lacking: 'Since 1974, owing largely to the economic crisis, it appeared indispensable that new tourist products be promoted to help France preserve its part of the world market in the domain of tourism' (Dupuis, 1990: 13). It was recommended that these new products should be taken from the works of industrial civilization: its history, its relics and 'all those cultural sites which are also elements used to promote the economic image of France' (ibid.). Besides, did not the Council of Europe, at a conference on the construction of an European identity revert to this directive, when it declared in an all-encompassing vision: 'We must think of integrating this technical world into a wider vision of Europe which will tempt the tourist back from his travels, and cause him to rethink his view of the world' (O'Driscoll, 1964). This is a far cry from the position held by academics.

It is the indispensable link between tourism and national heritage which is at stake, and not only the development of the latter. As for tourism, it is taking on a new mission, which it has in fact already long since included in its civilizing designs and its doctrine. From the start, national heritage is inscribed in the *very logic* of tourist operations, like any other newly exploitable asset.

That is why I think that the strategy of 'patrimonialization' opens the way to 'touristification'. By itself culture is never an 'asset': in order to transform it into one it has to be classified as part of 'heritage', and then enhanced by discourse. New agents will take over the process and, thanks to this added value, will take care to insert the items of national heritage into the system of international tourism. In order to touristify a site, several operations are required: institutionalization, classification, typologies and, above all, a doctrine which for educationalists turns culture/heritage into an indispensable element for the intellectual growth of a society, and for economists turns cultural tourism into an element just as indispensable for its economic development. The two doctrines, while mutually ignoring each other, are reunited in the same project of societal development.

Some reference points

On the one hand we have a former forge dating from the fifteenth century, situated in a remote area of the French countryside: the buildings are threatened with ruin following the cessation of economic activity since 1975. On the other hand we have the owners, of whom I am one, and whose family history forms an intimate whole with the premises. Indeed, from time immemorial their ancestors have always been *maîtres de forge* and have smelted metal on this spot. They felt a powerful attachment to this particular means of production. But the present economic evolution was threatening. The owners sincerely hoped to prevent the disappearance of the forge. They perceived themselves as being heirs to a part of history which they wished to prevent from falling into oblivion. Laboriously conserved for four centuries, the forge and its ancient workshops had to be saved, and the question arose: what had to be done?

The owners' first impulse led them to look for another possibility of production within an industrial framework. Discouraged by four years of failure, they concluded that the project was indeed utopian and gave up all thought of an industrial solution. It was then that, almost without hope, the owners appealed to the Ministry of Culture for the forge's classification as a 'historical monument' because classification as a historical monument in France definitely does save a monument or any architectural object of interest from the risk of ruin. But in such cases owners cannot undertake effective action by themselves. If they wish to gain official aid and recognition, they have to found an 'association'. The first step was therefore assured by the creation of a Rescue Association of the Forge of Savignac-Lédrier.

Saving the forge from the prospect of ruin became an urgent task. Moreover, the region was being deserted in a disturbing way. In a few years' time the beauty of the landscape would blend in with the 'ruin' so dear to strollers of the last century. But nowadays the prospect of ruin poses a threat: therefore there is a sense of urgency in any rescue campaign. This phenomenon is especially tangible in the field of conservation of industrial relics, which are expected to decay rapidly, the sense of impending ruin being the reason for the nervous tension experienced right from the beginning of the rescue operation. An urgent response to the question of classification was the mainstay of the argument put forward by the members of the association. That was why, in the space of a few months, the site was lifted from its apparent local modesty and classified in 1980 as a 'national historical monument'. As already mentioned, the moment was well chosen. Thus it was that a local and almost family initiative took its place with great ease in a novel societal trend.

But the mere fact of having sacralized a site as a 'historical monument' does not suffice. Several other operations are still necessary to guarantee its permanence and its takeover by the system of international tourism. As for our family forge, I was struck by the extent to which the process of touristification to which it was submitted followed the stages of tourist sacralization, so dear to Dean MacCannell: the phases of naming and framing, of mechanical and social reproduction (1976: 44–5). These phases fell into place in a synchronic rather than a diachronic fashion. Ten years after having begun conservation, this object of industrial capital completed its transformation. The result was mature enough for it to become an object of tourist capital. Accordingly, the site was included in the official *Guide to Industrial Heritage*, published in France in 1990, which presented no fewer than 1,000 museums officially listed in a country which had only counted one-tenth of that figure 15 years previously (de Ficquelmont et al., 1990).

Rescue operation: opposition

The implementation of such projects, and the completion of all these phases, require numerous agents drawn from various fields. Attached to their own network and belonging to different social bodies, their encounter in the field revealed numerous sources of divergence which provoked misunderstandings, shattering the original unifying idealistic vision.

The agents involved in the restoration and conservation of *buildings* will encounter a problem familiar to those dealing with historical monuments: 'How to intervene without modifying? How to resolve the antinomy conservation/restoration?' (Foucart, 1989: 7). Now these two terms, as I have already analysed in a previous publication, belong to two signifying chains whose relationship, when examined, refers back to two quite different projects within one and the same system of action (Bazin, 1987). On the one hand are agents engaged in *conservation*. Their approach is 'to return things to their former condition', as close as possible to the original. Their problem is to decide what was the original state, whether it is the last state before abandonment or that of a reconstruction based on what some documents can only hint at. On the other hand we have the agents engaged in *restoration*, advocates of transformation, who do not want to return things but intend to allocate a new function to the site. In our case, we found the former strongly opposed the architects in charge of restoration, when they took or proposed initiatives less committed to a restoration of the former condition and more directed at its outright transformation into a tourist site.

As for the agents in charge of reconstituting *history*, they would also be confronted with the dilemma of conservation/restoration 'at that dead end where memory hesitates between conservation or construction' (Merleau-Ponty, 1968: 71). A discourse has to be created as necessary for the recognition of the site, whose history is buried in archives and in memories. To elucidate the history of the site, various constellations of representations were called for. Besides those of academics, there would be those of workers, of heirs, of journalists and of local inhabitants. All these representations supported, conflicted with or ignored each other. So, which criteria should be chosen? Which convergences should be favoured? Conflicts of signification emerged; multiple and diverging discourses appeared. Each protagonist claimed to possess the 'original truth' as the basis of his construction, however, and thus gave rise to the need to discuss the notion of authenticity.

Academic discourse collided with lay discourse in its attempt to write history. A 'founding father' was called for, which this scientific discourse adopted and which quite often was neither that of the heirs of the place nor that of the local actors. It contradicted the stories which members of the same family had told to each other and which called for quite another representation of this 'father'. The passage from oral to written discourse froze the ever changing history of our memory.

Around our site, there would be frequent quarrels between the academics and the heirs, the latter going so far as to oppose each other on this occasion. Some were perpetually uneasy at the thought that the spotless image of their ancestors could possibly be undermined. Since this image transmitted to them was one forming an integral part of their identity, they persisted in provoking conflicts so as to hinder the task of the academics. As for me, being a sociologist interested in studying the process of transformation of sites into tourist products, I was in a position to follow the work of the historians in a different perspective. Even though I suffered because of these family conflicts, I was able to preserve my capacity for observation, aided by the distance provided by my professional interest. In any case, I was personally aware that the forge of my youth had disappeared for good and that the discourse constructed around this undertaking would never impair the identity forged along a genealogical lineage forever closed. The *maîtres de forge* were themselves already obsolete.

However, this schism was to be joined by another, that between academics and tourist promoters, whose task it was to present this history to the public. Unaware that any of their publications would be involved in that vast operation of the touristification of heritage, the academics came to see their discourse – serious, austere and technical – watered down and even metamorphosed by the seductive and attractive discourse of tourism.

As to our forge: which world should be evoked? Should it be that of 'Remembrance of things past', the title of an article published by the person in charge of the promotion of the site, which proposed a romantic ballad around the site permitting us to regain those bygone days, and which borrowed the title of Marcel Proust's major work to this end? Or should it be the world summoned by Yvon Lamy, the academic attached to our rescue association, who preferred the title of a book by Émile Zola 'L'Assommoir', because it evoked the hard labour of the previous century's workers in a more realistic fashion? Such was the polemic around this old forge, which brought into opposition the proponents of 'history' and the promoters of 'tourism', each accusing the other of the misappropriation of memory.

Heritage and/or patrimony

Since I became involved in this field of investigation, I have been confronted by the problem which is posed by the use of the notions of heritage and patrimony in public discourse. It was not merely by chance that my attention was drawn to this problem. Being myself concerned with this item of family heritage and consequently by its transformation into an item of national heritage, I was more liable to be sensitive about the confusion between these two notions. That is why, before going on to conclude this chapter, I propose to devote some time to the terms 'heritage' and 'patrimony', which are the foundations of the discourse about national heritage.

I will proceed to a reflection of an epistemological nature, certainly derived from the study of the particular case at hand, but which forms an intimate part of my analysis of the process of 'patrimonialization' as a whole.

It is striking to observe to what extent a rupture with the traditional concept of heritage is making its appearance. We know that the terms 'heritage', 'patrimony' and 'succession' have specific meanings within the domain of what the French call private law (*droit privé*), and that the legitimacy of transmission has been established within this framework. Until very recently in France, that which is nowadays called 'national heritage' was not designated as such by the state. In the eyes of the state these remained 'historical monuments and other artistic or cultural riches of the nation'. Similar procedures were adopted in England with the Royal Commission on the Historical Monuments of England, in Sweden with the National Board of Antiquities, and in the USA with the Historic American Engineering Record. The list of states which do not include the term 'heritage' in any official body concerned with the conservation of national monuments and other historical vestiges is lengthy.

In France it was only towards 1975, with the European Year of Heritage, that 'heritage' became linked to the definite article 'the' in order to become 'the heritage' (Jeannot, 1988). In this respect, 'the heritage' falls within the sphere of what the French call public law (*droit public*). It borrows from private law those notions of heritage, of patrimony and of succession, and the difficulties that ensue from borrowing these terms are conveyed by the fundamental vagueness of all their possible meanings. One cannot transpose concepts from one specific field into another in which their heuristic value remains to be demonstrated without bearing the consequences.

Indeed, on the occasion of a private succession, an inventory is taken of possessions and obligations transmitted to the heirs by the deceased. This inventory is then declared to be *closed* and final. It is frozen. It is only after receiving these possessions and obligations as his that the successor may incorporate the heritage into his own patrimony. The successor is then at liberty to use, liquidate or transform it, as he already does for his own possessions, the only barrier to this fusion being of a personal moral kind.

If one is talking of *heritage* or of an heir, the genealogy goes back from the son to the father, the root of the currently accepted notion being that heritage is 'that which one receives from the father'. If one is talking of *patrimony*, one's attention is directed towards the future, towards the son. The content of this term is not frozen, but fluctuates even during the life of the father. Therefore the movement goes from the father to the son. Later, the patrimony of the latter will not be composed of the same elements as that of the father, without necessitating a break in the *genealogical chain* which connects one to the other.

In the case of the former forge, it certainly involved industrial capital which was transmitted in order that it might yield profit. But its incorporation into the patrimony of the heirs, who had become fathers in their turn, and their concern to confer it not as the residue of the past, as an item of inheritance, but as something with a future, logically led them to transform it into tourist capital. A prerequisite for this was its sacralization as an item of cultural heritage.

Furthermore, the very concept of heritage itself as something which is closed after the death of the father is brutally challenged. We are faced with the curious proposal that the testament of past centuries be reopened in order to incorporate within it a multitude of possessions and obligations which were not part of the inventory at the time of death. It is not that they were unknown at the time, but, having *no value*, they were discarded as minor leftovers (archives or clogs), abandoned or negligently put aside, piled up into cellars and attics in a spirit of general indifference.

This operation involves a retroactive vision of heritage, where prescription is no longer possible. It is impossible in French private law to retroactively write into this inventory of the national heritage elements which were originally not part of it. In this process the frontiers became blurred between the past in relation to the heritage and the present in relation to the patrimony. This partly explains the actual tendency to consider the new discoveries which one incorporates into the public heritage as possessions transmitted through inheritance, whereas according to the Latin sense of the term, they are contemporary 'inventions'. But these inventions are not acknowledged as such. Their legitimization is looked for in the elsewhere of the present, in a past which has become the 'foreign'. In 'so working on the past, one transforms it into the Other of the present Society' (Guillaume, 1990: 16), and one displaces the markers of identity. Is it not this problem that the agents of 'the putting into heritage' confront?

But, even more so, it appears that all these vestiges of industrial society, at the time of their entry into the national heritage, suffered the same administrative fate as did cathedrals, abbeys, convents and churches in their day. The last, formerly under the Ministry of Religion and corresponding primarily to a religious function, became architectural prototypes of each great period of European history – Roman, Gothic, baroque or modern – to the detriment of their religious quality, when they were placed under the wing of the Ministry of Fine Arts. The same phenomenon is to be found in other countries under other guises. These monuments enter into another system of reference. A profound mutation takes place as regards the relationship to their origin with this new adherence. Thus factories left the Ministry of Industry, their natural father, when they were taken over by the Ministry of Culture in order to acquire the status of heritage.

Once this undertaking is completed, will we be able to recognize this national heritage? What will be left of it? Will not, in fact, the 'fabrication of a new site' have taken place? Would not new identification processes have by then emerged, rendering obsolete that which had functioned until that moment? Would not this struggle against obsolescence thus hasten an obsolescence which the ruins would have conserved in a more faithful manner? Since any undertaking of this sort is patrimonial, it cannot but convey profound changes, vectors of a dynamic other than the original one.

These institutional changes did not remain without their consequences because, thus patrimonialized, an inversion of their meaning emerges. These vestiges or signs of industrial society are perceived no longer as simple tools or products, rapidly and *luckily* obsolete, because of their natural evolution, but as 'relics' of a civilization to be protected, because they are *unfortunately* obsolete, and which should be frozen and admired as such.

It is thus possible for us to instantly seize the contradictions which from the start have visited this movement of putting items into the heritage of societies. From the very beginning, the patrimonial enterprise, which claims to be inscribed in continuity, demands a radical departure from the original purposes and values of all that is the subject/object of patrimonialization.

Furthermore, once these items of heritage have been appropriated by the tourist industry, what will remain of their original function – the prayer for salvation in ecclesiastical institutions, the labour for productive work in industrial institutions – in those brochures and leaflets destined for tourist information? What has then become of the search for the roots, of the return to the ancient, of the quest for authenticity, when such a schism installs itself in the system of filiation? If, according to Leroi-Gourand, 'tradition is as biologically indispensable to the human race as is genetic conditioning to insect societies' (1964–5: 24), what is the source of this peculiar tradition? What happens when communities, cities, entire regions become tourist curiosities, and, furthermore, when these communities turn a particular site or monument into identity markers of the region, in our case 'the region of forges'?

Indeed it was into that movement that the forge was borne. The site had acquired a history and consequently its name emerged from oblivion, all these operations being indispensable to assign it to the system of international tourism.

The heritage: administration

To understand how the project of turning our family forge into an item of public heritage had developed in that direction, we must put that forge back into its geographical and political context. I have already stated that it is situated in the Périgord, in the heart of an agricultural and forestry region which is declining economically and being depopulated rapidly. The department of Dordogne is divided into two by touristic enterprise. The south is rich in prehistoric and historic traces of Cro-Magnon man, the caverns of Eyzies, the caves of Lascaux, medieval walled towns, Renaissance castles, and battlefields on which fought the English and the French during the Hundred Years War: all sites which attract more than 500,000 tourists annually. The region is saturated. By contrast the verdant roads of the north, where our forge is situated, are only used by the rare motorist who might stop at the few places beginning to emerge from oblivion.

Aware of this imbalance, the local authorities have been trying to improve the situation for some years. It is here that the project of industrial archaeology, with this forge as its starting point, will serve to integrate this rural region by means of a tourist project of vast proportions. Dozens of abandoned rural forges, dating from the eighteenth and nineteenth centuries, line the rivers of this region. Tours based on this first lavishly restored site with its wealth of uncontested technological details could be introduced. The freshly awakened interest of tourists who have visited the first site might convince them to continue their tour along those rivers. The resulting activity would awaken the region, leading the local population to reaffirm their identity. Tourists would rediscover the long-neglected origins of our industrial civilization, from which they have been uprooted, in the ideally romantic sites transformed into recreation areas.

This policy of integration would eventually lead the state and its representatives to take a particular interest in our enterprise, prompting them to take it over completely. After all the association's efforts to promote the forge, it became the property of the department of Dordogne. The heirs relinquished their right to the property and the association ceased its activities: an operation which did not take place without some clashes and regrets for some of the initial promoters. When a site is elevated to the level of a historical monument in France, the state and local authorities can assume the right to appropriate it. It is common to see a monument classified as a historical monument against the wishes of its owners. UNESCO itself does not act differently when it decides, in accordance with the states concerned, to classify certain sites as part of the 'world heritage of mankind' without the assent of local populations and the modest associations concerned. The contradictions inherent in the local milieu risk being brutally exposed by such an event: 'What results can one expect from this dialectic between professional initiative, sometimes academic, often under state control, and goodwill, voluntary help and associations as a local tool?', asked social scientist Denis Woronoff during an international conference (Actes des Colloques de la Direction du Patrimoine, 1986: 13).

Viewed from this perspective, the strategies which are put into action rely on a wager, almost like taking up a challenge. The bet consists of uniting all the citizens of the state and of the planet in one common vision of heritage. This implies pairing together centralism and decentralization, state and democratic power, research and politics, specialists and amateurs, father and son. The question arises of how to cope with reconciling unity and diversity, local production and universalism, or tradition and modernity.

Perpetuating past divisions becomes reprehensible because it is destructive and prevents the emergence of feelings of identity. It has been said that the identity of a civilization is indivisible. Civilization forms a unique whole enabling contemporary societies to find their cohesion despite any division which, at times, undermines them by threatening their already fragile and constantly endangered sense of national identity. More fraught with danger is the effort to ensure that function in those sites which, in the past, were the field of battle between peoples or communities within one and the same nation. One of the tasks of national heritage is to resolve this grave problem, building on a collective memory pacified of the conflicts which originally were constitutive of it. Indeed, 'Memory is an essential element of what is now called individual or collective identity, whose quest is one of the fundamental activities of individuals and societies caught up in the fever and anguish of our day' (Le Goff, 1988: 174).

One, unique, indivisible: such should be heritage for a society.

International tourism has been entrusted with the task of ensuring the unity of heritage when it comes to rendering it productive: 'Tourism, a vital force for peace?' (D'Amore and Jafari, 1988).

(Translated by Kunang Helmi.)

References

Actes des Colloques de la Direction du Patrimoine (1986) *Les Inventaires du patrimoine industriel (Industrial Heritage Inventories)*. Paris: Ministère de la Culture et de la Communication.

Bazin, C. (1987) 'Capital industriel. Patrimoine culturel. Vers un capital touristique?', *Problems of Tourism* 10(2): 63–75.

D'Amore, L. and Jafari, J. (eds) (1988) 'Tourism: a vital force for peace'. First Global Conference, Vancouver.

Daumas, M. (1980) *L'Archéologie industrielle en France*. Paris: Robert Laffont.

de Ficquelmont, G.M., Blin, O. and Fontanon, C. (eds) (1990) *Le Guide du patrimoine industriel, scientifique et technique*. Lyon: La Manufacture.

Dupuis, J. (1990) 'Introduction', in G.M. de Ficquelmont, O. Blin and C. Fontanon (eds), *Le Guide du patrimoine industriel, scientifique et technique*. Lyon: La Manufacture.

Foucart, B. (1989) 'La Restauration au XXème siècle', *Monuments Historiques*, 161: 5–11.

Guillaume, M. (1990) *Patrimoines en folie*. Paris: Maison des Sciences de l'Homme.

ICCIH (1981) *4ème Conférence internationale pour l'étude et la mise en valeur du patrimoine industriel (4th International Conference on the Conservation of the Industrial Heritage)*. Paris.

Jeannot, G. (1988) 'Du monument historique au patrimoine local'. Thèse de doctorat de 3ème cycle, Université Paris X, Nanterre.

Lamy, Y. (1987) *Hommes de fer en Périgord*. Lyon: La Manufacture.

Lanfant, M.F. (1980) 'Le tourisme international, fait et acte social: une problématique', *Loisir et Société (Society and Leisure)*, 3(1): 135–60.

Le Goff, J. (1988) *Histoire et mémoire*. Paris: Gallimard.

Leroi-Gourand, A. (1964–5) *Le Geste et la parole II: la mémoire et les rythmes*. Paris: Albin Michel.

MacCannell, D. (1976) *The Tourist: a New Theory of the Leisure Class*. New York: Schocken.

Merleau-Ponty, M. (1968) *Résumés de cours. Collège de France*. Paris: Gallimard.

O'Driscoll, T.J. (1964) 'Remarques sur le tourisme culturel en Europe', *Rapport du Conseil de l'Europe sur le tourisme culturel en Europe*. Strasbourg: Conseil de l'Europe.

Querrien, M. (1983) *Pour une nouvelle politique du patrimoine*. Paris: La Documentation Française.

7

Tourism and Tradition: Local Control versus Outside Interests in Greece

Wendy Williams and Elly Maria Papamichael

A key concern emerging from tourism studies is the potential for social disruption from the use of 'tradition' as a tourist attraction. Disruptions often occur as host communities attempt to maintain their traditions as viable and marketable goods while living in (at least peripherally) and catering to a modern world. Disruptions also occur as a result of conflicts of interest between the host community and involved outsiders. If tradition is to be used as a marketing strategy, either explicitly or implicitly, some attempt must be made to select and define which aspects of the local tradition are to be promoted and how they are to be displayed. The various groups concerned – the tourists, the hosts, the developers, the government – are likely to have differing opinions. Certain aspects of tradition, which are considered important by the host population, may not be valued as a marketable commodity and, as in our current study, may even be considered by some outsiders as unattractive or undesirable. Some compromises may have to be made. Thus, an important element in the process of tourism development is the bargaining strength of the local community *vis-à-vis* outside interests.

In the town of Paláiá Epidhavros one aspect of tradition has been identified, defined and imposed on the local population by the Greek government. In 1984 a presidential decree was enacted which requires conformity to a traditional style of architecture. This imposed style of architecture is considered by government officials to enhance the appeal of Epidhavros as a tourist attraction, especially in relation to an important archaeological site in the area. However, the imposition of a style of architecture defined by outsiders and in contrast to the style of architecture preferred by the local population has interfered with certain traditional social values and work activities.

In this study we document some conflicts which have emerged as the control of tourism development shifts from the local population to the national government. We begin our chapter with a brief history of the town and a brief description of the main house designs in Epidhavros. Next we discuss the key elements of the presidential decree, including the building and zoning requirements, the motive for the decree and a brief outline of its development. We then analyse the impact of the decree on the lives of the people of Epidhavros. In particular, we study how the decree has constrained various traditional family relationships and activities such as: the provision by parents of separate living quarters for their adult children, the preference of related family households to live in the same neighbourhood or even in the same building, and the tradition of family members to work together in the same business and to assist each other in their separate businesses. We conclude with a summary of the study, highlighting the conflicts which emerged as a result of the government's intervention.

The town of Paláiá Epidhavros

Paláiá Epidhavros is situated on the eastern coast of the Peloponnese, across the Saronic Bay from Athens. By European standards it is a relatively new town. The few old buildings in the area are less than 200 years old. The land originally belonged to a monastery which began to sell off parcels in the early 1900s. Initially the area was undesirable for habitation because of a mosquito malaria problem. The flat-land area adjacent to the coast had once been a swamp. Following drainage and mosquito abatement programmes after World War I and especially after World War II the area grew rapidly, with most of the growth occurring in the 1930s and in the 1960s. At the time of this study, the population was approximately 2,000.

Paláiá Epidhavros is located just off a recently constructed highway which connects the town with Corinth to the north and the other areas of Greece beyond the Peloponnese. Prior to the construction of this highway only one main road connected Epidhavros with the rest of Greece. This road ran inland to Ligourion, a larger town a short distance to the south, and then from Ligourion to the western and southern areas of the Peloponnese. Before the new highway, travel to Athens was by way of Ligourion and then Náfplion, which is further west, a very indirect route. The new highway also connects Paláiá Epidhavros with the large ancient theatre of Epidhavros a few miles south. During the summer months, the weekend performances at the theatre drew many foreign and Greek tourists to the area. Since the construction of the highway Paláiá Epidhavros is now on the direct route between Athens and the theatre. The new highway and an improved ferry service from Piraeus, the port of Athens, has promoted closer ties between the town and Athens. The performances at the theatre are important cultural events attracting many prominent Greek citizens. Also, a growing number of Athenians own second homes in Epidhavros.

The very fertile land surrounding the town and an abundant supply of water support a thriving agricultural industry. Until recently agriculture provided the main source of income for Epidhavrans. Beginning in the 1960s the townspeople began to increase their investment in tourist-related businesses, mainly in small hotels, tavernas (small, informal restaurants) and souvenir shops and in expanding the small port which services visiting yachts, the ferry from Athens and a growing fishing industry. The investment in the tourist industry was influenced by and coincided with the improvements in transportation between Athens and Epidhavros and the growing importance of the theatre as a tourist attraction. Paláiá Epidhavros is the closest town to the theatre situated along the coast. Thus it was a natural location for attracting tourists. At the time of this study approximately one-third of the town income came from tourism.

The site of a large ancient city is directly adjacent to the town. Ruins are visible both on land and under water. The central site is currently covered with olive and citrus trees. While extensive excavation work has not yet begun, a small amphitheatre has been recently uncovered. The existence of this second though much smaller theatre, and the other ruins of the ancient city, prompted the issuing of the presidential decree. Government officials not only wanted to protect the ruins but also wanted to ensure the proper environment for their display. The Ministry of Civilization and Culture has plans for building a museum and a self-guided tour of the area and for sponsoring cultural events and performances at the little theatre.

The houses of Paláiá Epidhavros

A few of the original houses of the village are still occupied today. These houses are claimed to be between 150 and 200 years old. They all have tiled, gabled roofs. Originally, these houses had one room for living and one room for animals. They all had earthen floors and a hole in the roof from which smoke could escape. Today these homes have all been modernized with a concrete floor and a chimney. Construction was of stone with an earth-lime-water mixture used for mortar. The same mixture was used to cover the exterior and interior walls. A simple pattern resembling stonework was etched into the exterior surface. The walls were sometimes reinforced by mixing animal hair with the mortar and by strategically placing sticks between the stones. Generally, however, the walls were not strong enough to support a second storey Window and door openings were kept small so as not to unduly weaken the walls and as protection against the scorching summer sun.

The village remained very small until after World War I. Most of the early inhabitants rented land from the nearby monastery. After World War I, with the implementation of the mosquito abatement programme and the sale of prime agricultural land by the monastery, the population of Paláiá Epidhavros grew substantially. People moved into the town from other areas of the Peloponnese and from the north including Macedonia and Albania.

In the 1930s there was a notable increase in housing construction. Many of the houses in the town today date from this period. Most of these houses have two or three storeys, a square or rectangular shape and a tiled hipped roof. A few houses are L-shaped with a gable roof. Balconies are a fairly common element although many were later additions and are not typical of the period. Stone was still used as the basic building material but by the 1930s the townspeople had adopted more sophisticated construction techniques. These included the use of commercially prepared mortar, rather than the home-made lime and earth mixtures, and the use of metal reinforcement in the stonework. These improvements meant that walls were stronger and could easily support a second or third storey. Window and door openings were still kept small for structural reasons. Three distinct styles of etching patterns with their variations were used on the exterior surfaces and were often embellished with the use of colour. This style of house remained dominant in the village until the 1950s when construction technology changed again.

The second period of rapid population growth occurred in the 1960s. By this time stone construction had been replaced with the use of reinforced concrete. This type of construction prevails today, not only in Epidhavros but in all of Greece and in other Mediterranean countries as well. Reinforced concrete is used as the structural framework of the building which is then filled in with brick or construction blocks. The completed exterior and interior walls are covered with plaster. There is little of the traditional stonework-like etching on the exterior surfaces of these houses. Colour is freely used: different levels are often painted different colours to signify different owners. The reinforced concrete adds considerable strength to the framework so that the height of the building is no longer limited by structural constraints. Also, window and door openings can be very large as the walls are no longer required to bear the weight of the upper storeys. The roofs of the houses are flat reinforced concrete slabs.

The most recent type of construction – that of reinforced concrete – is the most prevalent and thus dominates the architecture of the town. For reasons we will explain later these houses are frequently left unfinished. The flat roofs are often cluttered with remnants of unfinished construction, with the storage of personal belongings and with building maintenance elements such as plumbing and solar water heaters. This cluttered and incomplete look is in sharp contrast to some of the more traditional island villages where the tidy and quaint red tiled roofs dominate the skyline. This contrast in rooftops was a key element in motivating the decree and the restrictions on roof construction are among its most controversial aspects.

The decree

A presidential decree of January 1984 sets forth specific building requirements and zoning regulations for the town of Paláiá Epidhavros. This decree places restrictions on Epidhavrans in addition to those of the general building code of Greece and the national laws protecting historic areas. The purpose of the decree is to protect the important archaeological site adjacent to the town as well as to promote a 'proper' architectural environment for the display of the ancient ruins, the future museum and the proposed productions at the little theatre.

The preliminary suggestion for the decree came from the Archaeology Department of the Ministry of Civilization and Culture in Náfplion, the administrative headquarters for the area in which Paláiá Epidhavros is located. The local ministry suggested a series of four zones surrounding the site of the ancient city which limits construction and agricultural use in the area. The zone which includes the site of the ancient city forbids most activities altogether except for minimal agricultural maintenance. In the next zone, limited construction is allowed for houses, for agriculture or for church purposes. In addition to these activities, the third zone also allows hotels but only as small bungalows. The fourth zone has the fewest restrictions and includes most of the commercial area of the town. In addition to the zones the city limits were changed so that the town itself is much smaller. In addition to limiting agricultural and building activities in the area, the Ministry of Civilization and Culture wished to prevent new construction in the surrounding zones from dominating the area and interfering with or blocking the view of the ruins. Thus in addition to the zoning restrictions the ministry suggested a building height limit of two storeys for the entire area.

Another government office, the Ministry of Town Planning and Environment, added still further building restrictions in order to promote a traditional style of architecture in the village which they felt would provide a more appropriate environment for the ruins and unify the visual impression of the town. The appropriated style of architecture was defined by a special committee which surveyed house types in Paláiá Epidhavros and the surrounding area, and is loosely based on the 1930 house designs. The building requirements of the decree are summarized as follows:

1 All buildings must be covered by a hipped roof.
2 The roof must be completed and covered with tiles immediately after the completion of the central structure and before occupation of the dwelling.
3 The tiles must be of the Byzantine type.
4 Only a chimney in the traditional style, and one TV antenna, may protrude above the roof.
5 Solar panels must lie parallel to the slope of the roof. All plumbing for solar panels must be under the roof.
6 Aluminium cannot be used in any architectural element on the house exterior.
7 The windows, the doors and their frames must be made of wood.
8 The width of door and window openings must not be greater than one-half the height.
9 The size and style of balconies must be traditional.
10 The colour of exterior surfaces, the wall that surrounds the yard, the placement of the house on the site, the general manner of construction and the overall impression must be traditional.
11 Existing buildings must be restored to their original form. This includes removing any 'foreign' elements: awnings, extra solar panels and TV antennas, any sort of tube installation, any object that causes pollution or creates a bad appearance.

These building requirements hold for shops as well as houses. There is also a list of restrictions regulating signs and advertising including size limitations, the degree of protrusion from the building, the use of foreign languages and the use of neon and similar lighting.

The people of Epidhavros claim that the decree was 'written on the knee', that is written without investigating the needs of the townspeople, and without investigating alternative options for protecting and displaying the ruins. Most of the townspeople agree that some sort of town plan is needed but feel the decree is not appropriate for many reasons. The main objections are as follows. First, the new town boundaries and zoning restrictions have severely limited the future growth of the village. Secondly, the references to tradition are too vague. In most cases there is no specific definition of 'traditional style' or 'traditional manner'. Some of the restrictions are controversial. For example, most townspeople point out the many three-storeyed older buildings. Also, not all of the older buildings have a hipped roof: some have gabled roofs, some have shed roofs. The vagueness of the decree and the differing opinions mean that what is accepted as traditional and what is not is left entirely to interpretation. This ties in with the third objection: no town resident sits on the Architectural Committee in Náfplion which must approve all building plans. At the time of this study there were two civil engineers and one architect living and working in Paláiá Epidhavros, all qualified to sit on the committee.

The issue of who interprets and enforces the decree is crucial. For example, one requirement is usually completely ignored: that requiring the use of Byzantine tiles. Roman tiles, which are less expensive and easier to install, are almost always used. This suggests there is some leeway in implementing the requirements of the decree. Points 9 and 10 of the above summary are very general and could be interpreted in many ways. For example, the traditional colour for the exterior surface is almost always interpreted to be white or off-white and plain. Yet our own observations of older houses show a wide use of colour and texture, especially the stonework-like etching patterns. The job of the architect or engineer then becomes one of guessing what the committee will accept and what it will reject. Once one type of design is approved by the committee there is a tendency for the architects and engineers to repeat the same style because they know it will be accepted.

At the time of this study, the town council and individuals acting independently had been campaigning for changes in the decree through various legal and bureaucratic channels and by generating public awareness and support.

The impact of the decree

Both the zoning laws and the design restrictions have placed constraints on local social and economic activities. The townspeople have voiced the greatest resentment over the zoning restrictions since they reduce potential building sites by about one-half. Also, since the town is very spread out and disconnected in parts there are no óbvious boundary lines. This has caused conflicts in defining acceptable town limits and is one of the key elements contested by the townspeople in their legal battle with the government. Before the 1984 decree most of the area was considered within the city limits. Now many people find themselves living or owning property outside the town boundary. Since the minimum plot size for building a house outside the boundary is much larger than within the boundary, they are now prohibited from building the home or business they had planned to build for themselves or for their children.

Obviously, the smaller town size has limited the potential growth of Epidhavros. This impacts upon the local community in two important ways: first, the potential for expanding the tourist sector has been limited; and secondly, it will become more and more difficult for younger generations of the local inhabitants to find housing in the area. These two impacts are considered in the following sections.

Tourism

The tourist industry is an important part of the town's economy. Families seeking to increase their income and provide employment for adult children often invest in tourism. For Epidhavrans, the tourist industry has many advantages. The small amount of uncultivated arable land limits any increase in the agricultural sector. Conveniently, the main crops, olives and citrus fruits, are winter harvest crops. Thus the peak work times and seasonal incomes between tourism and agriculture balance out over the year. The tourist industry provides opportunities for all family members to work, including children during the non-school summer months.

It seems natural that Epidhavrans would choose to become involved in the tourist industry. They are very friendly, outgoing people and gracious hosts. Many of the people in Epidhavros have learned to speak one, two or more foreign languages in order to converse with their guests. Many of the tourists who come to Epidhavros spend their entire vacation there and return year after year. They are seeking good food and lodging along the Mediterranean coast at reasonable rates. The townspeople provide it. Epidhavrans often offer services to their guests beyond those required of a business transaction. For example, one hotel owner makes arrangements with his fisherman brother to take his hotel guests on a boat to nearby beaches which are not easily accessible by car. On one occasion, when a guest had caught an octopus, the wife of the hotel owner volunteered to cook it in the Greek style.

The owner of the apartment we rented frequently came to have coffee with us in the mornings and often brought fresh fruit and vegetables from her garden. Of course these examples demonstrate sound business practice as well as expressing the natural generosity of the townspeople and their desire to relate to their guests on more than just a business level. Epidhavrans had not, as yet, experienced much disenchantment or frustration with the seasonal invasion of tourists.

The townspeople have also successfully integrated their domestic activities with many of the work activities in the tourist sector. For example, families with a young daughter will often build an extra flat or apartment to rent out to tourists until their daughter marries, at which time the apartment becomes her dowry. Women often cook at home, preparing food for use in the small restaurants. Some traditional home crafts are offered for sale. For example, a woman and her two daughters operate a small shop in the front of their home where they sew and sell embroidered household linens. In most hotels some refreshments are served from a small kitchen adjacent to the foyer. This area is often used as an extension of the living quarters of the family of the hotel owner. Here they entertain their neighbours and their personal guests while simultaneously serving their paying guests. It is not uncommon for the tourists to join in with the personal guests. On one occasion a group of us were invited to participate in a large family celebration which included dining, drinking, dancing and singing.

All of the tourist businesses except a very few are owned and managed by the townspeople. Thus the people of Epidhavros are not only hosts but also entrepreneurs, and as entrepreneurs they are able to control tourist activity in their town. For example, most businesses keep the traditional Greek hours, which means that all shops shut down for two to four hours in the afternoon. This is often inconvenient for tourists until they learn this local custom.

In considering the town layout, most of the hotels and restaurants border the small port. Tourists normally do not wander into the residential area of the town, yet Epidhavrans make use of the 'tourist areas' as much as do the tourists. For example, between the rows of hotels and restaurants and the water's edge is a new park. In the evenings, while tourists remain seated at the outdoor tables of the restaurants, the townspeople come down to the park. It is cool along the water and families – children, parents, grandparents and all – come to socialize. Epidhavrans often outnumber the tourists in this area. When the park was being built the local taverna owners were successful in preventing trees from being planted in it. Now the only shade in the area is provided by the awnings of the tavernas, and tourists must become their patrons in order to escape the sun.

Certain tavernas seem to be 'reserved' for the local population. Some of these are in the more residential areas, off the tourist track, but some are in the middle of town. Two elements which seem to signal to tourists not to enter are the architecture and the décor. For example, one taverna that only locals frequent is in the basement of an unfinished building. The taverna itself is unfinished and undecorated and rather dark. Another, located on the water-front, caters to both tourists and locals. Tourists generally sit at the outside tables while locals generally sit in the dining-room. The plainness of the building (lack of 'charm') and the openness of the kitchen, which is not hidden from the dining-room, seem to signal to tourists that the inside dining-room is private and that they should sit outside, which the tourists normally prefer anyway.

So, not only does the decree limit the growth of the tourist sector, it also disrupts the control the townspeople have over tourist development. It limits control in several ways. First, under the decree, it is harder to signal 'tourists welcome' or 'for locals only' since the architecture is necessarily becoming more uniform and more like the architecture which tourists, seeking a traditional atmosphere, find more attractive. Thus a certain level of privacy which the townspeople have been able to create may be threatened.

Secondly, with the growing emphasis placed on the ancient Greek culture there may be a shift in the tourist population. For the most part, the current long-stay tourists come for the hot climate and Mediterranean beaches. When the plans for the little theatre and the museum are realized, the town will attract more weekend or short-stay tourists. Broadly speaking, these tourists have different interests and come to Greece for different reasons. They are on a pilgrimage of sorts, seeking knowledge about the roots of their civilization, and normally prefer to visit numerous sites. This shift in the tourist population may have some effect on the relationships that townspeople establish with their guests.

Thirdly, at the time of this study two different large resorts financed by outside money were being considered for the nearby area. Perhaps the limitations placed on the local expansion of the tourist sector mean leaving further development to outside investors who have the capital and connections to negotiate at high govern-ment levels. If further development in tourism is by outside investors it is likely that the work activities of the townspeople will shift from entrepreneurial roles to more menial employee roles. As entrepreneurs it is Epidhavrans who are offering food and lodging to tourists. The tourists are *their* guests. As employees the people of

Epidhavros will be servants. In the former relationship there is a certain amount of equality between the host and the guest. In the latter this equality is lost. With development by outsiders, Epidhavrans will lose control over the extent of the tourist industry. Also, since development by outside investors is likely to be on a large scale, the number of tourists, particularly short-stay tourists, is likely to increase substantially. The lack of control and the change in the relationship between Epidhavrans and tourists may lead to frustration and disenchantment with the tourist population.

Housing

The second impact felt by the townspeople from the zoning restrictions and the smaller town size is the threat that their children, when they become adults, will not be able to live in the area. Many young Epidhavrans, unlike youths from other areas, prefer to remain in the town rather than move to Athens or some other larger city. The tourist industry provides both ample economic opportunities and amusement for local youth. Under the decree, town resources will be strained to meet the natural increase in population.

Both parents and adult children value living in the same town and especially in the same neighbourhood. Keeping the family close is important not only for social reasons but for economic reasons as well since family members often work together. In the agricultural sector fathers and sons, brothers and uncles all work together harvesting each other's crops. The production of olive oil is virtually a social event. Families bring their olives to the press – one of the oldest working presses in the area – and all pitch in to help as they wait for their oil. This tradition is extended to other business activities as well. For example, in the small restaurants many of the older women prepare large casserole dishes and desserts at home and a young child or grandchild carries these from home to the restaurant.

In another example, two cousins own businesses next door to each other. One owns a taverna, the other a butcher's shop. As is typical in most businesses, the family of the butcher lives above the shop. The slaughtering of small animals (lambs and goats) is often done in the back yard with the butcher's family and his cousin assisting. In exchange, the butcher stores the meat for the taverna. If the taverna is very busy or short of help, the wife of the butcher comes to wait on tables. Since she lives right next door her children are free to come and go or can call for her from the back balcony. Also, the grandmother lives in the same building and is available to watch the children.

In another case, one young unmarried daughter runs a hotel which is directly behind her parents' shop and house. She uses one of the hotel rooms as her own but frequently eats with her parents and uses their washing machine for doing her laundry. If her parents need to leave she takes over in the shop. The hotel guests know where to find her, and incidentally begin the habit of purchasing their supplies from the parents' shop. In this way there is a fluid and spontaneous movement between work and domestic activities and an exchange of responsibilities between family members, which depend on the proximity of family households. In many cases the distinction between work and non-work is very vague as many work activities are also an occasion for social intercourse.

The opportunity for building new shops or houses for one's children in Epidhavros has been drastically curtailed by the decree. Living in the same building or as neighbours is preferable, but as the number of empty plots within the town decreases families depend on building on the outskirts. However, as mentioned above, the minimum plot size requirements outside the town boundary limit this possibility. In addition, as more and more Athenians and foreigners build summer homes in the area, property prices will increase beyond the means of some of the families.

In addition to the zoning restrictions of the decree, the design and construction requirements also constrain social and economic activities in the community. The two-storey height limit has an obvious impact. Potential housing space is limited not only by zoning restrictions but also by height restrictions. Many Greeks wish to provide living quarters for their adult children especially, but not only, as a dowry. The two-storey height limit constrains fulfilment of this responsibility. It is less expensive to build an extra storey than to construct a separate house altogether. It also keeps the family close to have everyone living in the same building. Of course, two separate apartments can be built on the same floor but traditionally one floor represents one household. Also, with the smaller plot sizes that remain in the town, the size of the building is often not large enough to accommodate two apartments on the same floor.

The two-storey height also interferes with family work relationships. As mentioned above, it is typically the case that proprietors live above their shops. With a three-storey building, two households can live above the shop and share in the work responsibilities.

Another source of frustration from the design criteria of the decree comes from the roof requirements. With limited building sites and a two-storey limit on height, a flat roof could provide needed extra living space. Epidhavrans, like other Greeks, had taken advantage of the flat roof construction. In Greece outdoor space is frequently as important as indoor space for carrying out domestic activities. The yard is an extension of the house. Food preparation is often done outdoors. During the summer evenings chairs are moved outside to the front of the house for socializing. Daily house cleaning includes sweeping the area immediately in front of the house including the pavement and even the street. With the flat roof construction it was natural for people to make use of the roof area as a living space, especially as land values increased and yard areas decreased. Roofs are used as patios, for sleeping during the summer, for hanging laundry, for drying vegetables, for storage and so on. The only cinema in town is an outdoor theatre located on the roof of one of the downtown shops.

The main objection, however, is to the requirement that the roof be complete, with tiles, before occupancy. With the reinforced concrete construction it is possible to build multi-storeyed houses finishing only one storey at a time. Houses can grow as families grow and as finances permit. Before the decree families often began construction on a house knowing that it would be years before they had the finances or the need to complete it. Frequently only one storey of a two- or three-storeyed house would be occupied. The other storeys remained skeletal and unfinished until needed by an older child. If families didn't have the finances to build the framework for a three- or four-storey house they could plan to add another storey at a later date. To facilitate the addition of an extra storey it is necessary to leave re-bars, the reinforcing steel rods which are embedded in the concrete, protruding from the roof. The concrete framework for the later addition is then anchored on to the protruding re-bars. The requirement for roof completion disrupts the practice of having the house grow as the family grows.

The tiled roofs are also very expensive. While saving to finance the roof, a family could be living in the house, with the floor of the unfinished apartment above serving as a temporary roof. Now, families must wait before beginning construction until they have the finances to pay for the complete roof. In one case, two brothers planned to build a two-storey house with one level for each brother. The elder brother was ready and anxious to begin construction. The younger brother, however, was not as anxious and was not able to pay his share. Before the decree, the older brother could have completed his half of the building and let the younger brother build the second storey when he was ready. Now, since the roof has to be completed before occupancy, the older brother decided to wait as he did not want to be responsible for the entire cost of the roof.

Some families delay building for another reason. Many towns-people feel it likely that the height limit will eventually be changed either as a result of their efforts in petitioning the government or because of a change in the government itself. If families build now, adding on another storey at a later date will involve removing the tiled roof, a much more complicated and expensive procedure than just adding on to the flat roof.

While most Epidhavrans agree that the ancient ruins need to be protected and support the government's efforts towards these ends, they are often sceptical of the need for regulating house design. Most townspeople admire the charms of the older island villages but they do not think Epidhavros is unattractive or without its own charm. In fact the people of Epidhavros are fiercely proud of their town. For the townspeople, how an area is used is often more important than how it looks. For instance, the small park bordering the port was considered by some tourists as unattractive. The townspeople, however, while voicing some criticism, find this area very appealing. They relate to the park from the point of view not of design but of the activities which take place in the area.

Most people speak fondly of the past and of the lost traditions. For example, some of the older houses still have an outdoor oven. These are stone structures about 1.2 by 1.2 metres in plan and 1.5 metres in height in which a fire is built. When it is hot enough and the fire is reduced to coals, bread and other food dishes are placed inside for baking. Some families still use these ovens but only for special occasions and holidays. The ovens add a certain degree of that sought-after charm to the older neighbourhoods. No one, however, would think to require the families of Epidhavros to cook with these ovens. To many of the inhabitants the requirements for a traditional house design in Epidhavros are just as ludicrous. Epidhavros should not, many feel, be constrained by design codes which are more appropriate where a traditional and fairly uniform house design already dominates the town architecture. Some Epidhavrans feel that the design restrictions were included in the decree owing to the influence of some of the Athenians who own summer houses in the area.

Conclusion

The national government has explicitly decided to promote the ancient culture of Greece and its historical significance for tourists, most of whom live in Western societies. This aspect is stressed in the national advertising slogan, 'Come home to Greece'. The Epidhavrans, on the other hand, implicitly wish to promote their

Mediterranean village life-style, to share with tourists their food, lodging and festivities. This fundamental opposition has resulted in a series of conflicts between Epidhavrans and the Greek government. These conflicts centre on the design codes and zoning laws of a 1984 presidential decree.

For the government, the architecture in the town must provide the appropriate backdrop for the display of the ancient ruins. The government has chosen to enforce aspects of the local 1930s rural architecture as a way to affirm regional distinction and appeal to certain tourist expectations. The style of architecture chosen by the townspeople is universal and supports fulfilment of family responsibilities, social interactions and work relationships. There is no unique quality in this architecture to attract tourists and it is even considered by some outsiders as a distraction.

The government focuses on preserving house design as a finished product. For Epidhavrans house construction is an incremental social process tied to important life-cycle activities.

The zoning limitations attempt to establish a town centre with defined boundaries and to segment residential, commercial, agricultural and tourist areas. Prior to the decree, town growth followed social needs and local entrepreneurial incentives without concern for dividing the town into specific districts and without being constrained by artificial boundaries.

Epidhavrans were successful in finding a specific niche in the tourist industry – that of catering mainly to middle- and lower-income tourists – which allows them to combine domestic activities and responsibilities with their entrepreneurial roles, to control the dimensions of the tourist industry and to establish host–guest relationships based on equality and shared interests. However, the continuation of locally defined and controlled tourism is threatened by the interference of the government and the likelihood that future tourism development will be undertaken by outside investors. As entrepreneurs, Epidhavrans took advantage of their special location to create a viable tourist industry. Now, as outsiders become increasingly attracted to the area and attempt to impose their own standards, the legal and bureaucratic skills of the community will determine, in part, the final balance between local control and outside interests.

Note

The findings in this study are based on our observations and on a series of interviews with inhabitants of Paláiá Epidhavros and government officials in summer 1987 and January 1988. We would like to thank everyone who graciously agreed to talk with us. We would especially like to thank Tom Rosin for his support and encouragement throughout our project and the Marin Education Foundation for a special travel grant. The importance of the decree in the lives of Epidhavrans was brought to our attention while attending a joint summer field class in anthropology and architecture taught by Professors Jana Hessor and Eleftherios Pavlides and sponsored by Kansas State University. Relevant documents were translated by Ms Papamichael. All the usual disclaimers apply.

8

The Jewish Pilgrim and the Purchase of a Souvenir in Israel

MacCannell has claimed that the 'tourist consciousness is motivated by the desire for *authentic experiences*, and the tourist may believe that he is moving in that direction' when he travels (1973: 597). For MacCannell (1976) the search for authenticity is one of the outstanding characteristics of modern society, although he does not clearly define what he considers 'authenticity' to be. MacCannell (1973) proposes that we see the authenticity presented to tourists as 'staged', contrary to Boorstin (1964), who saw this authenticity as completely false, a 'pseudo-event'. An alternative theory is presented by Cohen, who proposed that we consider the authenticity of the tourist world in terms of 'the socially constructed nature of the concept' (1988: 374).

Following Cohen (1988) and Bruner (1989), we have chosen to deal with questions related to the representation and symbolization of authenticity. 'The question [we] ask is not if authenticity is inherent in an object . . . but how authenticity is constructed' (Bruner, 1989: 113), how it 'gradually emerges' (Cohen, 1988: 379) and is perceived.

The object of our study, the purchase of a souvenir, was chosen as, in our view, a souvenir does not simply serve as a 'messenger of the extraordinary' (Gordon, 1986). What is important about the souvenir is not what it is but how it is perceived by the individuals who are part of the social worlds connected with its production, sale and purchase (MacCannell, 1976; Appadurai, 1986: 44–7; Spooner, 1986) and how it acquires its meanings as a result of being taken out of one context and placed in another. 'From a theoretical point of view, human actors encode things with significance, from a methodological point of view, it is the things-in-motion that illuminate their human and social context' (Appadurai, 1986: 5).

We will attempt to relate two processes involved in the search for authenticity: the expression of personal identity, 'which has to do with our true self, our individual existence' (Handler, 1986: 3); and the endowment of authenticity to objects. Buying a souvenir is an act of acquisition of an object perceived as authentic. The process of the social construction of Israeli authenticity by which a material object is transformed into a souvenir, a symbol of identity, is the subject of our research.

Our main interest is, therefore, not in the object itself but in the world of meanings that emerge and define it through processes of social construction. This chapter, then, deals with the social processes which a souvenir undergoes within the context of buying and selling at Maskit, Israel's most prestigious store specializing in the sale of souvenirs.

Because Jewishness and Israeliness include three aspects – nationality, culture and religion – which are not necessarily over-lapping, there takes place in the space between the world of the sellers (Maskit) and the world of the buyers (primarily Jewish tourists) a discourse over the meaning of Israeli authenticity.

It appears that the boundaries of authenticity of the souvenir are the outcome of the negotiation of its symbolic meanings. The give-and-take moves between two poles: one is the search for Israeli authenticity by the Jewish tourist in the shop; the other is the creation and presentation of images of authenticity by Maskit.

To investigate this issue, field work was undertaken which concentrated on participant observation in Maskit's original Tel-Aviv shop, interviews with tourists, and interviews with Israeli and Arabic artists and artisans who create for Maskit. Maskit advertising copy written for its brochures and tourist magazines was also analysed. Although the purchase of souvenirs in Israel involves three groups of clients – local Israelis, Jewish tourists and non-Jewish tourists – this chapter focuses on the Jewish tourists who shop in Maskit.[1]

Our contention, that the purchase of a souvenir by a Jewish tourist is part of the search for authentication of identity, part of a pilgrimage, will be presented as follows. In the first section, a brief description of Maskit is given. In the second section, the manner in which Maskit socially constructs the reality in the shop will be analysed. The third section discusses Jewish tourism in the light of the modern pilgrimage. The relationship between the symbolic boundaries of identity and the sale of souvenirs is described in the fourth section. The closing remarks then summarize the argument.

Background

Maskit, Israel Centre for Handicrafts (the name *maskit*, meaning 'ornament' or 'beautiful and aesthetically exciting object', was taken from the Bible) was founded by Ruth Dayan (then the wife of Moshe Dayan) as a government project in 1954 under the auspices of the Ministry of Labour. Its stated purpose was 'to encourage artisans to continue their native crafts in the new surroundings . . . to retain and safeguard the ancient crafts and to present the crafts for sale' (Dayan and Feinberg, 1974: 152).

The artisans organized from among different groups of new immigrants were joined, in the 1960s, by well-known Israeli artists in order to add an 'Israeli artistic element' to the articles made under Maskit's patronage. The combination of modern imagination and creativity with ethnic and traditional craftsmanship gave a special and individual cast to the works sold by Maskit.

Maskit was highly successful and eventually opened a small chain of shops. With consolidation of its status, it began operating as, and was perceived as, an 'ambassador of Israel'. Dignitaries and delegations who travelled from Israel abroad were always equipped with gifts from the shop; official guests were likewise given Maskit gifts during their visits. Maskit became, essentially, part of the national ethos of the state of Israel, an institution not only involved in the production and sale of cultural objects but also, because of the role it took upon itself, a shaper of the Israeli culture presented to the public.

In the beginning of the 1970s, Maskit ceased to operate as a government enterprise and was sold to a Jewish-Canadian investor, which had little effect on the thematic content of the articles sold. Maskit has not lost its elite status over the years; it continues to use its history to grant legitimacy to what takes place in the shop.

The shop
Maskit's main shop, in which the field work was done, was located on a major thoroughfare near the Tel-Aviv beachfront hotel area.[2] The store had two floors. The entrance (on the top floor) was divided into five thematic areas. The bottom floor was reached only by an elevator, which brought the tourist down to the hall, which he or she actually entered by going down two steps. The bottom floor was especially large, almost a huge hall, also divided into different areas and looking more like a museum than a store.[3]

The customers
Maskit's customers comprise three social groups: local Israeli customers, non-Jewish tourists and Jewish tourists.

Of the Israelis who come to the shop, some are interested in purchasing gifts for the holidays, for rites of passage, and for other special events. However, most Israelis come to Maskit to purchase souvenir gifts for foreign visitors; their choice is prompted by their perception of the recipients of the gifts or how they want to 'represent' Israel to foreigners. The preference for Maskit, for these Israelis, comes from their perception that 'here one truly buys authentic items', that 'Maskit is Israel, without doubt.' We believe the elitist atmosphere expresses and supports that view.

As few non-Jewish tourists come to Maskit, they have not been included as part of the research population. We will only briefly mention them later in our discussion.

The Jewish tourists, Maskit's main customers, come to the shop on the basis of recommendations from local Israelis, other tourists who had been to the shop, or past experience. This is the source of their feeling that they have come 'to the right place', to a 'real place'. 'I know Maskit, I've been here before, I know Maskit very well': this statement by a tourist from Boston expresses the general relationship to the shop.

About 80 per cent of the Jewish tourists come from America, the rest from Western Europe, South America and South Africa. They are primarily 40–60 years old and middle to upper-middle class. Most have close relatives in Israel, which is the main reason behind the rate of their visits and one source of their close attachment to Israel.

At first glance, it may seem strange that two groups of customers (Israelis and Jewish tourists), with different desires and preferences, should find themselves together purchasing the same objects, yet defining them differently. In effect, however, each contributes to the other: Israelis enjoy the 'tourist' atmosphere and the tourists enjoy the 'Israeli' atmosphere. All this is the fruit of conscious creation and cultivation by the shop management and personnel.

The social construction of reality in the shop

Maskit is a cultural institution because of its stated purpose, the sale of cultural objects, but primarily because it has taken upon itself the creation, refinement and presentation of Israeli culture. Therefore, the essence of all its activities is related to the social construction of a reality which grants authenticity to the souvenirs sold within the shop. We will concentrate on the three central elements of that construction: women as sales personnel; Maskit as a museum; and presentation of images.

Women as sales personnel
The shop is almost exclusively controlled by women. Selling is done by 20 women whose average age is 50. All are married and have

families, except for two widows and one divorcee. They are carefully, even elegantly dressed, wear jewellery and use makeup, and
speak a number of languages (most were not born in Israel). These
women are middle class, usually lack formal professional education,
and have husbands who are either professionals or businessmen.

The reason for their working in the shop is not the salary (which
is very average for sales) but rather the flexible hours and especially
the character of the shop itself. As one woman said, 'If I am
already going out to work, it is important that the place be pretty
and pleasant. It is nice to work with tourists, and very important to
show them the beautiful side of Israel.'

The women gain status because they are Maskit employees and
they themselves contribute to Maskit's reputation for reliability and
respectability as a result of their appearance, age and manner.
Maskit is not satisfied simply with the benefits of women familiar
with the tourist world (Smith, 1979: 49--60) but demands an ideal
type of woman who can contribute to and complete the general
image of the shop.

Maskit as a museum

Maskit, especially on its lower floor, did not look like a typical
souvenir shop. It was organized by subject areas (such as the Bar-
Mitzvah Corner, the Holiday Corner, the Children's Corner), each
area having its own recognizable atmosphere and style of arrangement and decoration.

Maskit places great importance not only on the objects but
especially on the way in which it displays and offers them to
customers. This corroborates MacCannell's (1976: 78) emphasis on
the importance of the display of objects rather than the objects
themselves in the world of tourism. MacCannell differentiates (pp.
77–89) between two types of museums: those which present
collections and those which present 'representations' in order 'to
provide the viewer with an authentic copy of a total situation that
is supposed to be meaningful from the standpoint of the things
inside of the display' (p. 79).

The explicit effort Maskit makes to convert the shop to a
museum is intended to grant authenticity to the objects offered for
sale, as if the wares in the shop have previously undergone recognition and legitimation. The tourist in the shop has a unique
experience: he takes part in a 'guided tour' of the displays, accompanied by a saleswoman, in a space which is entirely characterized
by 'staged authenticity' (MacCannell, 1973). The tour is planned to
show great interest in the customer as well as to expose him or her
to the objects presented in a way that is interesting, pleasant and

convincing. No wonder that tourists themselves say that they have had a 'museum tour'.

Maskit nurtures the museum appearance of the shop by combining the two approaches. One is the display of different examples of the same category of crafts (such as jewellery, ceramics and carpets), often noting the name of the artist; the other is the theatrical display of objects against a background associated with their use. The first approach emphasizes the artistic element, and gives the impression of a 'collection'; the second emphasizes 'representations', by arranging the wares according to their supposed association and use, which is supported by the anonymity of the creators. The process of museumization thus serves to weave a web of unquestionable authenticity about all the objects, making the specific 'history' of the souvenir irrelevant to the tourist.

The construction of images

The 'self-image' Maskit presents influences the way in which its wares are perceived. It can be examined by an analysis of the written material which Maskit itself publishes and by the advertising copy appearing in the magazines directed towards tourists which are distributed primarily in hotels.[4] The analysis reveals four primary images:

1   The shop is not commercialized.
2   The shop is prestigious.
3   All sold items are hand-crafted.
4   There is no overt mention of Israeliness.

Maskit's low-key advertising serves the primary role of pointing out its elite status. We have noted above that most tourists come to the shop on the basis of personal experience and recommendations. No organized groups of tourists are ever present. The manageress of the shop stated that 'Everyone knows Maskit! There's no need to advertise.' But Maskit does assert its prestigious and international character: 'Walking into Maskit is like entering one of the finest stores in London, Paris or Rome.'

In addition, 'Maskit is associated with originality.' That is, more than prestige and style *per se*, 'originality', the 'something else' and the 'exceptional' which tourists seek are offered. This is accomplished by emphatically emphasizing the theme of hand-craftsmanship. Everything sold in the shop is described by expressions such as 'embroidered', 'handicrafts', 'hand-made', 'craftsmen', 'hand-knitted'. The absolute value of the item is thereby immediately increased and it is perceived as something which cannot be argued about or bargained over. The items gain value and legitimacy, unlike what the literature calls 'tourist art', 'airport art', or 'kitsch' (Dorfles, 1969: 155).

The emphasis on hand-craftsmanship permits avoidance of the direct mention of 'Israeliness', which is a problematic concept as a result of the variety of its definitions and interpretations. Maskit, by emphasizing such universal themes as reliability, anti-commercialism, prestige and handicrafts, about which presumably there is no question, sidesteps explicit designation of its content.

We will see that the multi-dimensionality of 'Israeliness' plays a central role in the interaction between the tourist and the saleswoman. During this interaction, the authenticity which creates the symbolic boundaries of the identity of the tourist is socially constructed.

The Jewish pilgrim

We propose that for the Jewish tourist, the purchase of a souvenir in Maskit is a process of confrontation with questions of identity and belonging, which begins with a tour of the shop and ends with the choice of a souvenir. Both Jews and non-Jews meet the requirements of the definition of the tourist as a 'temporarily leisured person who voluntarily visits a place away from home for the purpose of experiencing a change' (Smith, 1977: 2). Therefore, both groups are interested in a souvenir as 'an actual object [that] concretizes or makes tangible what was otherwise an intangible state' (Gordon, 1986: 135). However, the Jewish tourist purchases a souvenir not just as 'tangible evidence of travel' (Graburn, 1978: 28) but as an element of identity. Purchase of a souvenir for him or her is, in essence, a purchase of a symbol.

Different descriptions of the subject of tourism emphasize 'experiencing change' (p. 2), of going from one state to another (pp. 18–24), the change being not only in time and place but also in the passage from the secular to the sacred (Leach, 1961: 132–6). 'The tourist is one of the best models available for modern man' (MacCannell, 1976: 1–13) – and perhaps even for post-modern man – for whom travel is a type of ritual, although a ritual which is not necessarily related to religion (Moore and Myerhoff, 1977: 19–24). Nonetheless, concepts like the 'sacred' and the 'profane' are intertwined in the discussion on tourism, suggesting that we view tourism as a 'sacred journey' (Graburn, 1978: 24). This point leads us to argue that in order to better understand the phenomenon of Jewish tourism in Israel, we must relate to it as a pilgrimage, and to the Jewish tourist as a type of pilgrim.

As implied above, the debate over the nature of tourism has

often been fierce. Graburn sees a complete identity between tourism and pilgrimage because of three common elements: 'leisure ritual', 'outside of everyday life' and 'travel' (1983: 15). Boorstin (1964) claims that there is a loss and lack of authenticity in the phenomenon of tourism resulting from the transition from 'traveller' to 'tourist', while MacCannell contends that the 'touristic consciousness is motivated by its desire for authentic experiences' (1976: 101).

Cohen (1979) does not agree with Boorstin's point of view but he also criticises MacCannell for not making clear the distinction between tourism and pilgrimage. He would clarify and understand the phenomenon in Eliade's terms: 'Every inhabited region has what may be called a center; that is to say, a place sacred above all' (1961: 39).

Cohen classifies different types of tourism according to the tourist's social relationship to the 'centre'. The 'existential tourist' (1979: 189–93) is similar in certain aspects to the pilgrim in that he becomes connected and obligated to a centre which he himself has chosen. He 'is fully committed to an elective spiritual center, i.e., one external to his native society and culture'. Therefore, the role of the tourist in modern society fits, in a special and adaptive way, the role of the pilgrim. Graburn agrees with Cohen's approach and even confirms his conclusion: 'even when the roles of the pilgrim and tourist are combined, they are necessarily different but form a continuum of inseparable elements' (1983: 16).

Turner (1973) describes the stages of spiritualization that the pilgrim undergoes as he advances from the periphery to the centre. To him, the two are relative, determined according to the feeling and subjective relatedness of the pilgrim. 'Modern tourism is rooted not in one, but in two deep cultural themes, the center and the other' (Cohen, 1981: 11). The Jewish tourist lives in two worlds, withdrawing and approaching at the same time. His visit to Israel is in some ways a withdrawal from the other, diaspora world, and an approach to the centre (Israel). At the end of his visit he withdraws from the centre and returns to the other.

For those modern tourists who move in the direction to an 'elective centre', the transformation is into that of a type of pilgrim. This model suits the world of the Jewish tourists who move from the 'periphery' to the elective spiritual centre from which their identity emerges and on which it is dependent. This point is related, we believe, to the basic dilemma in the world of those Jews living outside Israel – the periphery – yet accepting Israel as their spiritual, cultural centre. It thus follows that the Jewish tourist undergoes an important personal experience in the elective centre, similar to the pilgrim; the purchase of a souvenir in Maskit becomes one of the elements of that experience.

The Israeli souvenir that the tourist purchases in Maskit is perceived in his eyes as an integral part of the centre, a symbolic expression of Israeliness and the spirituality of the place. The dialogue and the negotiations between the tourist and the saleswomen, to be described below, is a critical aspect of this experience, as purchase of the souvenir becomes the legitimate framework in which to ponder, debate, expose and declare one's position in regard to the question of identity.

There follow three examples of confrontations with the issue. One needs to understand that the tour in the shop, its atmosphere, is quite comfortable. The encouragement on the part of the saleswomen gives the tourists the feeling of security and encourages the desire to open their hearts. As one tourist put it, 'They really want to listen to me.'

Example 1 'My younger son does not want to live in Israel.' In this statement, a couple from Boston who visit Israel yearly complained that their younger son is uninterested in Israel despite the fact that their older daughter is living on a kibbutz. The kibbutz, to them, is the 'real' Israel.

Example 2 'To live in Israel is like being religious elsewhere.' A middle-aged brother and sister described their orthodox way of life as a protection from absorption into the secular, non-Jewish world of their native South Africa. They expressed regret, if not guilt, at not living up to a promise to their parents to come and live in Israel. To them, living in Israel, even if not with the same degree of religiosity, is the true 'Judaism'.

Example 3 'The children don't visit Israel and aren't interested in living here.' A widowed pensioner from New York rationalized his inability to make a decision to live in Israel with the fact that his children refuse to come, and that he is unable to leave them, even though he has already expressed his allegiance by fighting as an American volunteer during the 1948 Israeli War of Independence.

Although all three of the examples presented deal with different aspects of the relationship and the contact with Israel, they express a common dilemma: the 'duality of worlds', life in the periphery versus personal indebtedness to the elective centre, to Israel. We see parents disappointed that their son does not intend to come to Israel after the end of his studies; a brother and sister uncomfortable because they did not implement a family decision to come and live in Israel; and a pensioner that gave so much to Israel in the past prevented from fulfilling an old dream to immigrate to Israel.

This conflict between the periphery and the centre influences the two contradictory concepts which complete the foundations of the phenomenon of Jewish tourism in Israel – voluntarism versus obligation. The critical difference between the Jewish and the non-Jewish tourist is that for the first, voluntarism becomes obligation, which is the essential trait of the pilgrim (Turner, 1973: 200–2).

The souvenir that the Jewish tourist purchases creates a link between himself and the centre and, more than that, between himself and the cultural group to which he feels closeness and belonging. By purchasing the souvenir, the tourist expresses his loyalty and obligation to Israel during an experience which allows him to confront his identity. The obligatory links solidified with the aid of the souvenir resemble the idea of the mutual obligation woven with the giving and receipt of a gift (Mauss, 1950).

As the chosen souvenir, an integral part of the centre, is a symbol of this obligation, and of his identity, its purchase is also symbolic. Yet the logic behind the purchase creates a paradox. The fact of it being a souvenir expresses a relationship which permits both disengagement from the centre and return to the periphery with 'part of the place', with a symbol of authentic Israeliness as the tourist sees it. This authenticity, however, has been negotiated within the context of the sale.

The symbolic boundaries of identity

Jewish tourists, as we have seen, experience the purchase of a souvenir as a confrontation with one of the central dilemmas of their lives. Although they all arrive at Maskit with the purpose of purchasing symbols of Israeliness, each comes with an individual set of expectations regarding those symbols which reflect individual concerns with the issue of identity. Consequently, each tourist defines the souvenir in a way that suits those expectations. Because this confrontation is subjective, and thus different from tourist to tourist, the purchased Israeliness takes on a variety of meanings.

The purchase of a souvenir within the context of the discourse between the Jewish tourist and the saleswoman creates the possibility of defining and negotiating the authenticity of those meanings. 'Authenticity is not a primitive given, but negotiable' (Cohen, 1988: 379). Therefore, definitions, interpretations and the attribution of meanings are varied, different and changeable for the tourists because of their subjective 'ways of seeing' (Berger, 1972).

A number of approaches have been put forth which can help us to understand the role of objects in personal and social definitions of identity. 'The things that surround us are inseparable from who we are' (Csikszentmihalyi and Rochberg-Halton, 1981: 16) during the course of our lives. Objects are means of understanding societies: 'goods are neutral, their uses are social' (Douglas and Isherwood, 1979: 16). Not only the uses made of an object, but their meanings and the values applied to them are social. They are created, during negotiation of their purchase as souvenirs, in a way similar to that of the political value gained by commodities in the framework of exchange (Appadurai, 1986: 3).

Because a souvenir is 'partial' and 'an allusion . . . it will not function without the supplementary narrative discourse' (Stewart, 1984: 136). It appears that the saleswomen at Maskit have refined the techniques needed to use the objects sold as the starting point for the negotiation of meanings which are socially constructed during the discourse between themselves and the tourist.

The secret of the sale
At first glance, the impression received is that the definitions and the meanings attached to the object are known and exist as a stable repertoire. Maskit seemingly tries to indicate this consistency and stability of meanings in the display and presentation of the items to be sold. In practice, the situation is the opposite: the meanings of the objects are redefined in terms which vary from tourist to tourist as well as by the specific stage of the sale.

A certain article will be presented in one situation as 'a unique work', in another as 'really authentic', while in yet another as 'typically Israeli'; if the above are not convincing, the saleswoman will not hesitate to say 'something very authentic'. They try to present a 'range of Israeliness' whose expression relays nothing that is specifically Israeli.

In contrast to the expressions used by the saleswomen, the meanings of authenticity are more consistently formulated by the tourists. The five discerned tourist-desired categories (emic) of Israeli authenticity are:

1 hand-craftsmanship
2 art and aesthetics
3 local originality
4 cultural roots and the historic past
5 Judaica and ritual objects.

Thus, because there are no uniform definitions or criteria of Israeliness, everything changes according to those involved as the items undergo a process of attribution of meanings. This permits negotiation as well as manipulation on the part of the saleswomen. The following three examples elucidate the dynamics of the interaction at the end of which, and perhaps because of which, the tourist is satisfied and feels that his or her perception of Israeli authenticity is confirmed. The examples are first described and then discussed.

Example 1 Sylvia, an American tourist from California, was especially interested in a piece of art owing to her occupation, sculpture. She told the saleswoman a bit about her work and expressed enthusiasm for a particular piece of ceramics by a young Israeli artist. However, she found it hard to decide to purchase the item owing to, in her opinion, the extremely high price.

When the saleswoman discerned that the customer was enthusiastic but tentative, she suggested that the customer purchase two candlesticks from the same series of work by that artist. Sylvia then pointedly remarked that 'I've no intention to buy any religious object.' The saleswoman then paid the lady a compliment on her refined taste. In the end, the customer bought one of the objects that had originally interested her but in a lower price range.

Example 2 Julia, a tourist from Milan, comes to Israel almost every year and has purchased, according to her, many souvenirs for her family, her friends and herself. 'I really don't know exactly what I want; I have so many things from Maskit. Maybe this time I'll take a special, embroidered tablecloth.' The saleswoman accompanied her to the tablecloth area and offered her cloths of different types of embroidery and styles of weave.

Julia became excited about each but no one particular example 'caught on', as she said. 'I'll show you something you'll love immediately, something you haven't seen before; it's very authentic', said the saleswoman, and took out a number of placemat and napkin sets, upon which were printed archaeological motifs from different sites in Israel. The saleswoman opened one of the wrappings and showed the customer the included explanatory material. Julia, impressed by what was written, chose two sets in different colours and motifs, and said 'You see how ancient are our roots here? No one can take them from us.'

Example 3 A couple from New York request they be shown a talit and skullcap for an adolescent about to be bar-mitzvahed.[5] 'In a couple of weeks, the son of our good friends will ascend to the Torah, and we are very excited about it',[6] they explained to the saleswoman during the pleasant discussion about the reasons for the purchase and the degree of attention paid to their choice. Her husband added that he was the godfather at the child's circumcision, and continued with the comment that 'although we ourselves are not religious, we make a point of observing certain rituals.' After the couple chose two sets for the child and his older brother, the husband wanted to see a talit for himself, saying 'I never buy these things in America. I bought my talit in Israel a few years ago. To me, it has different meaning when you buy it here.'

Discussion, example 1   Here we are witness to an attempt by the saleswoman to convince a customer interested in artistic and aesthetic articles (category 2) to purchase a traditional-religious item. The offer was received with antagonism: 'I've no intention to buy any religious object.'

The saleswoman had adopted the manipulative strategy of totally changing the content of the sought-for 'Israeliness', as the offer of a traditional-religious object is almost always positively accepted by tourists: 'I already have a few of these but don't mind having another one.' This is not Sylvia's response, who actively opposed the offer and instead chose a type of item she had originally preferred while compromising only on price. Sylvia in effect refused to alter or negotiate her definition of authentic 'Israeliness' despite the attempts of the saleswoman.

Discussion, example 2   After being presented with various options, the opportunity was given to the tourist to choose an 'Israeliness' whose meaning is rootedness in the place, Israel, and the historic past (category 4): the saleswoman presents her with a 'really authentic' item, as verified by the documentation. But Julia was not satisfied with merely authentic ancient motifs and written explanations. She linked the purchased symbolic 'past' with her 'collective present': 'our roots [are] here . . . No one can take them from us.' By her statement and consequent purchase she reinforced her attachment to her membership group – although it is not clear if that group is 'Israeli' or 'Jewish'. In any case, rootedness and the past and, implicitly, continuity are the meanings of the souvenir which she chose to emphasize.

Discussion, example 3   We have before us an example of a couple from New York wanting to purchase ritual items for a religious service while emphasizing that, although they are not religious, they do observe some of the rituals. From the purchase of a gift the man turned to a purchase for himself and emphasized that 'I never buy these things in America . . . it has different meaning when you buy it here.'

The first question for us, then, is whether or not the meaning of the items and the participation in the rituals are predominantly religious or cultural based on the fact of conscious selectivity. In addition, and more pointedly for our discussion, the husband does not purchase ritual items in the United States, despite the richness of the variety, and the fact that many items are imported from Israel, because of the symbolic meaning and special importance for him of their purchase in Israel itself (a combination of categories 4 and 5). The place of purchase, of Israel as the centre, gives the item its 'different meaning'.

We see, then, that the 'authentic Israeliness' of the item is subject to negotiation of its boundaries and meanings, a process mediated by the intervention of the saleswomen. In effect, an 'Israeliness' that is not absolutely definitive is bought and sold; rather, it is only the perceived authenticity of the items that is the consistent element.

Closing remarks

We have concentrated on the manner in which 'a tourist makes a cultural product acceptable as authentic' (Cohen, 1988: 378). Cohen presents this as a question; we present it as an answer. That is, the tourist wants to see authenticity by means of the 'narrative discourse' during which he concretizes the meanings symbolized by the items he purchases through the ascription and confirmation of their authenticity.

The boundaries of the negotiation are, then, the symbolic boundaries of authenticity whose content varies with the subjective needs of the tourist. The authenticity searched for and perceived is the basic element of the search for identity which, in this case, he associates with themes of 'Israeliness'. The boundaries of authenticity are, in effect, the boundaries of identity.

Maskit, in its organization, choice of wares and style of salesmanship, serves as a 'reservation' of 'authentic' Israeli culture, providing alternative images and answers to the dilemmas of Jewish identity. This brings us to the conclusion that authenticity is confirmed during each and every purchase as a negotiation between the demands of the tourist in his or her search for identity on the one hand, and the images of authenticity Maskit produces and distributes on the other. The tourist, when purchasing a souvenir, selects those representations of authenticity which are meaningful to him or her.

A souvenir, then, is a symbol. It allows closeness and distance at one and the same time. Purchase of a souvenir expresses relatedness to the centre, to the group. Yet the souvenir, as part of the place, allows the tourist to retreat from the centre and return to the periphery in which he lives his daily life. The souvenir, as it represents the Jewish pilgrim's search for identity, allows him to solve temporarily his dilemma of identity and still continue his pilgrimage.

Notes

1 The majority of Maskit's customers are Jewish tourists; the proportion of Israelis who shop there was somewhat smaller. Almost no non-Jewish tourist bought souvenirs during the period of the research.

2 The research was conducted in the original main shop during 1984–5. A year later, the shop was moved to an adjacent street.

3 On the top floor of Maskit is found the Fashion Department. Displayed are women's clothing, wedding gowns, embroidered dresses, and other fashion items, but especially jewellery and artistic crafts made of silver, gold and Roman glass. In addition, there are areas containing religious items, glassware, ceramics, olivewood and metalware, and books on topics such as holidays, the history of Israel, archaeology, tradition and cooking.

On the lower floor are found embroidered children's clothing, games, hand-made dolls (camels, sheep), shirts printed with typical Israeli motifs (maps of Israel, duncecaps, cacti etc.), all in the Children's Corner. In the Embroidery Corner are found covers for bread and matzoth, bags, wallets, tablecloths embroidered and printed in a variety of styles, as well as skullcaps, prayer shawls and their envelopes. Glassware and ceramics, different from those found on the top floor, are also displayed. In other corners, antique-style copies of maps of Israel during different historical periods and hand-woven rugs designed by different artists are available.

4 The tourist magazines are primarily *Hello Israel* and *This Week*.

5 A talit is the ritual shawl worn by men during services in the synagogue.

6 The Torah contains the Pentateuch. Only males who have come of age, at 13, are allowed to read it. The bar-mitzvah service, performed at the age of 13, is the rite of passage from boyhood to manhood.

References

Appadurai, A. (1986) 'Introduction: commodities and the politics of value' in A. Appadurai (ed.), *The Social Life of Things: Commodities in Cultural Perspective*. Cambridge: Cambridge University Press. pp. 3–63.

Berger, J. (1972) *Ways of Seeing*. British Broadcasting Corporation and Penguin.

Boorstin, D. (1964) 'From traveler to tourist: the last art of travel', in *The Image: a Guide to Pseudo-Events in America*. New York: Atheneum. pp. 77–117.

Bruner, E. (1989) 'Tourism, creativity and authenticity', *Studies in Symbolic Interaction*, 10: 109–14.

Cohen, E. (1979) 'A phenomenology of tourist experience', *Sociology*, 13: 179–201.

Cohen, E. (1981) 'Pilgrimage and tourism: convergence and divergence'. Paper presented at the Conference on Pilgrimage: the Human Quest, Pittsburgh.

Cohen, E. (1988) 'Authenticity and commodization in tourism', *Annals of Tourism Research*, 15: 371–86.

Csikszentmihalyi, M. and Rochberg-Halton, E. (1981) *The Meaning of Things: Domestic Symbols and the Self*. New York: Cambridge University Press.

Dayan, R. and Feinberg, W. (1974) 'Maskit: Israel's center of handcrafts', in *Crafts of Israel*. New York: Macmillan.

Dorfles, G. (1969) *Tourism and Nature: the World of Bad Taste*. New York: Bell.

Douglas, M. and Isherwood, B. (1979) *The World of Goods*. New York: Norton.

Eliade, M. (1961) *Images and Symbols: Studies in Religious Symbolism*. New York: Sheed and Ward.

Gordon, B. (1986) 'The souvenir: messenger of the extraordinary', *Journal of Popular Culture*, 20: 135–46.

Graburn, N. (1978) 'Tourism: the sacred journey', in V.L. Smith (ed.), *Hosts and Guests*. Philadelphia: University of Pennsylvania Press. pp. 17–31.

Graburn, N. (1983) 'The anthropology of tourism', *Annals of Tourism Research*, 10: 9–33.

Handler, R. (1986) 'Authenticity', *Anthropology Today*, 2(1): 2–4.

Leach, E.R. (1961) *Pul Eiya: a Village in Ceylon*. Cambridge: Cambridge University Press.

MacCannell, D. (1973) 'Staged authenticity: arrangements of social space in tourist settings', *American Journal of Sociology*, 79(3): 589–603.

MacCannell, D. (1976) *The Tourist: a New Theory of the Leisure Class*. New York: Schocken.

Mauss, M. (1950) *The Gift: Forms and Functions of Exchange*. Glencoe, IL: Free Press.

Moore, S. and Myerhoff, B. (1977) 'Introduction. Secular rituals: forms and meaning', in S. Moore and B. Myerhoff (eds), *Secular Ritual*. Amsterdam: Van Gorcum. pp. 3–24.

Smith, V. (ed.) (1977) *Hosts and Guests: the Anthropology of Tourism*. Philadelphia: University of Pennsylvania Press.

Smith, V. (1979) 'Women: the taste-makers in tourism', *Annals of Tourism Research*, 6(1): 49–60.

Spooner, B. (1986) 'Weavers and dealers: the authenticity of an oriental carpet', in A. Appadurai (ed.), *The Social Life of Things*. pp. 195–235.

Stewart, S. (1984) 'Objects of desire', in *On Longing: Narratives of the Miniature, the Gigantic, the Souvenir, the Collection*. Baltimore: Johns Hopkins University Press. pp. 132–51.

Turner, V. (1973) 'The center out there: pilgrim's goal', *History of Religions*, 12(3): 191–230.

9

International Tourism and Utopia: the Balearic Islands

Danielle Rozenberg

Tourism and the incorporation of Ibician society

This study takes as its point of departure the specific example of the island of Ibiza in the Balearic group (Spain), and sets out to explore several general questions. How do visitors and the indigenous population represent the culture of the other? What kinds of material and symbolic exchanges take place between them? What part does culture play in the development of the tourist product and its commercialization? How are both individual and collective identities tested by the diffusion of international tourism? Our intention here is to use a case study to examine the analytical model of tourism, and its cultural implications.

The expansion of tourism on Ibiza has been rapid. In contrast to Majorca, Ibiza had no provision for accommodation prior to the arrival of tourism during the 1960s. A few family boarding-houses were sufficient to provide for the rare visitors. It was on the initiative of foreign investors, mediated by those from the Iberian peninsula itself, that the island began to build an infrastructure of hotels adapted to the needs of modern tourism. By the end of the 1960s Ibiza had become the archetype of the mass tourist enclave. With the advent of the tourism industry Ibiza passed from an agrarian to a capitalist mode of production, and came to be inserted into a widespread system of exchange in which the global process of modernization was only modified by a disproportionate inflation of the service sector. A specific social situation – tourism – linked the massive intrusion of foreigners into the archaic structures of the community, and defined the intensive social interaction which followed from this.[1]

The initial development of tourism in Ibiza from around 1960 was followed by an aggressive acceleration. In the crucial period 1964–7 the island acquired almost all of its endowment of accommodation. Since then, and despite both a world crisis (1974) and a national crisis (1979), Ibician tourism has become the principal factor which structures local life.[2]

The rise of tourism led to three types of mobility. There is *inter-sectoral mobility*, in which agriculture is abandoned in favour of construction, hotel-keeping and the tertiary sector in general. There is *spatial mobility*, involving the exodus from the countryside into urban centres, including also the immigration of workers from the Spanish mainland. Finally, there is *mobility in terms of social stratification*, involving an accentuation of inequalities in a hitherto very egalitarian society. In this process of mobility the islanders as a whole have risen socially.

These processes have had repercussions first of all for the system of succession, in that the inheritance of the estate by the eldest son has been abandoned in favour of an equal partition among all of the children. The farm no longer constitutes an integral unit of production and consumption. The extended family has come to be replaced by the nuclear and neo-local family. An end has been put to the former separation between spatially extended matrimonial areas, and there has been a growth in the number of exogamous unions between islanders and partners either from the mainland or abroad. For the Ibicenos caught up in these processes of change, their entire system of reference has broken down and been replaced by other relationships, both to their physical and to their human environment.

For as long as survival was dependent upon the land, peasant existence was given a rhythm by the agricultural calendar, and accorded to an elementary division of labour based upon age and sex. Economic rationality of the capitalist type was formerly experienced only indirectly through the activities of merchants. The industrial mode of production associated with tourism introduced notions of productivity, the quantitative evaluation of time, long-term planning and complex calculations of profit. Paid employment transformed the relationship between people and work. Parallel to these developments, the home came to be segregated spatially from the place of work, and a rift developed between time spent in production and that devoted to rest. This fragmentation of time and space corresponded to the anonymity of tasks within the enterprise.

With the augmentation of income came a growth in domestic consumption (equipment for the home, cars and various other expenditures), while money gave access to a whole range of services which had hitherto taken the form of mutual aid (tilling, harvesting, hauling, festive gatherings and so on). The new importance accorded to money, and the multiplication of the means of transport, initiated a process of the automation of social relations, and the development of individualistic attitudes among the younger generation (in terms of their residence, occupation, patterns of leisure and other choices relating to everyday life).

With traditional society the authority and prestige of the elders were at the heart of both the village community and the farm. Among collateral kin a hierarchy was established between 'the heir' and his younger brothers, who found themselves *de facto* in a position of inferiority to him. In the relations between men and women, the latter were characterized by a total submission first to their fathers and then to their spouses; and this went along with a withdrawal into the family and almost non-existent links with the outside world. By working outside the farm, however, the young became emancipated from the power of their elders. A greater income than that of their fathers conferred on them a new autonomy; while their greater receptivity to change pushed them towards the taking of more responsibility with respect to the choice of their occupation, place of residence or marriage partner. Hitherto synonymous with the wisdom of experience, age came to signify more and more a lack of adaptation to economic realities and to the new spirit of the age.

The competition between the value of land for agriculture and its value for tourism on the one hand, and the adoption of equal inheritance on the other, stripped the eldest brother of his privileges. Under the combined effects of a more liberal education, of mixed contact both in the workplace and during leisure, and above all the employment of women, the aspirations of men and women have come to be more convergent, more egalitarian, and characterized by a new division of labour between marriage partners. Above all, there has developed a duality of points of reference, and a diversity of coexistent ways of living and thinking. The speed of change has resulted inevitably in disequilibria, and in problems of adaptation in every aspect of life, whether it be at the collective or the personal level. In these and in other ways the rise of international tourism and the internalization of industrial culture have given rise to a bundle of changes which it is impossible to disaggregate.

These background observations present a picture which is familiar through the 'impact' model of tourism. Nevertheless, tourism development on Ibiza does have its own specific characteristics which have partly to do with the cultural contact introduced by foreign tourism. The study of these multi-faceted relationships provides the principal focus for the remainder of our case study.

During the period of the consolidation of tourism a colony of foreigners was also establishing itself on the island for whom the old world of agrarian self-sufficiency embodied the hope of an alternative way of life. From 1967 onwards dozens of young people, revolted by industrial society, disembarked every week from the Barcelona ferry. Pausing to break their journey along the road to Morocco and the East, they found in Ibiza a foretaste of an alternative way of living. Many remained on the island. Within 20 years or so these marginal social groups came to constitute a new social stratum on the island: the newcomers (about 4,500 people by 1987, or 8 per cent of the entire population) had become economic partners in Ibician life, creating for themselves a new social space. The contact between islanders and newcomers was extended and came to have a long-lasting mutual impact.

A game of mirrors and a subtle process of mutual acculturation were gradually substituted for the stereotypical reactions and the response of rejection which is usually regarded as inherent in the touristic encounter. The partial assimilation of one side met with a cultural inflexion on the other side, which went well beyond any kind of folkloristic reduction of their culture. Solidarities and alliances were woven together to give rise to a pluralistic society. It is this process which constitutes the primary point of interest in our study.

Conflict and the game of mirrors

In the period leading up to the mid 1970s the entire socio-economic activity of the island underwent a reorientation under the pressure of tourism, in which process marginal sectors of production were eliminated. The conditions of local life, however, allowed this community of new arrivals to live according to their own lights. Their stay on the island was seen at first as provisional. They made do with odd jobs and on a precarious income in order to give priority to a playful life-style, to creativity, to friendship and to the elevation of sensuality. The characteristics of the 'artificial paradise' in which these 'flower children' built their imaginative and playful counter-culture are suggested by contemporary reports in the mass media:[3]

> [The scene is] the woods, by night . . . Some make a fire; most of them light candles around a tree, and sing, smoke, talk and meditate. In this way, day after day, the months pass. (*Madrid*, reproduced in *Diario de Ibiza*, 6 September 1969)

> The little students of this world-without-frontiers are studying the laws of the universe in a refitted sheep fold. Here, in the dead of winter,

under almond and citrus trees heavy with fruit, they breathe the air of an endless holiday. (*Frankfurter Rundschau*, 9 September 1972; *Paris Match*, March 1972)

Hanno, who now 'lives the life of a simple Robinson Crusoe' because he was tired of 'prostituting himself in an artificial world to which he did not belong', affirms that 'everyone can take the plunge.' (*Handelsblatt*, Düsseldorf, 28 February 1974)

The cohabitation of the Ibicenos and these resident foreigners was, on the whole, peaceful, although it was not without mutual incomprehension and occasional clashes. At the peak of the hippie presence (1968–71) these relations did pass through a phase of conflict which everyone on the island still remembers.

For the newly disembarked urbanite the countryside was poetic – a Garden of Eden. One gathered ripe fruits along one's way without grasping that these were the results of the efforts of some farmer. When the young foreigners gathered in a pine grove to barbecue meat, or to celebrate the full moon around a bonfire, they aroused immense anxiety among the country folk, who knew how flammable the woodlands are during a period of drought. The long hair, jellabas and Indian robes, beads, turbans and other fantastic costumes adopted by the men did not fit at all the local idea of manhood. The short and transparent dresses worn by the women antagonized passers-by. Moreover, public expressions of tenderness, free love and communal living were all taken as confirming the view that the foreigners were immoral. Above all, in spite of their misperception of this phenomenon, the people of Ibiza thought they could discern the effects of drugs in the hyperactivity or delirious behaviour of the strangers. Toleration was sometimes difficult; and threats did not only exist in the imagination. The presence of naked young people on the beaches, where the Ibicenos were in the habit of taking their families, was experienced as an intolerable act of aggression.

There were other relationships between islanders and foreigners, some of whom had been settled there for a long time, such as archaeologists, architects, art dealers, painters and writers. These had established secure connections with the indigenous environment, demonstrated their interest in local culture and come to be accepted as Ibicenos. The sincerity of some of these newcomers, in making the effort to learn the local dialect and in deciding to send their children to school in the place, earned the respect of their neighbours.

In general, however, Ibicenos and foreigners lived in parallel worlds. With indifference the islanders were prepared to extend to the newcomers the rules by which native life was lived: hospitality towards visitors; discreet conduct in a world where everybody knew everybody else, and where one frequently had to cross the land of one's neighbour; and the solidarity which is necessary when living at some distance from urban centres. The immigrants were led to adopt all of these things through their own utopian mythology. That they were happy to describe their own relationship with the islanders in this way contrasted with the perceptions of the situation of the locals. The latter responded to this one-sided lyricism with indifference touched with mistrust or irony. Put down to pure chance, surprise visits by the police to the new settlers were often made at the suggestion of a worried farmer, who had been talking to the parson, who had been talking to . . . the police. At the moment when they came to ask for a residence permit a number of foreigners discovered, in the early 1970s, that without their own knowledge they had already acquired a dossier.

More usually ridicule was the preferred weapon of the Ibicenos. They made fun of the attempts at organic agriculture on the part of these townees, and gave them disparaging nicknames. In fact, their totally distinct daily rhythms and radically different sets of values were obstacles to any genuine communication between the two populations, although this did not prevent reciprocal cultural borrowing.

These two copresent groups found themselves at cross-purposes, each tending to evaluate the other in terms of real or supposed signs of a life-style to which they themselves aspired. For the islanders everything which indicated 'modernity', whether it be in the general manner or the behaviour of their visitors, was endowed *a priori* with positive connotations. In the eyes of the Ibicenos the village signified closure and submission to a constant social pressure. Agriculture was the symbol of backwardness and poverty, just as the town and paid employment meant entry into an ideal life. Inversely, in their quest for authenticity, the new arrivals glorified the rural world and island traditions, fastening on to various objects or the cultural traits which these symbolized.

These games of mirrors affected many areas of daily life, such as attitudes to technological progress, the approach to economic activity or to forms of sociability, one's understanding of the environment and one's tastes in clothing. The new immigrants sought to get back to the land, take up crafts, rediscover nature or simplify their own needs just as much as the islanders aspired to an involvement in the spiral of consumerism. There are plenty of examples of this contradiction between the orientations of foreigners and the Ibicenos. Three illustrations will suffice in this context.

At a time when the islanders were rejoicing in the development of modern hospitals on Ibiza, and it had become practicable to make the journey to Palma or Barcelona in order to consult a specialist, and when the battery of traditional medicines was falling into disuse, the foreigners were going crazy over natural products, giving a new lease of life to the herbalist on Ibiza. Several dozen young women were prepared to challenge the power of medicine to the extent of giving birth at home, and giving inspiration to the Californian movement of 'wild' wise women, at a time when not a single case of home confinement was recorded among Ibicenos.

In their rejection of the land and the way of life which tied them to it, the indigenous population got rid of their traditional furniture and farm implements which they now regarded as useless, in order to replace them with kitchen fittings in Formica, polished wardrobes and mass-produced dining-room and lounge suites. At the same time, the immigrants discovered with wonderment craftsman-produced chests, basins, mortars, millstones – all infinitely more precious in their eyes than any manufactured objects.

With regard to clothing, under the influence of tourism the Ibician people abandoned their traditional garb in favour of shorts, a transformation which they experienced as emancipation from the past. For the foreigners, however, to dress oneself in the country fashion was to deck oneself out poetically; and the long calico petticoats were dyed in various colours and turned into fashionable skirts. Learning of this change of use, dozens of country folk offered their wives' old clothes to the boutiques for a few hundred pesetas.

These borrowings cannot be reduced to a simple adoption of the elements of another culture. They are taken out of their customary frame of reference and filtered through a new scheme of interpretation. Thus 'going back to nature' involves making adjustments to the primitive life. If the newcomers praised the charm of lighting by means of candles, or of earth closets, or went into ecstasies about the aesthetics of old farm buildings, the modifications which they made to their environment before taking up residence were revealing. They would install electricity as soon as possible, and bring in lighting, refrigerators, cisterns and sanitation. They would fit supplementary heating, enlarge the windows with additional glazing, build on extra rooms, lay out terraces and dig swimming-pools. The country life took on the character of a bucolic game, with flowers grown more than produce for actual consumption, and animals such as goats, chickens, dogs and cats being cosseted to a degree which baffled the islanders.

Among the virtues of traditional society the visitors mentioned spontaneously the hospitality of the islanders, and the relationships of trust which made keys superfluous. Even so, it was the foreigners who introduced fences, and who put up notices saying 'private property', where the Ibicenos had been content to mark the boundaries of their land with a stone or a tree. The simplicity and frugality of the native life were often deferred to as a model. One made one's own clothes, adopted vegetarianism, or denounced the wastefulness of 'consumer society'. Nevertheless, the imitation of local tradition was transposed into the counter-culture in a playful way. While the life of the country people bore the stamp of austerity, scrimping and saving, the new arrivals gave pride of place to hedonism and the here and now.

The effects of these borrowings generated by the encounter between the Ibicenos and outsiders did not make for a convergent development, or contribute to a cultural melting-pot. If mutual acculturation did take place it was marked by discontinuities, a lack of coherence and the imaginary appropriation of the culture of the other. Above all, however, the dynamics of the encounter of these groups are embedded inextricably in the patterns of power which are typical of their global socio-economic context.

Local particularism and the tourist product

The contact between holiday-makers and the indigenous population was conditioned from the outset by the nature of Ibician tourism. This essentially took the form of charter tourism directed by the large European tour operators, especially the British and the Germans.[4] Located in hotels along the coast, summer visitors stayed on average for six days in the archipelago. This enclave character of the accommodation was part of the total package, which included lodging, meals and entertainment, of which the tourist industry took charge, and this limited accordingly the reciprocal contact of the islanders and their visitors. All the same, expectations about, and interest in, the host society on the part of the visitors seems to have been very limited, if one is to believe the various studies of motivation undertaken in the Balearic Islands.[5]

In a study of tourist motivation undertaken by the Instituto Español de Turismo in several destinations in the Balearic Islands, tourists were asked to indicate the principal reasons why they had visited Spain over the past five years.[6] Among the nationalities most strongly represented on Ibiza the percentage of response which mentioned cultural or artistic curiosity, or an interest in the Spanish language, varied between 1 and 6 per cent. If one adds together the two categories 'the climate and the countryside' and 'the sunshine', however, one arrives at figures between 64 and 85 per cent.[7]

In spite of the desire on the part of those who were promoting tourism in the Balearic Islands to offer an alternative to the famous 'four Ss' (sun, sea, sand and sex) on which the reputation of the Mediterranean resorts was based, the perception of Ibiza by its tourist clientele perpetuated this idea of holiday-making. The majority of excursions on offer (visits to the 'hippie markets' or 'pirate tours') took no advantage of any interest in discovering the culture. In 1987 and 1988 popular 'beach parties' drew hundreds of summer visitors before their suppression by the authorities.[8]

As for various folklore performances, to which were invited those visitors who were more or less eager to make contact with the vernacular culture, the rubric of 'entertainment' by which they were framed left little opportunity for more than a superficial mutual acquaintance. When songs and traditional dances which had hitherto normally been performed in the setting of rural churchyards were revived in an artificial manner, and detached from the contexts which had originally given them meaning, they lost the authenticity associated with their everyday use. Moreover, the way in which the locals presented them, doing their best to oblige with explanations of costumes or musical instruments, often provoked laughter among their audiences. For example, details of the petticoats worn by the women invariably triggered ribald remarks; and the invitation to try drinking from the *porrón* (which had the effect of making those who took it up splash themselves) only made for greater distance rather than genuine contact.[9]

Objects from the past were reproduced for sale to the tourists: but their very success resulted in their mass production, and by the same token led to the downgrading of craft workers. This was the case with glass-blowing, with ceramics, and with the copying of old jewellery in gold and silver. In this degeneration of specifically local creativity to satisfy the souvenir industry, syncretism reigned supreme. Dancers in Andalusian shawls, toreadors, bulls stuck with banderillas, guitars, plastic castanets and a flood of other gimcrack products which reflected clichéd views of the carnival, the flamenco and the bullring, drowned all that was specifically Catalan.

The tourist centres were conceived as dream worlds into which were allowed to filter only distant and stereotypical echoes of local reality. The only islanders met by the tourists (the tourist professionals) were within anonymous and interchangeable roles which discouraged all real interaction between foreigners and the native population. Other kinds of contacts were made more rarely.

Confronted by the importance of the economic issues, by the relationship of dependence which tourism entails with respect to the flow of foreign visitors, and above all by the development of international competition, the regional officials responsible for tourism set themselves the task of offering as original and competitive a product as possible.[10] To this end an emphasis was placed subsequently upon the richness of the heritage of the Balearic group, their sites of interest and the variety of their activities, alongside the considerations of climate and the opportunities for bathing which had been the foundation of their success.

After 1981, therefore, the tourism publicity of the Spanish islands accorded a central place to cultural activity and to the traditions of the islands, as much as to aspects of their contemporary situation such as fashion or crafts. By way of an example one might mention the short film *Island for Ever*, made available to travel agents and shown regularly at tourism fairs. It took as its theme a peasant dressed in the traditional way, taking a walk with his Ibician hound, and presented a succession of scenes in which tradition and modernity were combined: a statue of the goddess Tanit, the Phoenician protectress of Ibiza; a folk dance; a craft market; the atmosphere at night in the alleyways of the port; and the making of local costume. Showings of this documentary were typically followed by a second with an equally evocative title: *Ibiza is a Carnival*. As the occasion demanded, the presentation would be brought to a close with a show either of folklore or of fashion.

In this attempt to present an original tourism product several attractions of the island made their own contribution, such as the settlement of artists and craft workers, the creation of distinctive clothing and native tradition. It becomes apparent when one reads the guides and brochures put out by the travel offices and agencies, however, that along with these creative people 'marginals' were to an ever greater extent coming to play a supporting role in relation to promotion. Several extracts from the brochure 'Ibiza and Formentera', available in all the tourism offices, illustrate this process well:[11]

> *The isles of youth* Ibiza and Formentera are two islands which exercise a powerful attraction over young people the world over . . . Thanks to these, Ibiza and Formentera are certainly two islands found in the avant-garde of all the youth movements, from the time . . . of the existentialists and the beatniks to the hippies and neo-hippies.

Food and the crafts   You can get things made by the good craft workshops of the islands – leather goods (bags and belts), pottery, hangings, fantastic jewellery and lacework, among others. Above all, there is fashion – the spontaneous fashion of Ibiza; the fashion of an island with a vocation for spontaneity; fashion which could only be born in an island like Ibiza.

The travel agents employ a similar line of argument:

Ibiza is the island of fashion, of landscapes, of beaches, and above all of people. It is the island of all those who want to spend their holidays in another way. Come to live with writers, artists and hippies in the Ibiza style. (leaflet of the Club de Vacaciones, summer 1980)

From marginality to tourist activity

At the moment when the marginal foreigners found themselves constrained by the industrialization of the island to modify the ways in which they participated in the life of the island, they opted for economic activities which were as remunerative as possible, such as the purchase of a boutique or a shop, entry into salaried employment, art or craft work, or trade in the public markets. In these ways they brought into play the financial and/or educational capital which had always been at their disposal – or putting it another way, the social differences which immigration had hitherto blurred.

For those who were most hard-up, craft work of the most commercialized type and direct sale to the public offered enviable opportunities of access to the endless procession of tourists, bearing in mind the small investment which was necessary, and their reluctance to become engaged in regular hours of work and the rigidities of the legal framework. The market 'hippies', whose anarchic growth had at first been tolerated by the authorities, were brought under municipal control. Besides the nightly market at Eivissa, four other weekly markets brought together several hundred vendors. The most famous of these, the fair at Es Canà, used to attract a considerable crowd of up to 4,000 tourists every week, according to its organizer. Several tourist agencies used to offer organized excursions to the 'hippie market'. To this ritualized activity several other specific events came to be attached, in which the new arrivals agreed to take part. In this way the discothèque KU, one of the most famous on Ibiza, organized on several nights each year a 'hippie night'. The craft traders were invited in massive numbers to display their wares during the course of the evening, in an area set aside for their use. The possibility of substantial takings was held out to them in return for their lending a tone of exoticism through their own clothing, ornaments and makeup.

In this way the economic integration of the foreigners served a double function. It provided economic activity; and the tourist success of the 'hippie markets' turned them into the principal attraction after the beach. Thus one can see the incorporation of the counter-culture taking place at two levels. On the one hand there is the symbolic use made of the presence of 'freaks' in publicity films, guide books, the brochures of travel agents and postcards. On the other hand this tourist activity, whether permanent or occasional, comes to be seen as an extra cultural asset in relation to the touristic value of the destination.

The crisis of identity

The rise of international tourism confronted the islanders, their values and behaviour, with a test of their own identity. A succession of phases leads from the rejection of local tradition to the reappropriation of vernacular culture, and then to the reaffirmation of Ibician identity.

The rejection of tradition and cultural colonization

Very often contact between Ibicenos and foreigners led the natives at first to devalue themselves, and at the same time to accept the imposition of a tourist diktat concerning norms, and behaviours which were contrary to local usage.

Decked out in the prestige of urban life and European fashion, the visitors often served as models for the young islanders. The latter set out to copy the freedom of morals of the tourists, the free and easy behaviour which held sway in the discothèques, while the young girls went in for slimming and a sun-tan. Among the bourgeoisie of the island several members of the free professions or businesspeople themselves adopted behaviour which they considered appropriate to an elite, such as the use of marijuana or nudism. The rejection of the attributes of the traditional way of life in the name of modernity – clothing, furnishing, and so on – has already been mentioned.

The process of massification associated with tourism entailed a 'colonization' of culture.[12] Innumerable signs appeared in foreign languages, such as 'Jaime's', 'Pedro's', or 'Angel's Shop'. In order to satisfy the holiday-makers, meal-times were brought forward ahead of those which were usual in Spain by two or three hours. French, Italian and German restaurants, and stalls selling crêpes or hamburgers, multiplied in order to meet the needs of a clientele which was rather conscious of the fact that, gastronomically speaking, they were in a foreign land. In several areas it became easier to buy foreign newspapers than the local dailies.

Some residential or leisure areas took on the atmosphere of occupied territory, as the crowds, the soaring prices, the disco music played at full volume and the aggressiveness of drunken strollers steadily emptied some quarters of their residents or those who traditionally had taken a walk there. Some beaches became virtual British or German enclaves.

This instrumentalization of the host society had an impact, at the level of everyday life, in some particularly sensitive areas. This was the case with the practice of nudism. For a long time forbidden and punished, this was legalized for several Spanish beaches in 1978 – including two on Ibiza which were officially designated for naturism. The question for the legislature was how simultaneously to establish these 'reserves' in order to satisfy nordic demand, without damaging local susceptibilities. This toleration proved powerless, however, to restrict the spread of nudism into neighbouring areas. In exasperation, the inhabitants of one of the affected areas banded together to form a self-defence association. Failing other means, armed with sticks and stones they organized anti-nudist raids, following which they managed to obtain a prohibition against nudism on the beach which had been the occasion of conflict. Nevertheless, in spite of this partial victory, the Ibicenos could only resign themselves to the spread of foreign mores.

The most serious problems to threaten the island of Ibiza were the growth of petty crime and the use of drugs. These phenomena, common throughout Spain, took on alarming proportions in a society which had been used to relationships of trust. Thefts and acts of vandalism multiplied. Hitherto the actions only of foreigners or those from the mainland, the use of drugs and delinquency began to occur among the indigenous youth, to the consternation of the adults.

The islanders were powerless to affect the distinctive reputation which Ibiza acquired, at the same time as the development of charter tourism, among targeted groups of holiday-makers: homosexuals of all nationalities, Spanish celebrities, people connected with the arts and entertainment, as well as a cohort of younger summer visitors typical of fashionable resorts. Several agencies abroad played upon this identity, in particular classifying Ibiza as a 'gay' destination.[13] Meanwhile a succession of 'crazy nights' announced by the discothèques added to the procession of nightly events, and fuelled this scandalous image. The Ibicenos themselves were more and more inclined to lay all their ills at the door of the summer invasion.

The rediscovery and reappropriation of the past

Yearning for the urban life the Ibicenos got rid of their rustic furniture and other objects and clothing which symbolized the past. As these items of popular culture came to be elevated in the eyes of 'other people' to the status of antiques, however, the islanders began to re-evaluate their own culture. The hand-made chests and musical instruments, the heavy golden ornaments of women's costumes, were jealously cared for by those families which still possessed them. Several folklore groups were created during the 1970s. These latter did indeed take part in tourist activities, but they had their origins primarily in an emotional attitude towards the preservation of tradition. The recognition which they gained through performances for foreigners, on account of the originality and antiquity of the vernacular culture, awakened a feeling of pride among the islanders.

This movement towards the recovery of the past extended to everything which bore the specific stamp of local society, from the Ibician hound to rural architecture, and including costume and folk wisdom. A new generation of singers began to collect the old couplets which had formerly enlivened social gatherings, and added them to their repertoire. The *Diario de Ibiza* published a course in the Ibician language for the benefit of its readers. It printed long interviews with elderly craft workers, and reproduced the techniques for making traditional musical instruments and the construction of the old sailing boats. Among the comfortable middle classes there was a movement to restore the ancient family farms which they had inherited, converting them into second homes or even principal residences. Associations were created for the protection of the architectural heritage.

The reaffirmation of identity and the Balearic Statute of Autonomy

Confined at first to the initiatives of literati anxious to preserve the linguistic and historical heritage of the islands, this movement for the reaffirmation of Ibician identity steadily gained ground among the wider strata of the population, benefiting the more from a socio-economic context which encouraged the expression of regional specificity in Spain. Thus the Institut d'Estudis Eivissenos took on the task of consciousness-raising. By means of the journal *Eivissa,* and various other publications, the Institute applied itself to the evaluation of the resources of popular culture, through ethnographic works, the collection of local history, courses in the Catalan language and a series of conferences. A spectacular effort was organized with the support of the public authorities, as much with an eye to the museums as to the conservation of monuments, with a renewed effort at excavation, the classification of Punic and Roman collections, the restoration of the city walls of Eivissa, and care of the watchtowers and fortified farmhouses which were vestiges of the struggle against pirates.

With the passing of the Balearic Statute of Autonomy a new impetus was given to the process of re-evaluating Ibician culture.[14] Important funds were released by the Govern Balear and the Consell of Ibiza for the restoration of historic buildings, and for the publication of school texts, since at the same time the official acknowledgement of bilingualism made obligatory the teaching of Catalan in schools.

After a long decline which seemed to herald their final disappearance, the village fêtes recovered their former dash, partly because of the credits made available by local authorities, but more especially because of the enthusiasm of their participants. On the occasion of various popular activities the celebrations were marked by the performance of *ball pagès* by the local folklore group. To the extent that the dancers and musicians were native to the village (as indeed were most of the onlookers) these patronal festivals could not be reduced to the level of mere theatrical displays of old costume. They consisted at one and the same time of a recovery of memory, and a rediscovery of the reference points of local culture, interpellating the individual by means of landmarks both distant and familiar.[15]

Conclusion

Ibiza appears today to be a plural society, oscillating between rootedness and cosmopolitanism. Despite the obvious administrative and material problems the new arrivals on the island, who have provided the primary focus of this study, did develop a fond attachment to, and came to identify with, the place which they had discovered for themselves and its 'real' life. For the Ibicenos of the old stock, there was a return to their origins, which was brought about through a reaffirmation of Catalan identity and through the investigation of their own development. At the same time, the successive waves of immigration, amplified by the flow of tourists, gave to the place an international flavour. Working with these heterogeneous groups and currents of ideas, which were tied into an informal network of relationships with foreign countries, and utilizing its own experience of social division and diversity of origin, the island concocted something of a cultural brew.

A double crisis of values tended from the outset towards contradictory consequences. The indigenous system of reference was shaken both by the impact of mass tourism, and by the implantation of an enclave of hippie culture. While offering a radical challenge to elements of traditional Ibician identity, this latter came to take on a double role of a more positive and adaptive kind. The 'utopian' re-evaluation of tradition by the newcomers, reflected back upon the local population, fed the movement towards the reappraisal and reappropriation of local identity. At the same time, the playful adaptation of elements of tradition, and the initially tentative integration of the new arrivals into the economy of tourism, served the creation of a distinctive Ibician tourist product. In this process an original micro-society was forged, distinguished by the diversity and plurality of its life-styles.

(Translated by John Allcock.)

Notes

1 I have borrowed the notion of 'situation' from George Balandier (1963: 3–37) and his reflections on colonization. It seems appropriate to speak of the 'tourist situation', in that there is 'a particular conjunction which imposes upon the agents a certain orientation and a process of transformation . . . which constitute a whole, and prepare the way for the construction of a society'. This kind of approach has the merit of underlining at one and the same time the dynamic of change and the relationships of dependence which exist, involving both the tourist receiving and the sending centres.

2 The figures are eloquent: in 1960, 30,000 visitors were accommodated in the hotels of Ibiza; in 1965, 102,000; in 1970, 350,000, in 1987, 648,000. Source: Ministerio de Transportes, Turismo y Comunicaciones, Comunidad Autónoma de Baleares et Conselleria de Turismo de Ibiza y Formentera.

3 The fieldwork upon which this study is based included an analysis of 145 dailies and weeklies from Germany, Austria, Switzerland, Belgium, Britain, France, Portugal and Spain, published between 1969 and 1974. One should also mention here Barbet Schroeder's film *More*, shown in the USA and in the majority of European countries in 1969 and 1970, the impact of which among young people was considerable (Rozenberg, 1990).

4 The Servicio de Estudios Económicos del Banco de España (1985) estimates that the operators handled 96 per cent of foreign tourism to Ibiza. F. Afiza, the island's delegate to the Secretariat of State for Tourism, suggested in 1980 an appreciably lower figure: 'The foreign charter companies deal with 63% of Ibiza's tourists' (reported in *Diario de Ibiza*, 26 November 1980). The British and the Germans alone account for two-thirds of the demand for hotels, followed by the Spaniards (14.7 per cent), the Italians (6.2 per cent), the Dutch (2.7 per cent), and

the Swiss, the French and the Belgians (figures of the distribution by nationality of travellers accommodated in the hotels of Ibiza in 1986, according to the Consell Insular de Ibiza y Formentera).

5 One survey undertaken in 1974 in 16 new leisure villages in Spain (which included the two most touristified areas of Majorca and Ibiza) showed that cultural concerns ranked at best fifth among the reasons why holiday-makers had chosen the country – below by a long way considerations of climate, tourist activities, economic reasons and the beach (Gavira et al., 1975).

6 Estudios Turísticos (1979).

7 'Nearly 40% of the tourists who visited Majorca in 1979 made no significant trips at all but preferred to remain during the ten or twelve days of their stay within the very same locality in which they had been dropped by the bus which brought them from the airport': Pere Morrey, of the Consell General Interinsular, in *Empresario Balear*, 42, 1981.

8 These 'beach parties' typically took the form of a sea trip to some less frequented creek where a convivial *paella* would be served – together with excessive amounts of alcohol – followed by what an indignant press called 'obscene games'.

9 A carafe with a long neck used in Catalonia and the Balearic Islands, from which the whole company is expected to drink in turn without touching the lips.

10 Several studies of the market were undertaken 10 years ago when the Balearic product came into competition with other Mediterranean areas. Price, quality of service, waiting times and customer satisfaction were all considered. Assured for a long time of its own leading position by virtue of its superior receptive capacity, the archipelago had to take into account henceforth the competition of other regions, principally in Italy, Greece, Tunisia and Yugoslavia. See in particular Subdirección General de Comercialización de la Secretaría de Estado de Turismo (1979); Agrupación de Cadenas Hoteleras de Baleares (1979).

11 Published by the Ministerio de Transportes, Turismo y Comunicaciones.

12 Some idea of the extent of this can be gained from the fact that the ratio of tourists to local inhabitants in 1987 was 10:1. The normal method of calculating this relationship, using the number of visitors accommodated annually in hotels, does not take account of non-hotel and auxiliary accommodation. The real measure of the density of tourism is well in excess of these figures. One should note that the island of Ibiza, which has 66,000 inhabitants, takes in during any day at the height of the peak season more than 100,000 visitors.

13 One such is the tourist agency Lambda Tours from the USA (*Diario de Ibiza*, 6 December 1980) and another the French agency Iltours (*Nouvel Observateur*, 26 August 1983).

14 The Autonomous Community of the Balearic Islands, by virtue of the transfer of the powers of the state to the regions (Articles 137 and 143 of the Constitution of 1978; Statute of Autonomy, 1982–3) now disposes of decision-making powers in various domains, such as culture, the language of the region, the protection of the natural and cultural heritage and the promotion and organization of tourism.

15 Abeles (1980).

References

Abeles, M. (1980) 'Le local à la recherche du temps perdu', *Dialectique*, 30: 31–7.

Agrupación de Cadenas Hoteleras de Baleares (1979) *Estudio sobre los mercados turísticos de la competencia*. Consell Insular de Mallorca.

Balandier, G. (1963) *Sociologie de l'Afrique noire*. Paris: Presses Universitaires de France.

Estudios Turísticos (1979) *Estudio de motivaciones para el turismo en España*. Madrid: Estudios Turísticos, 61–2.

Gavira, M., Iribas, J.M., Sabbah, F. and Sanz Arranz, J.R. (1975) *Turismo de playa en España*. Madrid: Turner.

Rozenberg, D. (1990) *Ibiza: une île pour une autre vie*. Paris: L'Harmattan. Spanish translation 1990, Madrid: CIS, Siglo XXI.

Servicio de Estudios Económicos del Banco de España (1985) *La economia de Baleares a la hora de la CEE*. Madrid.

Subdirección General de Comercialización de la Secretaría de Estado de Turismo (1979) *Estudio comparativo de los precios de los 'packages' turísticos del área mediterráneo, 1978–9*.

10

Life as a Tourist Object in Australia

Meaghan Morris

My interest in tourism derives from a research project on the cultural politics of 'development' – that whole nexus of real estate speculation, industrialized leisure, tourist promotion and environmental conflict constituting what is called (not without a touch of irony) the 'hospitality sector' – in Australia between 1972 and 1988. These dates serve as a guide to the periodization made necessary by tourism's ongoing importance to the Australian economy, and its effects in the social landscape. Without historical parameters, critical discourse in a project such as mine risks consigning itself to the role of descriptive chronicling of apparently endless change.

The year 1972 represents a threshold in modern Australian history: our first Labor government since 1949 was elected in a climate of euphoric political radicalism and desire for social change, but also in the last year when it was possible to assume that our post-war economic prosperity was now 'natural' to Australia. In 1988, another Labor government (driven by economic rationalism and political pragmatism rather than any form of euphoria) supervised the celebration of the Australian Bicentenary, a huge touristic-historical spectacle which lasted all year and had considerable impact on the social structure of major cities, especially Sydney (Morris, 1988b).

During these 16 years, it became part of the common sense of our media culture that Australia is not a secure, wealthy 'European' society marooned in Asia, but a strange and vulnerable hybrid. It has something like a Third World economy dependent on natural resources and tourism (with a structurally underdeveloped manufacturing sector) sustaining a society with First World expectations of living standards, and a white majority culture with an inherited, but increasingly inappropriate, First World *self-image*. No longer a European outpost, Australia had become, in the 200 years since the British invasion of Aboriginal land, one of the minor countries of the Pacific Rim, economically dominated by Japan.

Within this historical framework of enormously conflictual

change, I use tourism as a focus for studying how change is worked through in the everyday life of particular communities. I do this by analysing representations of space, time and movement (in other words, of transformation) *at work* in the related touristic practices of shopping, driving, sightseeing, using museums, malls, motels and theme parks, carried out in particular places. I examine not only the discourses involved in the material production of tourist places (government reports, media stories, architectural and planning features, promotional literature), but also those which circulate as gossip, myth or opinion between the 'users' – residents as well as visitors – of a place. I then consider the ways in which these practices inflect older Australian *narratives* of travel and histories of 'place', changing the terms of our understanding of the relations between 'home' and 'the voyage' (Morris, 1988a).

This involves some comparative research into the histories of places in different regions and socio-economic contexts. Most of the East Coast places I am studying (an urban telecommunications tower, three suburban shopping malls, a country town motel, an ageing highway, a Captain Cook memorial park) are invested in some way by working class communities, and most of these are now, in response to economic and ideological distress, reconstituting themselves and their histories as tourist landscapes. It is therefore in a double sense that I study 'life' as a tourist object: I am concerned not only with the commodity promotion of an image of past and present social 'life', but with the effects of this process for the human communities who may now find themselves living *as* 'tourist objects' – their ways of life spectacles to be visited, experiences to be consumed. My purpose is not to denounce this development (which promises 'survival' to many communities), but to ask how people *live* on a day-to-day basis with other-oriented images of their *life* (Morris, 1988c; 1990).

With this context in mind, in this chapter I want to take up an invitation by Marie-Françoise Lanfant to present a single *question* arising from this research. My question can best be framed by the puzzlement I felt at a certain moment during Alain Touraine's keynote address to the 12th World Congress of the International Sociological Association. His lecture emphasized practices of consumption considered in isolation from issues of production, and thus in polemical distinction from the traditional objects of Marxist political economy. When asked why he seemed to be returning to the model of the 'consumer society' at the end of a decade in which, at least in Britain and the United States, the great public debates had rather been about *production*, Touraine replied that a feature emerging from the global restructuring of capitalism and the collapse of communism was a *dissociation* between the 'economic' (playground of transnational corporations) and the 'cultural' (field of the new social movements) such that the latter could be considered in absolute, rather than relative, autonomy from the former.

Now this is a move which, in all its details (including the collapse of the complex concept of 'mode of production' into a binary opposition whereby the term 'production' becomes metonymic of 'the economic' in general, while 'consumption' is used as a metonym of 'culture'), is familiar to scholars in my own discipline, which is not sociology but cultural studies. Indeed, it is possible to argue that some such gesture of reduction has been foundational for that dominant strand of cultural studies which, distantly inspired by the work of Raymond Williams (1958), and more recently by Michel de Certeau (1975), has taken as its object of study those popular cultural *practices* which appropriate and transform the meaning of the commodities disseminated by the mass culture industries.[1] The oppositions then line up in a suspiciously neat (and manifestly incoherent) order: production versus consumption, mass culture versus popular culture, passive versus active, bad versus good, exchange value versus use value and so on, culminating in economy versus culture. Recent books by John Fiske (1989a; 1989b) demonstrate this tendency very well.

One of its effects in cultural studies has been to create a political cosmology whereby on the one hand there is an Olympian realm occupied by global corporations (working in mysterious ways that mere mortals can do nothing about), and then a secular world of culture, full of warmth, human practice and possibilities for action. Touraine's argument has a different genealogy, deriving from an interrogation of the categories of classic sociology (and of Marxist theory) in response to the political changes in both Western and Eastern Europe over the past few years. Nonetheless, it seems to be heading for much the same conclusion – and the same mythic universe – that cultural studies reached in the early 1980s (that is to say, during the peak years of the consumer-driven 'miracles' of Margaret Thatcher and Ronald Reagan).

Criticisms of this approach in cultural studies have become more insistent in recent years (Grossberg, 1988; Mellencamp, 1990). Here, I simply wish to pose a question. *If*, as Touraine suggests, the economic and cultural realms are now effectively dissociated, why is it that, throughout the 1980s in Australia, our corporate leaders, our politicians, our managers and bureaucrats, and even our trade unionists, began to preach *cultural* change? I offer just one example from a thick dossier I have of statements by businessmen defining the relations between economy and culture. It is a quotation used as a headline for a personality profile of a corporate leader, Don Swan, in one of the most widely read of our Sunday tabloid newspapers: 'Changing the culture is not a quick process in something as old and as large as ARC.' ARC is not a nation undergoing a revolutionary transformation, or a class or a subculture undergoing an ideological reform. Smorgon ARC is Australia's largest producer of concrete reinforcing steel (Australian *Sunday Telegraph*, 26 November 1989).

By 'changing the culture' men like Don Swan mean altering the work habits, industrial protocols and attitudes built up during the decades when Australia had a hyper-protected economy regulated by a strong welfare state. But to speak of habits ('work practices') is to begin to speak about the minute organization of everyday experience; to question industrial protocols is to question the very foundations of traditional Australian society; to challenge attitudes is to challenge values, expectations, desires – the very terms of personal and social identity. It is to begin to suggest, in other words, that improved economic performance can *follow* from 'changing the culture' in a rather broad sense.

By 'changing the culture', such men certainly also mean 'getting people to do more work for less money'. Their 'cultural' strategy is in fact an economic one, with strictly economic goals, narrowly conceived, in mind. The interesting thing, however, is the increasing frequency with which a culturalist *rhetoric* has been employed, and is assumed to be effective, in the public sphere as a means of negotiating solutions to economic problems, and securing ideological assent if not always to solutions, then to the *terms* in which problems are posed. Far from dissociating economy and culture, the corporate Olympians seem inclined to predicate a *convergence* between them, and to count on a public agreement that cultural change, and economic action, are now more intimately related than ever before under capitalism (Morris, 1991).

Tourism is at once a paradigm *economic* strategy in which this convergence develops, and the *cultural* field in which its operations, and its effects, can most immediately be studied. Indeed, the study of tourism may provide a better ground for rethinking the conditions of social action today than an immediate critical revision of the history of sociological theory. To make the point schematically: wherever tourism is an economic strategy as well as a money-making activity, and wherever it is a policy of state, a process of social and *cultural* change is initiated which involves transforming not only the 'physical' (in other words, the *lived*) environment of 'toured' communities, and the intimate details of the practice of everyday life, but also the series of relations by which cultural identity (and therefore, difference) is constituted for both the tourist and the toured in any given context.

Following from the work of MacCannell (1976), researchers have studied ways in which this process can involve the production of a 'designer reality' inhabited, in different and asymmetrical ways, by tourists and toured alike. For example, Wai-Teng Leong (1989) shows how tourism policy in Singapore participates in a 'nation-building process' whereby images of the country's 'diverse ethnic traditions' are manufactured and promoted in an international market – in ways that change how actual cultures of ethnicity are henceforth to be *lived*. Toured communities are increasingly required to live out their (manufactured) ethnicity for the gaze of the other, with the result that the destruction of some traditions and their replacement by others is required by the state, and then negotiated in various ways by those whose bodies and practices are thus required (but do not necessarily directly consent) to incarnate policy.

Clearly, 'manufacturing traditions for tourism' is a complex business with ambiguous effects, in which it is misleading to assume that the toured may be treated as the *victims* of a process beyond their control. I am interested in the ambiguities of tourism policy in Australia (much less systematic, less efficient, and so perhaps more fantasmal than in Singapore) as it affects, and is revised by, communities whose 'inherited' traditions – like xenophobic white racism, for example – cannot always be considered as intrinsically good things. Part of the interest of studying tourism in Australia is that it is simultaneously *post*-colonial, having been both a British dominion and an American satellite, and *neo*-colonial, retaining a role in American Pacific policy even as it gravitates increasingly towards Japan. Consequently, the strong distinctions drawn between 'self' and 'other' in Australian historiography often turn out to rest on shaky compromises and acts of wishful thinking; the history of national 'identity' has traditionally been written (usually by white men) as a history of desire, uncertainty and fear of a *lack* of 'difference'.

The development of a national tourism policy both extends and breaks with this history. It is an extension in that while the 'policy' may be Australian, much of the tourist *industry* is already foreign-owned; among the most difficult issues facing the environment movement today is how to mobilize opposition to destructive coastal resort developments without fostering anti-Japanese sentiment. On the other hand, the sense of a 'break' can be read in our literature and cinema by tracing a shift in the narrative positioning of the Australian (white, male) subject from *tourist* to *toured*. In spite of the differences between colonial exploration and organized mass tourism, the figure of the tourist has fitted easily into a rich tradition of travel writing (a privileged genre for thinking the experience of imperial conquest) in Australia – sometimes helping, in fact, to efface the travel/tourism difference.

For most of the twentieth century, the 'quest for national identity' was a defining theme of white Australian historiography and political discourse, and this ideal quest was commonly narrated as a story of nascent national subjectivity (Clark, 1979). Such narratives, however, usually ended in more or less transcendent *failure* for the white male hero, as in Patrick White's famous novel from 1957, *Voss* (Gibson, 1985). As Kay Schaffer (1988) has pointed out, intensely ambivalent relationships were also constructed by this masculinist tradition between 'the Land' and the figure of 'Woman' – with attendant racial and sexual anxieties being projected on to Aboriginal men and women.

However from the 1950s to the 1970s – when increasingly accessible air travel made it possible for more Australians to leave the continent – an identity question was more often posed in popular culture by tales of the Australian *tourist* abroad (for example, Bruce Beresford's film *The Adventures of Barry Mackenzie*, 1972). The Australian in these stories was often a Candide figure – bumbling and naïve, or obnoxious and insecure – and thus an agent of a satire directed more at Australians than at others encountered *en route*. This tradition ranges from Murray Bail's merciless novel *Homesickness* (1980) about suburban Australians on a package tour in Europe, to the pop song by the band Redgum which pillories the 'home' culture of the ugly Australian tourist ('Been there, done that, I've been to Bali too').

Alongside this continuing tradition, a different theme emerged in the 1980s as Australia became more popular as an international tourist *destination*, and as conflicts arose in policy-making and in local communities about whether to privilege international or domestic tourism – and which cultural images would suit the former rather than the latter (Craik, 1988). Australian culture now is debated as a potential tourist *object*: 'identity' is predicated no longer in romantic terms as a goal to be achieved, but as a commodity to be produced, an image to be promoted. The film *Crocodile Dundee* was in many ways at once a manifesto of this shift, and its canonical expression; indeed, the film itself can be read as an allegory of 'export drive' logic underpinning tourist policy (Morris, 1988d).

The representation of Australia to Australians as a *destination* for international tourists reached a peak of intensity during the Bicentennial celebrations of 1988, when some of the long-term implications of the shift from tourist to toured became more obvious in the public sphere. On the one hand, thousands of poor, aged and invalid people were evicted from low-income housing in Sydney to make way for hotel development and luxury accommodation, and this, in combination with a property boom, helped to destroy the ideal of home ownership for (almost) everybody that once identified with 'the Australian dream'. On the other hand, the federal government was forced into symbolically initiating some hasty and inadequate measures to compensate for its own years of broken promises towards Aboriginal people, for fear that the presence of prying television crews from other countries (who might well be more interested, as are many tourists, in Aboriginal rather than in non-Aboriginal Australian cultures) could make Australia 'look bad' internationally for its treatment of indigenous people.[2]

The implications of these developments, and these wishes, fears and fantasies about what the gaze of the other might see, are enormous. Economically motivated *cultural* restructuring involves not only a revision of the past, but a deployment in the conflictual spaces of the society being 'touristified' of desiring and *polemical* images of identity and alterity in *future*. To indicate something of the complexity of this deployment in Australian contexts, I shall offer three examples of cases in which self/other relations are renegotiated through tourism in different, even incompatible, ways. My point here is to demonstrate the difficulty of deriving general theories about the 'effects' of tourism from such cases, rather than to develop in this restricted context an analysis adequate to each.

I have discussed the first of these, Sydney Tower, at length elsewhere (Morris, 1982; 1990). Sydney Tower is a major tourist-shopping-telecommunications complex in downtown Sydney. First opened in 1981, it was one of the first architectural declarations in Sydney of what Jacques de Weerdt has called a 'vocation' for tourism (de Weerdt, 1990). At the beginning, Sydney Tower explicitly interpellated domestic tourists and residents of Sydney. Visible from all over the city, the tower was a monument to progress in the classic imperial sense: not only was it celebrated in the media as a sign of Sydney's modernity but, with a scandalous lack of sensitivity, audiovisual displays in the tower turret narrated (to whites) a 'history' of Sydney's tourist vocation by representing a primal scene of first contact between the British and the Eora people in touristic terms. The key image was a simulated naïve painting of a sailing ship in Sydney Harbour, with natives *pointing* at the ship from the shore. While this gesture defined the

Aborigines themselves as potential 'sightseers', the audio track specified that the addressee of this discourse on the genesis of tourism, and on tourism as genesis, was a non-Aboriginal tourist only: '*You* can imagine *their* surprise', said the voice, 'as the settlers sailed in to *this* [not their] magnificent harbour.'

It is an irony of history that by 1988 this whole narrative had vanished from the turret, which had been 'renovated' to appeal to a different clientele. Not only had Aboriginal people disappeared from the field of touristic address, but so had *all* Australians. The gallery spaces of the tower were now devoted to ads for duty-free shopping, and to full-colour photographs of the transport systems (Qantas jets, buses, hire cars) bringing international tourists into the country, then shuttling them between the anonymous resort locations (motels, swimming-pools, zoos, cocktail bars) also promoted on the walls as future sites to visit. In seven years, the tower had been transformed: a monument designed to attract local shopper-tourists back to downtown Sydney by symbolically unifying the city and celebrating its modernity had become a 'first stop' on an *itinerary* for tourists from elsewhere. All signs of local history – offensive and otherwise – had been effaced from the turret space, which now became a monument to international tourist time.

This vision of tourism as a process which progressively destroys the mediating signs of 'real' locality, history, ethnicity and nationality probably still defines many people's worst nightmare of what international mass tourism can mean for local cultures. It also captures, however, the ambiguity of a moment in which a society that has, like modern Australia, produced its own identity historically by dispossessing and excluding others now finds itself subject in turn to fears and fantasies of displacement.

The example of Sydney Tower, however, functions for me not as a metonym of a supposed general 'problem' posed by international tourism, but as a way of framing another story of encounter and exchange which cannot be, I believe, quite so easily diagnosed.

This is the strange tale of 'Crocodile Shoichi' – the name that an Australian journalist gave to the hero of a 200-page manga (adult comic) published in Japanese by the Australian government in 1989 specifically to maintain Japanese tourist interest in Australia (Hartcher, 1989). At the beginning of the story, Shoichi is a young executive complaining about having to travel to Australia on business for the fifth time: 'Just once, I'd like to go somewhere with a bit more character.' But his plane crashes in the desert where he encounters Aborigines, the Flying Doctor (an airborne medical service for isolated families and remote communities), bush hospitality and – oddly, to an Australian reader – a horse-riding Japanese wanderer who explains to Shoichi what wonderfully 'warm and open people' Australians really are.

Thus far, the narrative appears to be projecting on to Japanese readers certain historic *Australian* fears about the flaws and failings of Australian identity: for example, an anxiety that the culture is somehow dull and its attractions too quickly exhausted, along with a concern, which is sometimes a nostalgic *wish*, that authentic Australian life may not be found in the sprawling coastal cities where most people actually live, but only in the (to whites) mysterious and forbidding 'dead heart' – in myth a source of historic white Australian identity, but in social practice an entirely exotic other for the majority of non-Aboriginal and urban Australians. At this level, the manga can represent not only a product of market research into Japanese preferences, but also a discourse on what *some* Australians think that *most* Australians would think about Australia if they were Japanese thinking like Australians.

But things soon become more complicated. Shoichi becomes so enamoured of Australia that he decides to abandon the project which brought him to Australia – a *tourist development* that his company plans for Tasmania – in order to protect the wilderness. This will mean instant dismissal, but 'so what if I am sacked, I *will always have my agriculture*'; it turns out that Shoichi's father is a farmer who has always wanted his son to maintain tradition by taking over the farm.

This is a discourse of desire so impacted that it is difficult indeed to interpret. On one level, it seems to be a sophisticated response to a market-researched perception of Australia as attractive to Japanese tourists because of its 'natural' and 'unspoilt' wilderness area, which those same Japanese tourists are likely to realize must shrink because of Japanese tourist developments. So it represents a (perfectly reasonable) projection by the Australian government of a Japanese other who is consciously subject to, and a knowing subject of, much the same contradictions as any Australian tourist in those same wilderness locations. In representing a fantasy solution through Shoichi's renunciation, of course, the manga paradoxically aspires to be part of the *problem* – by attracting still more tourists to the wilderness.

At the same time, the manga also represents an attempt to exploit a much-discussed nostalgia among younger Japanese for the good old days of the 'real', agriculturally based, Japan – and to bring this into equivalence with dominant forms of *Australian* nostalgia for the good old days of rural Australian life. However there is a difference being reworked here: however much Australia's national wealth in the past may have derived from 'our agriculture', most Australians have *never* lived a rural life. Our rural history has long been both industrial (not arcadian or subsistence) and environmentally destructive: mining, savage clearing of the land for massive cattle and sheep grazing lands (Bolton, 1981). Furthermore, the production of unspoilt wilderness as a source of Australian cultural authenticity is a relatively recent development – connected as much to the economic imperatives of tourism itself as to the rise of global ecological awareness.

The final twist is that in offering potential Japanese tourists a fantasy in which, by coming to Australia, they can help to destroy global tourism, the manga uses an allegory about avoiding one of everyone's worst nightmares (environmental catastrophe) in order to express a uniquely *Australian* nightmare. If the tourist industry collapses, we could face an economic crisis in which 'we will *only* have our agriculture'. This is, in fact, the very possibility which leads many of our gloomier economists to compare Australia now to Argentina some decades ago, and which has prompted so much desperate enthusiasm for a national tourism policy – and for supporting 'tourable' ways of life ('warm and open people') that might in future help to sustain it.

In order to refer this back to my original question – why, if economy and culture may be dissociated in contemporary societies, should corporate leaders be promoting cultural change? – I would like to stress that I have not (and could not) read the manga itself. My speculations concern only the media report *about* the manga – a report addressed casually to me, as to all Australians likely to read a newspaper, as a text about the stakes of our cultural identity in the present, and for ways of life in the future. So I suspect that the story (addressed to Australians) of the story of Shoichi (addressed to Japanese) contains the beginnings of an answer to my question.

I want to conclude, however, with a text that points towards another set of questions altogether. *Ngukurr: Weya Wi Na* (*Ngukurr: Where Are We Now?*) is a videotape produced in 1988 as a programme for broadcast on Aboriginal television in central Australia (see Michaels, 1986). Made by several members of the community at Ngukurr in the Northern Territory, the tape is both a history of a multi-lingual Aboriginal community that developed *after* white settlers, missionaries and teachers arrived in the north, and an argument for a cultural politics to sustain that community's autonomy in the present and the future.[3] The tape is a complex and visually beautiful polemic on behalf of a practice of self-determination by Aboriginal people enabling them to appropriate on their own terms technical knowledge and cultural goods from other societies. The argument of the film is that it is possible for the community to maintain its own languages and cultures while ensuring that future generations have greater access to non-Aboriginal societies, and thus further to secure their independence from both welfare bureaucracy and political pressures towards assimilation.

One segment of *Ngukurr: Weya Wi Na* is of particular interest to me here. As part of a policy discussion about how to teach English as well as Aboriginal languages to their children, a group of people connected to the community's school (including some children) go to Singapore to look at an example of a multi-lingual society where English is used in schools, while other languages are spoken at home and in social life. The segment documents a tourist expedition, one in which there is more mutual exchange between cultures than most tours commonly require, or even permit: as well as a Chinese school where the children sing in English for their Aboriginal Australian visitors, there are scenes from the airport, the zoo, the city streets and the markets, and a visit to a Portuguese-speaking community. In return, the tourists perform traditional music for their Singaporean hosts, and teach some local children how to dance. The trip – an auto-didactically motivated practice of 'cultural tourism' with quite precise aims in mind – is considered very successful, and its story is incorporated into a lesson at school back home at Ngukurr.

As a white urban Australian viewer, and one for whom the white as well as the black communities of the Northern Territory inhabit a far-distant, legendary space that I have only ever imagined visiting precisely as a tourist,[4] *Ngukurr: Weya Wi Na* challenged my thinking about tourism in three fundamental ways.

One was to confront me in practice with something that I thought I already knew: that it can be quite misleading to think of tourism and touristic encounters in terms of a dyadic relation only between what Dean MacCannell calls the 'international middle class' (usually assumed now to be European, American or Japanese) and its exotic – and often 'underdeveloped' – others. While this may be a useful model for thinking about structurally and politically dominant *forms* of international industrialized tourism, it is inadequate to a study of tourism as *practice*.

What was disconcerting to me in *Ngukurr: Weya Wi Na* was not the representation of tourism as an encounter between Aboriginal and Asian societies unmediated by significant European agents, but rather the irrelevance of my own concept of 'Australia' to the cultural and political map constructed by the film. As an American viewer pointed out to me, white Australia only figures seriously in the film as a sign of the past (archival footage of a missionary school), or as a technological 'membrane' – represented by a Qantas jet – through which people can pass to an elsewhere in the present.[5] An important link between these figures is provided by an older man's comment, in voice-over as the group boards the plane, that he had always wanted to travel overseas, but had been refused a passport in 1966.[6] The tourist industry then appears as one of a number of enabling mechanisms for a kind of social action defined without reference to the values and fantasies of white Australia – including the myth of the other. While Singapore itself certainly figures as *different* from Ngukurr, this difference is conceptualized as a basis for constructing *limited* and thus non-specular similarities (for example, multi-lingualism) from which the tourists can derive their own 'use value'.

The second challenge follows from this. For several years now in Australia, there has been a debate about the status of Aboriginal culture as an *object* of tourism. It is a debate in which Aboriginal intellectuals, bureaucrats and community leaders have participated, and it has involved an argument for preserving 'traditional' culture by 'manufacturing' (in Wai-Teng Leong's phrase) versions of it for tourist consumption, transforming its status in contemporary Australian society by increasing its prestige, and using tourist revenue as a basis for economic independence from the state. Traditional culture in this sense is not a pure remainder of some pristine and untouched ancient cultural source, but is in itself already a hybrid product historically developed in response to, as well as in spite of, generations of dealing with white invaders and functionaries (advisers, bureaucrats, ethnographers). An influential argument has therefore been that maintenance of tradition can best be ensured by building on existing practices of *transforming* tradition through appropriating elements from other (not 'other') societies.

As I have suggested, *Ngukurr: Weya Wi Na* endorses this strategy. At the same time, however, it is *not* about Aboriginal culture as a tourist object. It is a film about Aboriginal people as *subjects* of a tourist practice (as well as of pedagogy, and of running the cattle industry on which the community's livelihood may depend). In this sense, it goes beyond the analysis of how manu-facturing culture can change the ways in which culture is henceforth to be lived – since this process is taken for granted as a given historical experience. Instead, it asks how the processes of change can be planned and managed by the people whom change will affect. It also goes beyond, or rather 'beside', the critique of Australian historiography as a dominant white male narrative of becoming – and of passage from tourist to toured – in order to tell a story in which a discrete tourist narrative is incorporated into an ongoing Aboriginal history of survival and struggle.

However the third challenge which I see in *Ngukurr: Weya Wi Na* concerns the doubts I have about my formulation of the first two. It would be easy to take the next step and declare that, in terms of my argument about the relations of economy to culture as defined by contemporary tourism, the Ngukurr community tape represents an exemplary case in which culture *is* economic, and in which we can see possibilities for self-determination by small and once historically marginalized societies opening up under the conditions provided by tourism which might not have been possible without it.

To some extent, that may well be so. Nevertheless, I suspect that this reading of *Ngukurr: Weya Wi Na* also represents my own impacted 'discourse of desire', and may articulate for me some of my own anxieties about the past, present and future of Australia – in much the same way that I claimed the story of Shoichi did for the discourses of Australian state bureaucracy and economic planning. If it is historically tempting for white Australians now to idealize Aboriginal ways of life without effectively supporting their struggles, it is also all too easy to look selectively at the symbolic success stories of Aboriginal tourist practice, and then to appropriate these as so many reassuring promises of 'Australian' cultural survival in a global tourist age. It is this aspect of my work on tourism which, I think, most immediately calls for further research.

Notes

1 The term 'popular' here is not taken in a folkloric or a class-specific sense. Since this kind of cultural studies has flourished in mediated societies where traditional peasant and community-based working class cultures are now vestigial, 'popular' tends to refer to something like a cross-class willingness to appropriate the products of mass culture. Perhaps for this reason, the privileged figure of popular culture in this tradition has not been the peasant or the worker, but 'youth' (Chambers, 1986).

2 One site of tension has been Australia's refusal, through the doctrine of *terra nullius*, to recognize the prior existence and ownership claims of Aboriginal societies (Reynolds, 1988). At the Barunga festival in the Northern Territory in 1988, Prime Minister Hawke was moved to promise a treaty or a 'compact' to redress this situation. Federal cabinet approval of a plan to begin negotiations towards a formal 'instrument of reconciliation' was obtained in December 1990.

3 Directed by Ronald Thompson, Andrew Joshua, Kevin Rogers, Raymond Geoffrey and Brian Burkett, *Ngukurr: Weya Wi Na* was produced by Ngukurr School Council, Ngukurr Adult Education Committee, and Yugul Manggi Media.

4 Most of the population of Australia lives in a few south-eastern cities. On the history of the Northern Territory as an imaginary site of the other, see Stratton (1989).

5 James Hay, University of Illinois at Champaign-Urbana, private conversation.

6 Aboriginal people were only granted full citizenship rights in 1967, following a referendum approving an amendment of the constitution.

References

Bolton, G. (1981) *Spoils and Spoilers: Australians Make their Environment 1788–1980*. Sydney, London, Boston: Allen and Unwin.

Chambers, I. (1986) *Popular Culture: the Metropolitan Experience*. London and New York: Methuen.

Clark, M. (1979) *The Quest for an Australian Identity*. Brisbane: University of Queensland Press.

Craik, J. (1988) 'Tourism down under: tourism policies in the tropics'. Cultural Policy Studies Occasional Paper 2, Brisbane: Institute for Cultural Policy Studies.

de Certeau, M. (1975) *L'Invention du quotidien*. Paris: UGE.

de Weerdt, J. (1990) 'L'espace rural français: vocation touristique ou processus de touristification?'. Paper presented to the World Conference of Sociology, Madrid.

Fiske, J. (1989a) *Reading the Popular*. Boston. Unwin Hyman.

Fiske, J. (1989b) *Understanding Popular Culture*. Boston: Unwin Hyman.

Gibson, R. (1985) 'Yondering: a reading of *Mad Max Beyond Thunderdome*', *Art and Text*, 19: 25–33.

Grossberg, L. (1988) *It's a Sin: Politics, Post-Modernity and the Popular*. Sydney: Power.

Hartcher, P. (1989) 'Bound for Tokyo: Crocodile Shoichi', *The Sydney Morning Herald*, 24 November.

Leong, W.T. (1989) 'Culture and the state: manufacturing traditions for tourism', *Critical Studies in Mass Communication*, 6: 355-75.

MacCannell, D. (1976) *The Tourist: a New Theory of the Leisure Class*. New York: Schocken.

Mellencamp, P. (ed.) (1990) *Logics of Television: Essays in Cultural Criticism*. Bloomington: Indiana University Press.

Michael, E. (1986) *The Aboriginal Invention of Television in Central Australia 1982–1986*. Canberra: Australian Institute of Aboriginal Studies.

Morris, M. (1982) 'Sydney Tower', *Island Magazine*, 9 October: 53–67.

Morris, M. (1988a) 'At Henry Parkes motel', *Cultural Studies*, 2(1): 1–47.

Morris, M. (1988b) 'Panorama: the live, the dead and the living', in P. Foss (ed.), *Island in the Stream: Myths of Place in Australian Culture*. Sydney: Pluto Press.

Morris, M. (1988c) 'Things to do with shopping centres', in S. Sheridan (ed.), *Grafts: Feminist Cultural Criticism*. London: Verso.

Morris, M. (1988d) 'Tooth and claw: tales of survival and *Crocodile Dundee*', in M. Morris, *The Pirate's Fiancée: Feminism, Reading, Postmodernism*. London: Verso.

Morris, M. (1990) 'Metamorphoses at Sydney Tower', *New Formations*, 11: 5–18.

Morris, M. (1991) 'On the beach', in L. Grossberg, C. Nelson and P. Treichler (eds), *Cultural Studies*. New York: Routledge.

Reynolds, H. (1988) *The Law of the Land*. Ringwood: Penguin.

Schaffer, K. (1988) *Women and the Bush: Forces of Desire in the Australian Cultural Tradition*. Cambridge: Cambridge University Press.

Stratton, J. (1989) 'Deconstructing the territory', *Cultural Studies*, 3(1): 38–57.

Williams, R. (1958) *Culture and Society*. London: Chatto and Windus.

11

Sex Tourism and Traditional Australian Male Identity

Suzy Kruhse-MountBurton

The description of sex tourism simply as 'tourism whose main or major motivation is to consummate commercial sexual liaisons' (Graburn, 1983: 438) masks the complex process by which individuals choose to seek sexual gratification, first within prostitution, and secondly as a part of the tourist experience. Observers have suggested that the 'cheaper' sex available in South East Asian prostitution is an inadequate explanation for the persistence of sex tourism, since the impetus for blending travel with the consumption of commercial sex can be distinguished from the employment of prostitutes within the normal environment of the individuals involved (Wyer and Towner, 1988: 35; Hong, 1985: 73). Clearly, both 'push' and 'pull' dimensions of motivation must be considered in gaining an understanding of the inclination of men towards sex holidays (Dann, 1981: 191).

Therefore, as Truong suggests, the features peculiar to the societies where the demand is generated represent an important, and yet neglected aspect of research (1989: 342). With this view in mind, the chapter will endeavour to provide a brief profile of gender relations in Australia, a Western country from which thousands of men embark every year for sex holidays in South East Asia, and in so doing will detail the crises facing men in their efforts to sustain the traditional masculine identity.

The phenomenon of sex tourism in South East Asia

An undeniable correlation exists between tourism and the growth of prostitution in South East Asia, a fact which has resulted in some critics intimating that prostitution in that location was caused by tourism. (Putschogl-Wild and Krawenkel, cited in Cohen, 1982: 404; Prahl and Steinecke, 1979: 98). However, historical evidence indicates that the institution was a traditional feature of most societies in the region (Jones, 1982: 113; Phongpaichit, 1981: 15–23) and that prostitution catering to European clientele first developed just after the Second World War. The demand resulted from a heightened military presence in the region, as personnel, unaccompanied by women, were stationed on bases like those in the Philippines (Renschler, cited in Maeder, 1982). Later the R&R programme was instituted by the military authorities as a means of maintaining the morale of disenchanted troops caught up in the unpopular Vietnam War.

This policy entailed the visit of tens of thousands of men on leave from the war zone to cities such as Sydney in Australia and Bangkok, Thailand (O'Grady, 1982: 38). Yet, the end of the conflict did not mean the demise of the thriving districts which catered to the foreign market for sex. The King's Cross red light district in Sydney remains as the Australian legacy. However, in Thailand the burgeoning tourist industry grasped the opportunity opened up by the attraction of gaudy massage parlours and bars, and with the blessings of a government eager for foreign currency, arranged for Japanese and Western European tourists to replace the dwindling military personnel ('Human toll of a red light zone. The geography of prostitution. Part 1: The East', *The Geographic Magazine*, March 1988; Yap, 1986: 59).

The accessibility of cheap travel to the workers in developed countries, in combination with the seductive marketing of South East Asian holidays, helped to publicize the region as a specialist tourist destination, catering to the erotic fantasies of men. The massive expansion of prostitution in South East Asia therefore represents the outgrowth of the indigenous industry to cater for a mass market.

The South East Asian sex tourism experience: contrasts with prostitution in Australia

Gail Sheehy made the observation that, for a man, prostitution represents an opportunity of 'buying the nostalgic illusion that things are how they were when he was a boy' (1971: 3). The support role of prostitution for the 'male ideal' of ready sexual access to women and the possibility of playing out fantasies cannot be denied (Prieur, n.d.: 6–7). However, prostitution in the Australian context is often appraised by clients as deficient, in that prostitutes are criticized for being emotionally and sexually cold and for making little effort to please, or to disguise the commercial nature of the interaction. Men appear to find the latter aspect particularly demeaning since it highlights the failure to find a willing and satisfactory free partner.

At best, prostitution in Australia offers only a temporary and extremely limited means of seeking sexual identity confirmation, although the popular belief in the 'whore with a heart of gold' and the prostitute who falls in love with her client still persists within male mythology (Winick and Kinsie, 1971: 206). But in reality, a measure of professional distance, combined with severe time restrictions and considerable expense, limits the extent to which men are able to indulge their fantasies or to interact with the prostitutes in any meaningful way. Australian sex workers are also usually in the position to demand safe sex practices and to set boundaries on the sorts of services which they are willing to supply to clients. A minimum age for prostitutes is another restriction which many men, socialized to glorify youth in the female, find unacceptable in their access to commercial sex partners.

In contrast to the perceived failings of prostitution at home, many of the participants of sex holidays stressed that the warmth, affection, femininity, youth and beauty of Asian prostitutes, combined with an aptitude for disguising the mercenary aspect of the arrangement, were the features which held most appeal. One participant, a man in his late 40s, explained his feeling towards the prostitute he had hired as a companion on a three-day Indonesian holiday in the following way:

> You could have just lifted her out of an Asian *Playboy* centrespread. She was magnificent. I found out later that she was 19 and she was just gorgeous. She didn't look that young. She didn't look as though she was a child bride or anything. Even on the boat we sat close and I thought she had taken to me. We got to the island and were shown our little thatched cottage. She knew enough English that we could get by and have a reasonable conversation. We warmed to each other very quickly so it was probably only about 30 minutes before we were in bed. She looked attractive with her clothes on but when she took her clothes off I said to her, 'I could just stand you up in a corner and look at you.' I mean she had a magnificent body, not an ounce of fat, golden dark skin, she was just perfect.

The same man rationalized his involvement in the commercial sex transaction with the comment that:

> It's true there is no chance of rejection. But now maybe I'm a bit idealistic in the sense that I think, wouldn't it be nice if during that day, and that encounter, that there developed a genuine friendliness. So that what I would like to do, and maybe I'm a bit of a romantic or a bit naïve or something, but I'd like to think that we got on well together to the point that she just actually liked me and enjoyed my company. So when the time comes and we've had a good time, we maybe kiss and cuddle and go to bed, and that it is an enjoyable experience for her even though she's guaranteed of making some money.

Other participants of sex tourism explained that they particularly enjoyed the tempering of commercial sex in combination with personal services like laundry, cooking and companionship in that it approximated a sort of ideal temporary marriage without responsibility. The low cost is clearly an attractive feature of these arrangements which may run for days, weeks or even months, and may be renewed on subsequent holidays. A sex tourist in Indonesia explained the particular appeal of this style of contract, and the technique which is commonly used by Australians to negotiate a reduced price:

> You can get a girl quite cheap. You can bargain with them so that when they tell you they want 50,000 rupes [sic], which is $45 to $50 Australian, you can turn around and say but you're very young, not very experienced, 25,000. Then you'll argue 30,000, 35,000, or whatever, until you arrive at a fee. But it's going to be under $50 and that girl will act as a companion and in fact there's no set time limit. You can eat and drink with her and take her anywhere you like, and she'll be your companion all along. This arrangement gives the whole sex business some sort of decency.

Some participants commented on the possibilities of gaining free sexual attention, either for economic motives or as a symbol of the authenticity of the relationship. A considerable number of Australian men maintain a correspondence with one or more women, and after a few trips some men opt for Asian wives, often with the belief that these women will be easily controlled and dominated. But popular male mythology nevertheless warns against marriage to an Asian prostitute with the expression, 'You can take the girl out of the bar, but you can't take the bar out of the girl.'

Unquestionably many of the limitations present in Australian prostitution are not features of the organization of South East Asian sex tourism. Girls of all ages are readily available and a variety of services, referred to by one client as a 'sexual smorgasbord', can be cheaply and readily purchased in many tourist ports. Commercial sex, in league with tourism, has an added appeal in that it removes participants from normal role obligations and frees them from the mores which restrain their behaviour at home, while it simultaneously places them in an environment in which they are able to indulge anonymously in puerile activities reminiscent of boyhood behaviour (Dann, 1981: 191; Crompton, 1979: 416–19).

The consuming of copious quantities of alcohol is of significance as a means of further encouraging disinhibition whilst on a sex holiday, since the Australian cultural expectation of intoxification is that it allows emancipation from social rules, increases sexual confidence, and frees the individual from responsibility for his actions (Reinarman and Critchlow, 1987: 435–60). This generalized state of euphoria can be maintained over many weeks in a haven catering to sex tourists where the alcohol is cheap, bars are always open, and drinking partners abound. Some prostitution establishments cater especially to Australian drinkers, and name the premises accordingly. In Bangkok the employees of a bar called the Kangaroo Club offer oral sexual services to clients at the table, so that the men are free to continue to chat and drink with their friends.

Sexual myths nurtured in the all-male environments of mining camps, oil rigs and cattle stations back in Australia, and exploited by the mail-order pushers of pornography, find their fulfilment in these South East Asian holiday destinations. The lost paradise of natural sensuality is embodied by the youthful, petite and gracious Asian women who are believed to enjoy pleasing men. Running parallel to this mythology is a desexualization of white women, who may even be referred to by the derogatory term of 'white bellies', creatures who are deemed to be spoiled, grasping and, above all, unwilling or inferior sexual partners.

One man in his 60s explained the romantic appeal of women in the Philippines, as opposed to the reluctance of young Australian women to respond to the advances of a man of his generation, with the following anecdote:

> The attitude of Asian women is free and open, not like in Australia where women are very wary of an unwanted involvement. In the Philippines a man could be idly standing at the bus stop and a bus approaches packed with people. A pretty girl by the window catches your eye and continues to smile as the bus moves on. It's an instant romance of a sort, and can happen a few times every day in the Philippines, even to a man my age.

Rites of reversal, celebrated to highlight these contrasting views of womanhood, give rise to bizarre sexual spectacles (Jafari, 1985: 122–3). For example, in Manila, a bar catering to Australians is furnished with a central stage which resembles a boxing ring. Intoxicated men are thrust in one at a time by their friends, to be titillated by up to half a dozen nubile naked girls, while onlookers shout encouragement. The clients apparently gain vicarious pleasure and a sense of solidarity from the events, the popularity of which can be argued to indicate that such rituals have an important function in celebrating ideals of manhood and in facilitating the reconstitution of male bonds placed under stress within the hierarchical and competitive labour market (Tiger, 1969: 136, 141, 147).

Sex tourism as play

Within Western societies the concept of play has a direct relationship with the work ethic, in that powerful moral notions surround
the perceptions of 'proper' conduct in time and place (Norbeck,
1971: 48–53). Work is an activity which one does in the familiar
environment, while the state of play is best achieved in another
location. Travel is therefore unique in providing individuals with an
opportunity for freedom from the ethical constraints dictated by
work, and from moral and other expectations imposed by the
conventional social environment (O'Grady, 1981: 38).

Available material on sex tourism indicates that it is a practice
well patronized by the working class of many nations, and even
encouraged by management (Korean Church Women United, 1984:
12–13; Giarelli, 1981: 21). This fact may reflect the popular conception of tourism as a state-of-being, diametrically opposed to the
condition of work, a form of play which allows a reconstitution of
the individual both physically and mentally (Graburn, 1977: 18).
However, sex tourism has an added rejuvenating potential for the
worker in that the personal sense of power it provides may act as a
compensatory behaviour for an individual unable to exercise any
real authority within his daily existence (Schmidt, 1982: 94).

Hantover points out that 'traditionally, men have looked to
work, the family and sex as arenas for masculine validation' (1981:
94). Frustration at the restrictions placed on actualizing these
avenues of role fulfilment appear to constitute a 'threshold factor'
which motivates men towards sex holidays (Iso-Ahola, 1982: 258;
Hantover, 1981: 95). Certainly, the working lives of contemporary
men allow little scope as a proving-ground for the idealized
masculine qualities of self-reliance and independence. Instead the
modern work environment offers limited opportunities for self-
expression, compounded by the often demeaning requirement of
subserviency within a bureaucratic organization.

Fullerton's observations on the connection between male
sexuality and feelings of power further elucidate the attraction of
sex tourism. He asserted that: 'For men, sexual potency and socio-
economic-political power are intertwined: the economically and
politically powerful male can command the sexual favours of the
most desirable women' (1972: 52). In sex tourism, one of the
appeals for the common man is undeniably that he is free to
experience the exhilaration usually open only to the wealthy, that is
of having sexual access to many women of youth and beauty, a
situation which would be highly improbable at home.

The Australian Navy recognized the potential of a recruiting drive which glorified sexual access to attractive young women of Asian race as a form of recreation, in association with the Australian pastime of beer drinking. In 1989, an advertisement illustrated with images of Australian sailors and beautiful Asiatic girls walking arm in arm narrated:

> Aussie sailors are experts on the local brews from Bangkok to San Diego and have a well deserved reputation for really knowing how to enjoy themselves . . . After work they are just as likely to find themselves in some exotic new place and then it's on with the freshly laundered best blues and off with your mates to make a close study of the local wild life. All work and no play makes Jack a very dull boy, but not in the Australian Navy. ('Blues', recruitment advertisement authorized by the Department of Defence, Australia, *People* magazine, 1989)

The extreme youth of many South East Asian prostitutes appears to have a particular appeal, since it has been estimated that in Thailand between 20 and 50 per cent of prostitutes are under the age of 13 years ('The spoils of tourism', *The National Focus* (Thailand), 2 August 1989; Pangiliman, 1986), while in the Philippines children may constitute an even larger percentage of those employed in prostitution ('Spare us children', *The National Bangkok*, 1 August 1989).

The provision of virgins is a speciality offered by brothel keepers to foreign clients in Thailand. Some of the men interviewed in Australia on their return from holidays reported having employed sex partners as young as nine years of age, with the comment that the services of these children cost up to seven times the price of a grown girl. The price ranged, in 1988, from about $190 to $270 Australian, depending on the attractiveness of the girl ('Savage truth of one night in Bangkok: tragedy of the seedy sex scene', *Northern Territory News*, 28 May 1988). Yet, like the American men interviewed by Hite (1981: 775), the participants denied tendencies towards paedophilia as an expression of their sexuality back in Australia, and were able to rationalize their activities with Asian children as acceptable, in the alternative moral milieu of a holiday in that part of the world.

A similar logic appeared to be in operation for the patrons of homosexual tourism. One client commented that his workmates, who were conventional in disapproving of homosexuality in Australia, had been regular patrons of the 'hiki girls', the transvestite male prostitutes of Singapore. The men apparently did not perceive an inconsistency in their behaviour when they returned from holidays brandishing photographs of the seductively clad but male prostitutes who had been their bedfellows in Asia.

Social change: the family, sex and the threatened sense of male identity

Role identity has been described as a man's 'imaginary view of himself as he likes to think of himself being and acting as an occupant of that position' (McCall and Simmons, 1966: 67). The work environment of the majority of Australian men appears to offer only limited opportunities for the validation of traditional masculine role expectations, while the changing nature of family life seems to be placing further stress on the male identity. It has been observed that an individual's identity is threatened:

> when the processes of identity, assimilation-accommodation and evaluation are, for some reason, unable to comply with the principles of continuity, distinctiveness and self-esteem, which habitually guide their operation. The reason for this obstruction of the processes of identity constitutes the threat. (Breakwell, 1986: 7)

In the case of the Australian male, a variety of factors have converged to endanger the individual's sense of his place in the world. Improved contraception, combined with economic pressures, have ensured that large families, a traditional means by which working class men were able to demonstrate masculinity, have not been a viable option for several decades (Rainwater, 1960: 85). In the 1960s the Australian family was described as a 'matriduxy', that is a family dominated by the mother (Adler, 1965: 149–55). But even though he was marginalized in the domestic realm, the 'Australian dream' was realized for a man if he could demonstrate his ability as breadwinner by having a wife who was financially dependent (Game and Pringle, 1979: 10).

However, in the 1980s and into the 1990s, with better education, equal pay, and opportunities opening up for women in the workforce, wives increasingly seek economic autonomy and personal accomplishment outside the home. This reality confronts the provider role traditionally occupied by man, a position of responsibility but also privilege, which bolstered masculine self-esteem and ensured a place as head of the household. A working wife is also less likely to uncomplainingly provide all the home comforts which men have been socialized to expect, so placing considerable stress on the relationship between spouses ('Husbands still say no to housework', *Northern Territory News*, 25 January 1989: 20) and constituting the major source of conflict within the family (Helen Glezer, cited in Arndt, 1986: 52).

In the event of divorce, of which Australia experienced 41,007 in 1988, an increase of 3 per cent over the previous year, men are faced with a severe emotional and economic crisis ('Living without a woman: the brave new world of the single dad', *New Man* (Australia), May 1990: 41; 'Year saw 41,007 divorces', *Northern Territory News*, 26 August 1989; 'System encourages couple to split up, says counsellor: marriage in state of crisis', *Northern Territory News*, 12 August 1989: 5). According to a recently published exposé on men and divorce in Australia today: 'More women are walking out of unacceptable relationships and leaving men marooned and bewildered. Splits frequently result in custody battles, financial hardship and alienation, which may lead men to physical and mental illness' (Townshend, 1990: 43). In fact, 65 per cent of separations are initiated by women (Family Court of Australia, cited in Arndt, 1986: 55) and wives generally maintain custody of children and are able to claim financial support against their husbands through the courts and more recently the Tax Department. After divorce men are faced with the loss of their children, the end of family life and a reduced appeal in the marriage market, since they must bear the economic liability of the previous wife and children.

Symptomatic of the stresses confronting men in Australia, heart disease, cancer and illnesses related to high blood pressure continued to be the main causes of death. The male suicide rate is four times higher than that of women, and in 1989 was triple that for men in the 1950s. Life Line, a personal crisis phone-in service, reported that men contemplating suicide often indicated to counsellors that they were wracked by feelings of inadequacy at not being able to fulfil the traditional role expectation of providing for their families, and that as a result they suffered from low self-esteem and a sense of failure ('Men pushed over edge by despair', *Northern Territory News*, 31 January 1988: 9).

The changing nature of gender relations is particularly disconcerting to men socialized to keep their emotions in check. In Australia it has not been considered acceptable for men to cry, or to share insecurities with other men, and so they depend almost entirely on women to provide comfort and reassurance. However, communication between the sexes appears to be increasingly problematic (Williams, 1988: 37). At a time when social change has caused the collapse of other values and so placed more reliance on the importance of close personal relationships, sexuality is rapidly becoming a battleground.

After decades of advice from sex manuals recommending that women take more responsibility, the ideal of the passive woman, which allowed men the role of teachers and initiators, has been replaced by the expectation of female sexual expression and fulfilment. This transformation in female sexual requirements has diminished the definition of sexual masculinity down to an emphasis on prowess designed to meet the demands of the 'new woman' (Teifer, 1986: 592–3). Anxiety about performance has predictably resulted in many men retreating into impotence (Boyer, 1981: 162). Recent findings estimate that one in ten Australian men suffer from the condition and that psychological stresses accounted for about half of these cases (Grimwade, 1990). The problems are considered to be so severe that, in an attempt to pre-empt relationship difficulties, marriage guidance councils have set up discussion groups designed to help men to meet the changing expectations of women (Townshend, 1990).

Reflecting male confusion about the new role requirements, magazines abound with advice on solving relationship difficulties between the sexes. One of the top Australian current affairs magazines, *The Bulletin*, printed the results of a survey entitled 'What women want', with the conclusion that most women stated a preference for a caring man who would be sensitive to their needs (2 August 1988: 45–6), a difficult requirement for men socialized not to be demonstrative about their feelings. In May 1990 a magazine called *New Man* came on to the market, and featured yet another article trying to reach an understanding of what women are really asking of men and wanting from sex. The format also included segments giving advice to men who hoped to relate to the 'new woman' in the age of equality, on men and coping with the traumas of divorce, and on single-father families (of which Australia now has an estimated 100,000). Perhaps as an encouragement to readers, the magazine included an exposé entitled 'A sex addict repents', the confession of a promiscuous man who was able to reform and begin to appreciate the new woman.

Sex tourism: an endeavour to sustain the male identity?

Buck observed that:

> When an existing social order fails to provide for the emotional needs of large numbers of people – fails to provide them ways to meet social expectations and to feel loved – significant social movements with emotionally loaded mass appeal may ensue. (1976: 529)

Therefore, sex tourism can be understood to constitute, in Smelser's terms, a 'norm-oriented movement', that is a collective behaviour oriented towards the restoration of the 'generalized belief' of what it is to be male. He interprets this form of group behaviour as: 'uninstitutionalised collective action, taken to modify a condition of strain on the basis of a generalised reconstitution of a component of action' (1962: 73, 270). In the most visible form, the ritualized and public sexual conduct which is often a feature of sex holidays appears to be an attempt to reaffirm, if only temporarily, the idealized version of the masculine identity and mode of being (Hantover, 1981: 96; Kirkendall, 1972: 56; Fromm, 1956: 63).

Conclusion

A number of features of contemporary Australian society predispose thousands of its male members to seek sexual fulfilment in commercial sex havens outside the country. The popularity of sex tourism for these men can be perceived as a foil for their alienation in the workplace, and as symptomatic of stresses on the family and on gender relations back in Australia. The changing role of women, although grudgingly accepted by some men, and expounded in the official government rhetoric of equal opportunities, appears to have posed a considerable threat to the male identity, particularly at a time in history when men are increasingly restricted in opportunities for masculine expression, and so place substantial emphasis on the sexual realm as a venue for the demonstration of identity. The attraction of sex holidays for Australian men must accordingly be perceived in relation to the loss, within the normal social environment, of the support audience for the conventional male role of financial supporter and sexual authority.

References

Adler, D. (1965) 'Matriduxy in the Australian family', in A.F. Davies and S. Encel (eds), *Australian Society: a Sociological Introduction*. Melbourne: Cheshire.

Arndt, B. (1986) *Private Lives*. Australia: Penguin.

Boyer, K.D. (1981) 'Changing male sex roles and identities', in R.A. Lewis (ed.), *Men in Difficult Times*. Englewood Cliffs, NJ: Prentice-Hall.

Breakwell, G.M. (1986) *Coping with Threatened Identities*. London: Methuen.

Buck, R. (1976) *Human Motivation and Emotion* (2nd edn). New York: Wiley.

Cohen, E. (1982) 'Thai girls and Farang men: the edge of ambiguity', *Annals of Tourism Research*, 9.

Crompton, J.L. (1979) 'Motivation for pleasure vacations', *Annals of Tourism Research*, 6(4).

Dann, G. (1981) 'Tourism motivation: an appraisal', *Annals of Tourism Research*, 8(2).

Fromm, E. (1956) *The Sane Society*. London: Routledge and Kegan Paul.

Fullerton, G.P. (1972) 'Watered-down passion', in G. Neubeck (ed.), *The Myriad Motives for Sex. Sexual Behaviour*, vol. 2.

Game, A. and Pringle, R. (1979) 'Sexuality and the suburban dream', *The Australian and New Zealand Journal of Sociology*, 15(2).

Giarelli, A. (1981) *End of 'Sex Tours'*. World Press Review, no. 21.

Graburn, N.H.H. (1977) 'Tourism: the sacred journey', in V. Smith (ed.), *Hosts and Guests: the Anthropology of Tourism*. Philadelphia: University of Pennsylvania Press.

Graburn, N.H.H. (1983) 'Tourism and prostitution', *Annals of Tourism Research*, 10.

Grimwade, D. 'Impotence strikes one in ten men', *Northern Territory News*, 27 May 1990.

Hantover, J.P. (1981) 'The social construction of masculine anxiety', in R.A. Lewis (ed.), *Men in Difficult Times*. Englewood Cliffs, NJ: Prentice-Hall.

Hite, S. (1981) *The Hite Report on Male Sexuality*. New York: Knopf.

Hong, E. (1985) *See the Third World While it Lasts: the Social and Environmental Impact of Tourism with Special Reference to Malaysia*. Palau Penang: Consumers' Association of Penang.

Iso-Ahola, S.E. (1982) 'Towards a social psychological theory of tourism motivation: a rejoinder', *Annals of Tourism Research*, 9(2).

Jafari, J. (1985) 'The tourism system: a theoretical approach to the study of tourism'. Unpublished doctoral thesis.

Jones, D.R.W. (1982) in F. Rajotte (ed.), *The Impact of Tourism Development in the Pacific. Papers and Proceedings of a Pacific-Wide Conference Held by Satellite*.

Kirkendall, L.A. (1972) 'Non-sexual motivations', in G. Neubeck (ed.), *The Myriad Motives for Sex. Sexual Behaviour*, vol. 2.

Korean Church Women United (1984) *Kisaeng Tourism: a Nation-Wide Survey Report on Conditions in Four Areas, Seoul, Pusan, Cheju, Kyongju*. Research Material Issue, Centre for Responsible Tourism, 2 Kensington Road, San Anselmo, CA-94960.

Maeder, U. (1982) *Fluchthelfer Tourismus: Waerme in Der Ferne?* Basle: Arbeitskreis Tourismus und Entwicklung.

McCall, G.J. and Simmons, J.L. (1966) *Identities and Interactions*. New York: Free Press.

Norbeck, E. (1971) 'Man and Play', *Natural History*, special supplement *Play*.

O'Grady, R. (1981) *Third World Stopover: the Tourism Debate*. Geneva: World Council of Churches, Risk Book Series 12.

O'Grady, R. (1982) *Tourism in the Third World: Christian Reflections*. Maryknoll, NY: Orbis.

Pangiliman, L. (1986) 'Child prostitution in Asia: no kid's stuff', *Balai Asian Journal*.

Phongpaichit, P. (1981) 'Bangkok masseuses: holding up for the family sky', *South East Asia Chronicle*, no. 78.

Prahl, H.W. and Steinecke, A. (1979) *Der Millionen Urlaub*. Darmstadt: Luchterhand.

Prieur, A. (n.d.) 'The male role, prostitution and sexual assaults'. Department of Sociology, University of Oslo, Box 1096, 0317 Oslo, Norway.

Rainwater, L. (1960) *And the Poor Get Children*. Chicago: Quadrangle.

Reinarman, C. and Critchlow, L.B. (1987) 'Culture, cognition, and disinhibition: notes on sexuality and alcohol in the age of AIDS', *Contemporary Drug Problems*.

Schmidt, G. (1982) 'Sex and society in the eighties', *Archives of Sexual Behaviour*, 11(1).

Sheehy, G. (1971) *Hustling: Prostitution in Our Wide-Open Society*. New York: Delacorte.

Smelser, N.J. (1962) *Theory of Collective Behavior*. London: Routledge and Kegan Paul.

Teifer, L. (1986) 'In pursuit of the perfect penis', *American Behavioral Scientist*, 29(5).

Tiger, L. (1969) *Men in Groups*. London: Nelson.

Townshend, D. 'The big split: how men cope with divorce', *New Man*, Melbourne, Australia, May 1990.

Truong, T.D. (1989) 'The dynamics of sex tourism: the case of South East Asia', in T.V. Singh, F.M. Theuns and F.M. Go (eds), *Towards Appropriate Tourism*. Berne: Peter Lang, European University Studies, vol. 11.

Williams, D. 'The Hite of controversy', *The Sunday Mail*, 24 July 1988.

Winick, C. and Kinsie, P.M. (1971) *The Lively Commerce*. Chicago: Quadrangle.

Wyer, J. and Towner, J. (1988) 'Tourism in the Third World: developmental issues', in R. Millman and A. Hutchinson (eds), *The UK and Third World Tourism*. Tonbridge: Tens, ECTWT.

Yap, V. (1986) 'The context of prostitution: tourism', in *The Third World People and Tourism*. Ecumenical Coalition on Third World.

12

The Anthropologist as Tourist: an Identity in Question

Malcolm Crick

A tourist is always the other person.
J. Krippendorf, *The Holiday Makers*

The anti-tourist deludes only himself. We are all tourists now.
P. Fussell, *Abroad*

The last 25 years have witnessed a staggering growth in mass tourism; it has also been a period of considerable change within the discipline of anthropology. With the collapse of the colonial framework which provided the opportunity for so much of our field research, combined with a number of general theoretical shifts, anthropology has entered a period of reflexive anxiety which has brought to the fore the problem of the anthropological identity. Much recent work which has addressed the issue of the representation of the 'anthropological self' has focused on the field work experience and the process of textual construction. It also happens that, besides studies which analyse the role of tourism in processes of socio-cultural change, a leading area of tourism research in which anthropological contributions have been notable centres on representation (Graburn and Jafari, 1991: 6). One topic requiring attention in this respect is the identification of different types of tourist, whose behaviour and motivations vary considerably. For anthropologists who do field research on tourism, yet another question of identities arises: in what ways is the anthropologist studying tourism like or unlike the tourists being studied?

It is suggested in this chapter that there is a partial overlap in identities here and that anthropologists and tourists may be regarded as distant relatives. Given its brevity, this is necessarily a fairly broad-brush discussion. Clearly, anthropological field research can differ considerably in length and intensity. So too are there several very different types of tourist: ethnic, cultural, environmental and recreational in Smith's schema (1989: 4–6);

recreational, diversionary, experiential, experimental and existential according to Cohen (1979: 167–8). This chapter does not attempt to give rounded descriptions of different types of anthropological field work or of different types of tourism, but merely assembles some reminders which have surfaced during the last 20 years of reflection in anthropology. These suggest some points of commonality, and so suggest that it may be worth pursuing further the issue of overlapping identities rather than resting content with the notion that the two identities are worlds apart. After all, if anthropology is presently attempting to cope with a 'crisis of representation' (Marcus and Fischer, 1986: vii) over how we portray the objects of our discourse (the other), pondering on how we represent ourselves can scarcely be regarded as a luxury since the images of 'self' and 'other' are interdependent; indeed, perhaps the other represents precisely those aspects of self which we wish to disown. Whilst this chapter concerns itself solely with the anthropologist/tourist relationship, far more general issues are potentially involved. For previous ages it might well have been the case that the 'tourist gaze' was distinct from other forms of experience, but in our present post-modernist, mass communications world we have very much seen a universalization of a mode of perception and being which might be termed 'touristic'. In other words, it has become increasingly difficult to differentiate between tourism and other socio-cultural processes (Urry, 1990: 2, 82, 132), as so many of us are now tourists for much of the time.

The notion that anthropologists and tourists have something in common has been remarked on by a number of anthropologists over the past few years (for instance, van den Berghe, 1980: 378; Hamilton, 1982: 103; Mintz, 1977: 59; Rosaldo, 1986: 96; Leach, 1984: 359; Dumont, 1977: 224; Albers and James, 1983: 124). Unfortunately, such comments have seldom been adequately developed. Indeed, there seems for some to be a desire to avoid dwelling on the comparison at all. Thus, for Errington and Gewertz, the very justification for doing anthropology virtually vanishes if it is contended that anthropologists and tourists are fundamentally alike (1989: 39). For others, the idea cannot be held in consciousness. Thus, in a discussion of anthropology in the context of other adventurer/travel roles, Peacock can list 'spies' and 'missionaries' but fails to mention tourists (1986: 51–4, 58–65; cf. Pearce, 1982: 32–6 for a detailed empirical consideration of a range of travel roles including anthropologists, missionaries, migrants, pilgrims and explorers). What is so forgettable or appalling about tourists that provokes these over-reactions and avoidances? After all, in our recent reflexive phase, we have been likened to other identities such as con-men, voyeurs and clowns (Boon, 1982: 6; Rose, 1982: 219, 272) which might, on first glance, appear to be even less palatable than the tourist comparison. How is it that Lévi-Strauss can achieve international fame with *Tristes Tropiques*, which among other things is an account of his travels, and yet commence by stating baldly that he hates travel and travellers (1976: 15)?

The avoidance of the suggested overlap in identities between anthropologists and tourists is the more curious given the very obvious fact that almost anywhere anthropologists go to do research nowadays there are likely to be tourists, and, indeed, an anthropologist is likely to be classified as one by locals (Nuñez, 1978: 207, 212; Pi-Sunyer, 1981: 272). Despite this ubiquity of tourism, however, anthropologists are still prone to producing monographs about societies as if the international tourism industry did not exist. Anthropologists and tourists are travellers and collectors – both literally and metaphorically – in the space of the 'other', yet there seems a reluctance to admit the presence of these other travellers. Indeed, given our nineteenth-century origins when armchair theoretical speculation was largely divorced from the ethnographic data collection role performed by explorers, missionaries and so on, our modern discipline has, in fact, climbed on the back of travellers and adventurers (Fabian, 1983: 82). Naturally, we may need to distinguish between such earlier travel, when learning and even discoursing were frequent motives, and modern mass tourism where gazing and playing are dominant (Adler, 1989), but even so professional anthropologists are often reluctant to grant the full ethnographic value to those records created by 'amateurs'. The Malinowskian myth of field work is, in fact, very much tied up with a systematic debunking of the efforts of other kinds of Europeans (Payne, 1981: 421-2).

We might be able to explain the lack of attention of anthropologists to contemporary tourists if tourism itself could be construed as of only marginal interest, but the fact is that it 'fits easily into anthropological concerns' (Nash and Smith, 1991: 13), such as the process of culture contact and patterns of social change. Lett has even claimed that since tourism represents the largest peacetime movement of human populations across cultural boundaries, 'anthropology cannot ignore the phenomenon of tourism and retain its identity' (1989: 275-6). Despite such statements about the anthropological significance of tourism, anthropology has, like other social sciences, been tardy in regarding tourism as a legitimate object of study (Nash and Smith, 1991: 13). If there is any substance to MacCannell's contention that the tourist *is* 'modern man' in general (1976), this must clearly be reckoned an awful oversight.

How can we explain the anthropological avoidance of tourism and tourists? Is it that anthropologists fail to define tourists as 'other' since they largely come from their own society, and so have just overlooked them? Is it that academics have a more general difficulty in taking play, leisure and fun as serious topics for research (Pearce, 1982: 1–2)? Is it that anthropologists share the widespread cultural bias that tourism is inherently inauthentic and trivial? Is it simply a reluctance to display any interest in travel and observation that is, compared with their own, supposedly unauthoritative (Nash and Smith, 1991: 14; Bruner, 1989b: 439)? Should we be looking for an intellectual source for the avoidance or are we in the presence of a deep emotional aversion? The safest thing we can say is that the matter is over-determined, and the argument of this chapter is that one component may be a dim perception that the anthropological and touristic identities overlap, which causes anxiety, and so a desire to leave the whole issue unexplored.

Just how over-determined the avoidance may be is well illustrated in Kottak's (1983) *Assault on Paradise* – an account of social change in a small Brazilian fishing village from the 1960s to the 1980s, when Arembepe had become a 'tourist town' (p. 159) surrounded by the effluent from a nearby multinational chemical factory. Kottak did several periods of field research in Arembepe, and despite the advent of a hippie colony in the late 1960s, during his field research in the early 1970s he ignored this foreign presence entirely; he never even visited the hippie enclave (p. 41). He gives a number of reasons for his disinclination to include these tourists in his study. He resented intruders queering a pitch he had staked out years earlier. He resented the fact that some of them spoke to him as if they were the experts on the local community (p. 40). It is thus with great pride that he exposes the basic lack of understanding of the local social system revealed by a well-educated, multi-lingual hippie who had married one of the wealthiest local fishermen (p. 181). He acknowledges that there is an overlap between his own somewhat romantic notions of 'unspoiled natives' and the hippie quest for a simple way of life, but he, middle-aged and married with dependants, envies them their 'youthful adventurousness' (p. 41). By the 1980s, Kottak tells us that he was less jealous and possessive, and so able to include tourism in his account of the processes of change going on (pp. 42–3, 171–3), but in the 1970s he hoped by ignoring the hippies 'to magically rid the community of their presence' (p. 42) – a strange exorcism ritual when the whole point about field work is that 'being there' enables one to see what is going on on the ground. A sense of jealousy, competitiveness and defensiveness is present whenever the tourist presence is discussed, and clearly people do not compete with or attempt to deny the existence of others who are of no significance. It is suggested, then, that the reactions discussed by Kottak may have something to do with a sensing that tourists are our relatives, and hence that their motives for being overseas, their activities, their experiences, might tell us something, albeit obliquely, about our own practices.

Kottak's experience is by no means unique. Errington and Gewertz, for instance, describe vividly their competitive encounters with tourists and travellers in Papua New Guinea (1989: 37). They even admit that they were motivated in some of the same ways as the tourists (p. 46). Nevertheless, they repudiate the proposition that anthropologists and tourists are similar, especially if the suggested connecting thread is the ludic nature of both research and much touristic behaviour. The reason they give is that anthropology is 'serious' (p. 51); anthropologists have a serious obligation to discharge, to present their systematic, socio-historically well-contextualized understanding of world political economy and the vulnerable position of some groups within it. Anthropologists have the serious role of speaking for the oppressed, at least until such times as they find their own effective voice (p. 52). So, if we 'cannot easily differentiate our personal motivation from that of tourists, we can differentiate our politics from theirs' (p. 46). Tourists do not have sufficient knowledge to understand world political economy; some do not want to understand; some are even unilinear evolutionists; some do not even want to hear what anthropologists have to say about local culture (p. 51).

This contrast between the ignorant, fun-loving tourist and the serious anthropological stance would be very easy to swallow were it not for the level of generalization present at both ends of the contrast, quite apart from the obvious point that the 'ludic' and the 'serious' are not necessarily mutually exclusive; some games, after all, are deadly serious. One simply cannot caricature all tourists as being ignorant of the world in which they move and as uninterested in learning more. To do so, in fact, is to indulge in that form of loathing and snobbery which very much forms part of the tourism world itself, whereby every type of tourist feels superior to some other supposedly less sophisticated type of tourist (Pearce, 1982: 17; MacCannell, 1976: 10, 94; Krippendorf, 1987: 41). Perhaps anthropologists defining themselves as 'sophisticated' compared with other travellers is merely one more example of how different types of tourist distance themselves from each other. Likewise, speaking for the oppressed in the Third World is not something that all anthropologists do, perhaps because from the safety of academe in the affluent West such pronouncements may be seen more as inflating self-indulgence than as a serious intervention in the politics of the real world, as a variety of 'protected', inauthentic involvement of precisely the kind tourists are meant to be expert in. At the very least, a disparagement of tourists, and thus leaving tourism out of the picture, is injurious to the very task which serious anthropologists have conferred upon themselves. Errington and Gewertz admit (1989: 53, n.2) that they have omitted references to tourists in their publications, and in so doing they considerably weaken their contribution to the serious task of understanding world political economy. The tourist industry is, in dollar terms, probably the largest industry in the world already, and it is widely predicted that it will easily be the largest in the next century (Richter, 1989: 3). In many areas of the Third World, two decades after colonial rule, affluent Westerners return, not this time as administrators and missionaries, but as tourists, where, as in the colonial period, areas of the country are put aside for their recreation. Meanwhile international capital and the ideology of 'development' ensure that peripheral economies are tied to the needs of the centre, just as they were as suppliers of primary product exports during the colonial era. Some argue that the international tourism industry necessarily re-establishes essentially colonial labour relations and attitudes. In short, nowadays one cannot be serious or systematic about world political economy if one leaves international tourism out of the picture.

Anthropologists may find tourists embarrassing and emerge from their encounters with them feeling that they know more than tourists, have more authentic experiences, are less harmful than tourists, and so on, but the stark fact is that in many areas anthropologists and tourists now literally stare at each other. There are the anthropologists engaged in scientific colonialism (Galtung, in Fabian, 1983: 177, n.18) in their 'ethnographic periphery', collecting data (Clifford, 1988: 215, 220, 230–1) for export back to their university where they can manufacture it into publishable products in order to advance their careers. And there are the international tourists indulging in hedonistic neo-colonialism in their 'pleasure periphery' (Turner and Ash, 1975), collecting souvenirs, photos and other things they find of value in the culture of the other which constitute symbolic capital which they transform into status back home. Both travel to collect and expropriate what they value from the other and then tell of their journeys. Are the motivations and experiences of these two identities totally different? Can we responsibly refuse to examine the issue?

In a perceptive review of MacCannell's *The Tourist*, Dumont has contended that tourism is a good model for meta-inquiry; the book, he suggests, 'ought to be frightening to anthropologists' (1977: 225). One reason for this is that if a tourist is, in MacCannell's words, 'modern man' both exploring and representing modernity, the same can be said of anthropologists and social scientists more generally. In a more political vein, anthropologists, for Dumont, are metonyms of the Western world (1978: 44), and in this day and age, so are tourists. Consequently, irrespective of any individual motivations, 'structurally' anthropologists and tourists are over-lapping identities. In fact, the anthropological denial of similarity here might well be seen simply as the latest in a long line of denials of points of commonality with others from our society. In the colonial period, for instance, anthropologists distanced themselves from administrators, missionaries and the like, despite the fact that their own presence, even if they were critical of the colonial set-up, was underpinned by the same political and economic forces which brought about the colonial system as a whole; indeed, it was often the colonial authorities themselves which provided their research funds. Well might we say, then, that just as colonial power made the world safe for ethnography (Caulfield, 1974: 182), today entrepreneurial influence and the collaboration of local elites makes the world safe for tourism (Fussell, 1980: 390). In a previous period the anthropologist claimed to be different from a whole range of other Europeans who made up the colonial apparatus; in the present day it is the tourist from whom the anthropologists distance themselves. In actual fact, not only is the denial equivalent, but so perhaps is the context, for the international tourism system may well be represented as neo-imperialism in action (Nash, 1978). For Krippendorf, for example, tourism has a colonial character 'everywhere and without exception' (1987: 56), and for many commentators, tourism can be regarded simply as the latest manifestation of the expansive cultural energies of the West which in previous ages led to geographical exploration and imperial conquest (Graburn, 1983: 16). Tourists, in other words, are only finishing off a process commenced by the travellers of yesteryear – the conquerors and colonists (Cohen, 1972: 182). In Bruner's terms: 'colonialism, ethnography, and tourism occur at different historical periods, but arise from the same social formation, and are variant forms of expansionism occupying the space opened up by extensions of power' (1989b: 439).

If it is conceded that there are certain socio-historical forces which mass tourism and anthropology jointly express, it might still be argued that an industry involving so much fantasy and hedonism is not significantly related to a scientific enterprise which aims to present an accurate portrayal of other cultures. When one examines what anthropologists actually do in the field and compares that with what tourists do, any areas of overlap disappear, it might be argued. This chapter argues, to the contrary, that recent insights into the actual practice of field work, combined with recent discussions about the nature of ethnographic writing, suggest that we cannot convincingly maintain the proposition that anthropologists and tourists are worlds apart. Tourists are essentially strangers temporarily residing in other cultures; they are normally more affluent than those among whom they stay; they have quite circumscribed interests in the other, interests which are formed in advance and which derive from their own culture; they are awkward and essentially marginal while in the field, and communicate less than effectively; they use their economic resources to obtain the experiences and relationships they value; not 'belonging' in a fundamental sense, they are free to leave at any time; on returning home they re-establish their more permanent identity and relate their experiences, enhancing their status with every telling. All these traits, it is contended, characterize anthropologists.

There can be little dissent from the view that the tourist industry creates and then sells images of other peoples and their cultures (Britton, 1979). The industry 'spectacularizes' and 'commoditizes' cultures, and then sends the tourist to consume what it has created. Because of these well-constructed sets of representations of touristic paradises, tourists have well-formed expectations as to the sort of people they will meet and the experiences they will have. Imaging tourist destinations in the Third World is often a matter of how to 'mystify the mundane; amplify the exotic; minimise the misery; rationalise the disquietude; and romanticise the strange' (Weightman, 1987: 229). But, anthropology has not been free of romantic motives: it too has indulged in exoticism and camouflaged unsettling forces. Simply because the motives are 'scientific' does not automatically or completely change the way in which the geographically remote is symbolically represented (Helms, 1988); scholarship too betrays a 'geographical unconscious', 'geopolitical imagination' or 'national imaginary' in its portray of the other (Bishop, 1989: vii, 179; Hamilton, 1990: 16). Thus, if the arguments of Said (1978) are accepted, 'the Orientals' and 'the Orient' are no more real than the 'friendly natives' who inhabit various tourist 'paradises'. Anthropology itself, through the nineteenth century, viewed geographical space as the equivalent of historical time, so that a contemporary savage was also a distant ancestor (Fabian, 1983). In this century, field workers have studied societies as if they were coherent wholes, dwelling in a harmonious, stable equilibrium. Moreover, they have depicted them as living in a fictional timeless time, largely divorced from history, called the 'ethnographic present'. It is also obvious that anthropological expectations are significantly shaped in advance by classic texts of our most authoritative portrayers in the discipline, an influence which extends to how a field worker writes up the data collected (Bruner, 1987–8: 16). None of this is at all surprising, for if scientific research normally proceeds within a paradigm, then experience and interpretation are bound to be substantially structured in advance. Even if this were not so, anthropology remains inherently semi-autobiographical. If one were to say that tourist brochures tell one as much of the outlook and values of the society from which the tourists come as about the cultures to which they travel, then likewise anthropology is self-referential for the simple reason that any image of the other is partly dependent upon an image of the self. Not surprisingly, therefore, just as Third World tourism critics have complained loudly at the unsavoury ethnic stereotypes and other distortions found in tourist literature, so Third World anthropologists have alleged that the Western images of African societies, for instance, have been little more than self-serving, misleading, self-indulgent fantasies (Owusu, 1978), masking the political interests of the Western societies which have produced the anthropologists, just as the touristic images contribute to the process of touristic exploitation by people from those self-same societies. It needs no demonstration today that power and knowledge are intimately related, that representation is a political act. If international political economy lies behind the touristic depictions of holiday destinations, anthropological insight into the status of its portrayals of otherness also requires acknowledging that their 'right to write' is political.

Does not what an anthropologist actually does in the field remove all thought of parallels with tourism? The past 20 years have created a sizeable literature on the experience of field work. The 'conspiracy of silence' is now well and truly over (Crick, 1982), and the substantial gap between methodological pronouncements of the kind set out by Malinowski in *Argonauts* (1961) and the daily reality of the research process as set out in his diary (1967) is now common knowledge. In the light of such demystifications, we can now accept that what ends up as ethnographic fact in our monographs often starts life as a temporary agreement on meaning in a fragile inter-subjective context, by two people engaged in a

liminal mode of communication, with neither fully understanding
the intents or assumptions of the other party. Despite this, the
tourist parallel escapes the consciousness of many commentators.
Thus, in his humorous account of field work among the Dowayo,
Barley confesses that at the start of his research he did not really
know what to do or what 'being an anthropologist' actually
entailed (1983: 51). He describes the way he passed time travelling,
being ill, reading trashy novels, trying to avoid encountering 'them',
his joy when it was time to go home so that he could 'be done with
the Dowayos' (pp. 97, 112, 180). These activities and sentiments are
typical of the tourist world, yet Barley refers only to those periods
when bureaucratic holdups prevented him from getting on with
things as 'playing tourist' (p. 20). Other anthropologists have seen
things in a similar way, that they are tourists before their real
research gets under way, despite the fact that such 'incidental
ethnography' is also published in scholarly journals (Halpern and
Halpern, 1972: 149). A most striking case of this blinkered vision is
Turnbull's moralizing tale about tourists in Bali. He describes the
frenzy of tourists taking photographs at Balinese cremation
ceremonies, the tourists displaying all the cultural insensitivity one
has come to expect of people who regard other ways of life as mere
spectacles (1982: 26, 30). Clearly Turnbull regards the anthropologist as a very different kind of animal, but it is arguable that he
was behaving in exactly the same way. While the tourists were
photographing the Balinese, Turnbull was photographing the
tourists (p. 32); they were his spectacular other. The tourists left
with their photos and memories, to tell tales at home and to show
the photos collected in their albums; Turnbull leaves with his
photos and memories and gets a publication to add to his
curriculum vitae as well.

There is, of course, one distinction we might insist on here:
tourism is about fun and play, whilst field work is precisely that –
work. Thus tourists exist in their 'environmental bubble' (Cohen,
1972: 166), safeguarded from genuine experiences of 'them',
helplessly reliant on guides to mediate their encounters. By contrast,
anthropologists 'immerse' themselves in the other culture, participate in its activities, learn the language, and so on. Two facts serve
to weaken the suggested contrast here. First, not all tourists do
cherish a protective bubble; many are exploratory and self-reliant.
On the other hand, much anthropological field work falls far short
of anything which could be called 'immersion'. Malinowski's
portrait of landing on a Kiriwina beach, himself alone among
savages, is a palpable nonsense. There were other Europeans there
whose company he often sought out, and his diary and monographs

make it very unclear in what sense he was a 'participant' in the lives of the locals. Margaret Mead, who uses the term 'immersion' (1977: 1), lived with fellow Americans while in Samoa, eating familiar food. Few anthropologists have anything like the 'inner transformation' which Peacock suggests is part of the field work experience (1986: 55); a transformation in the sense of 'going native' is, indeed, the very reverse of professionalism for some. Many anthropologists are also reliant for considerable periods during their research on translators and research assistants, who perform for them a role similar to that performed for the tourists by their guides: all three are professional 'culture brokers' who know enough about our wants to make our desired experiences possible.

Furthermore, if the tourist is in a non-social state, without any real sense of community, without long-term ties (McHugh, 1974: 138, 141–7), the 'participant observation' of the researcher is not entirely different. Indeed, the opposition work/play itself even breaks down: for what is participant observation if not 'playing' for a short spell at being a member of another society? Also, even if 'work', the academic sabbatical when much research is done is very much an activity performed away from the normal work routines of teaching and administration. But there is another problem here, too, namely whether the play/work opposition is usefully employed within the tourism context at all. There are analyses which very much depict tourism as a matter of play, ritual, the sacred, pilgrimage (Graburn, 1983: 11–23); in other words, as a separate, inverted unstructured realm out of normal time and space away from routine commitments (Wagner, 1977) and following rules different to those of the normal workaday world. The concept of 'free time' in much sociology of leisure literature is one expression of this sort of view, but it is a perspective to which serious objections can be made. Leisure is, of course, made possible, and perhaps necessary, by the nature of that workaday world. Furthermore, because the merchandising of leisure has become so vital a part of advanced industrial capitalism, the nature of that system expresses itself through the leisure activities themselves (Rojek, 1985). Much of the organization of leisure actually eliminates the senses of freedom and play (pp. 173–5), the heightened anxieties, regulation and pressures of holiday-making being well known. As Habermas has expressed it graphically, a vacation is the 'continuation of work by other means' (cited in Krippendorf, 1987: 63). The analytical value, and certainly the universality of application, of any general model of social reversal in the tourism context must clearly be questioned.

Richardson has argued that what makes anthropologists different to tourists is the relationship established with informants (1975: 520, 527). Tourists normally have short-lived relationships with people in other cultures, and invariably of an essentially instrumental kind, in which they use their resources to purchase the experience they desire. Tourists also spend much of their time wondering whether they are being deceived by guides, con-men, and other locals they come into contact with. Although anthropologists frequently represent themselves in the field as 'participants', 'friends', 'quasi-kin' and the like, the relationships they set up are also very much matters of 'mutual exploitation' (Hatfield, 1973). Anthropologists are in the field for quite explicit aims; they deliberately forge relationships in order to obtain data; they have their eyes on publications even before they embark on their field work; in some cases they quite literally buy their data by paying informants. Anthropologists are also conscious of the fragility of their position, living with the 'working fiction' (Geertz, 1968: 151–4) that they share a world of understanding with their informants, but aware that at any time that world may be shattered and their situation disintegrate into one lacking trust, lacking understanding, in fact, exploded into two mutually non-communicating worlds.

There is one other aspect of what anthropologists actually do in the field which needs to be mentioned. Quite apart from what research project one designs in advance, the reality is very much more that what one does in the field is determined by what other people allow one to be. In other words, the anthropological self is significantly shaped by the interests, attitudes and understandings of the other. Any question about the anthropological identity clearly needs to take into account this vulnerability of the self to the semantics of the other, as I myself became acutely conscious of when a novice monk addressed me one day with the words 'Hello, hippie' (Crick, 1989). Even after seven months of field work in Sri Lanka, I was still not sure of what understandings and rules my chief informant, a pavement hawker in Kandy called Ali, was bringing to our relationship. It might well be that for him I was simply a kind of tourist, to be manipulated like any other relatively ignorant foreigner in the tourist arena. How can one establish an identity for oneself as a researcher interested in gaining reliable information, if the other insists upon treating this interest as just another basis upon which to do business with a peculiar type of tourist? The anthropologist, after all, is not in a superior epistemological position. The meanings which Ali brought to our relationship were just as valid as those I brought, and if those meanings were very different, that too is typical of what happens between tourists and locals.

The reality that one's identity is significantly determined by others is of general import. In her study of witchcraft in the Bocage, for instance, Favret-Saada's establishment of an identity 'ethnographer', simply intent on getting information, was impossible because any communication on this subject could only be part of the mechanics of witchcraft itself; a researcher, therefore, could only find out anything when actually caught up in a situation of accusation or counter-magic (1980: 9–11, 25, 95, 167–8). Similarly, we might argue that in the touristic arena an identity just based upon a desire for information is not possible, that the researcher must become part of the system of tourist–local relationships in order to find out anything about the system. In other words, an anthropologist has no practical alternative to being subjected to touristic rules in order to undertake the research; in that sense, an anthropologist simply is a type of tourist. In actual fact, irrespective of the particular topic of research one is doing, local people frequently experience and portray tourists and ethnographers in a comparable manner (Bruner, 1989b: 439). There are a good many unsavoury caricatures of anthropologists and their behaviour produced by those we study (Howe and Sherzer, 1986). Tourists, of course, besides being spectators are also spectacles in their own right, and many cultures have negative stereotypes for them, and may even burlesque their unacceptable behaviour, just as other varieties of foreigner have been symbolically incorporated into local cultures (Sweet, 1985: 10, 22–3, 66; Evans-Pritchard, 1989: 79–80, 87). What seems to be less widely known is that anthropologists may be mocked in exactly the same way as tourists, some people only recognizing the difference between a camera for the one and a tape recorder for the other (Sweet, 1985: 32–5; Evans-Pritchard, 1989: 92).

Some commentators might acknowledge that there are similarities in the behaviour of anthropologists and tourists, but that the end results of their experiences and encounters are entirely different. Tourists come home and *tell travellers' tales*; in fact it might be argued that many go overseas precisely in order to be able to tell tales on their return. Anthropologists, however, return to *write scientific reports*. For a start, however, there are significant overlaps between ethnographic monographs and other travel writings (Wheeler, 1986; Pratt, 1986); indeed, of late, anthropology has even been described as a species of 'story telling' (Webster, 1983), even as a matter of 'persuasive fictions' (Strathern, 1987). Over the past 20 years, as the demythologizing of field work practice has proceeded, it has become increasingly obvious that anthropologists have a second basic task, namely to write, so that anthropology is, among other things, a species of writing (Marcus, 1980; Marcus and Cushman, 1982; Webster, 1982; Boon, 1982: 20, 263 n.2, 264 n.7). This new literary consciousness, directing attention to the fabrications which are part and parcel of the construction of ethnographic authority and the representation of the other, has made problematic the notion of ethnographic fact. We also now live very much in a world of 'blurred genres' (Geertz, 1980); in fact, 'dedifferentiation' in general, the widespread collapse of distinctions, is very much part of the post-modern condition (Urry, 1990: 84). Anthropologists maintaining a unique identity by insisting on a battery of differences may thus be quite out of keeping with the spirit of the times.

In the pages above I have queried a number of the ways in which we might wish to radically separate an anthropological identity from that of tourists. But clearly if it is suggested that an anthropologist is a type of tourist, the nature and extent of the overlap will depend considerably upon which type of tourist one is referring to. Despite the great increase in social science tourism research over the last 20 years, we are still very much in the dark about tourist motivation, what tourists experience, how their travels affect their knowledge, their attitudes and conceptions of themselves. Our taxonomies of tourist types are not only rudimentary, they are not much employed at all. The explicit links between anthropologists and tourist types which have been made, in fact, have not employed these taxonomies but have proposed new categories. Thus, anthropologists are seen as 'serious tourists' (Mintz, 1977: 59–60), as 'in-depth tourists' (van den Berghe, 1980: 370), as 'part-time tourists' (Albers and James, 1983: 124), as 'third-order tourists' as distinct from 'mere' or 'critical' tourists (Redfoot, 1988: 299), as 'refined', 'sophisticated', 'elite' tourists (Dumont, 1977: 224). Bruner (1989a: 112) states the overlap in terms of anthropologists being interested in Geertzian (1973) 'thick description', whereas tourists will accept 'thin description', which implies, perhaps, only a quantitative difference. Dumont's own depiction of the anthropologist as a 'refined, sophisticated, elite' tourist certainly indicates a merely quantitative difference. If we further admit that there is now possibly a new species of tourist, the 'post-tourist' (Urry, 1990: 11, 100), who displays role distance, is aware of inauthenticity, but who nonetheless enjoys playing the tourist role, then we have narrowed the gap even more. Is there a basic difference between the tourist gazing at a spectacle and the theoretical gaze of the anthropologist? Even etymology fails to protect our professional pride here, for the terms 'theory' and 'theorist' are, in fact, related to those for 'spectacle' and 'sightseer' (Abbeele, 1980: 13). All science, in this sense, is intellectual travel.

When Dumont stated that MacCannell's book ought to produce problems for the anthropological identity, he added that anthropologists had a choice (1977: 225). Anthropologists could recoil at the suggested parallels between anthropology and tourism, or they could explore that anxiety and, in the process, gain some insight into what they themselves do. In this chapter the second course has been followed, and it may well be that travelling through such potentially embarrassing territory might not only produce a more viable self-concept for anthropologists in the contemporary world but also refine our understanding of the diversity of touristic activities and thus aid the social science comprehension of tourism. If van den Berghe can seriously ask whether an anthropologist is an 'in-depth tourist or an entirely different breed of sensation seeker' (1980: 367), Dumont's first course simply is not an option. When MacCannell himself suggested – no doubt with a hint of irony – that the difference between anthropologists and tourists is that anthropologists are not mystified as to their motives for going overseas whereas tourists are (1976: 179), he errs in two directions simultaneously. In the first place, our comprehension of the diversity of the touristic phenomenon simply does not allow us to utilize the notion of 'mystification' in such a blanket manner. Secondly, the reflexive trends of the past 20 years have shown that anthropologists possess a somewhat less than immaculate self-understanding. Our insights into our activities have increased, and with them the anthropological identity has changed; these processes will inevitably continue.

Anthropologists have long been interested in the process of symbolic classification in the societies they investigate, but according to Bourdieu academics are themselves the supreme classifiers (1988: xi). One classification of considerable importance to academics is that set of contrasting identities through which academe establishes its characteristic methods, authority, knowledge and so on. To many an anthropologist, the touristic world may be one of deception and inauthenticity, but for Bourdieu (1988: 19) few worlds offer as much scope for self-deception as academe. Our professional habitus, the shared but less than fully conscious sets of practices, values, types of knowledge and modes of perception, is, to some degree, sustained by powerful blinkers. It is in neither a nihilistic nor a narcissistic spirit that the suggestion is made that valuable self-knowledge may derive from seriously playing with the sets of contrasting others which constitute the field within which the anthropological identity exists. The suggestion in this chapter is that the overlaps between the anthropological and touristic identities may be a deeply entrenched blind spot. No doubt such a tampering with our sense of identity will not be universally welcome, but then 'enlightenment is on the side of those who turn their spotlight on our blinkers' (Bourdieu, 1990: 10). Anthropologists, like others, may well be reluctant to abandon a comfortable, because more familiar, identity, but this resistance is itself part of the anthropological identity and so is also worthy of serious anthropological attention.

References

Abbeele, G. van den (1980) 'The tourist as theorist', *Diacritics*, 10: 2–14.

Adler, J. (1989) 'Origins of sightseeing', *Annals of Tourism Research*, 16: 7–29.

Albers, P. and James, W. (1983) 'Tourism and the changing photographic image of the Great Lakes Indians', *Annals of Tourism Research*, 10: 123–48.

Barley, N. (1983) *The Innocent Anthropologist: Notes from a Mud Hut*. London: Colonnade and British Museum.

Bishop, P. (1989) *The Myth of Shangri-La: Tibet, Travel Writing and the Western Creation of Sacred Landscape*. Berkeley: University of California Press.

Boon, J. (1982) *Other Tribes, Other Scribes*. Cambridge: Cambridge University Press.

Bourdieu, P. (1988) *Homo Academicus*. Cambridge: Polity Press.

Bourdieu, P. (1990) *In Other Words: Essays towards a Reflexive Sociology*. Cambridge: Polity Press.

Britton, R. (1979) 'The image of the Third World in tourism marketing', *Annals of Tourism Research*, 6: 318–29.

Bruner, E. (1987–8) 'Introduction: experiments in ethnographic writing', *Journal of the Steward Anthropological Society*, 17: 1–19.

Bruner, E. (1989a) 'Tourism, creativity and authenticity', *Studies in Symbolic Interaction*, 10: 109–14.

Bruner, E. (1989b) 'Of cannibals, tourists and ethnographers', *Cultural Anthropology*, 4: 438–45.

Caulfield, M.D. (1974) 'Culture and imperialism: proposing a new dialectic', in D. Hymes (ed.), *Reinventing Anthropology*. New York: Vintage and Random House.

Clifford, J. (1988) *The Predicament of Culture*. Cambridge, MA: Harvard University Press.

Cohen, E. (1972) 'Towards a sociology of international tourism', *Social Research*, 39: 164–82.

Cohen, E. (1979) 'A phenomenology of tourist experiences', *Sociology*, 13: 179–201.

Crick, M.R. (1982) 'Anthropological field research, meaning creation and knowledge construction', in D. Parkin (ed.), *Semantic Anthropology*. London: Academic Press.

Crick, M.R. (1989) 'Shifting identities in the research process: an essay in personal anthropology', in J. Perry (ed.), *Doing Fieldwork: Eight Personal Accounts of Social Research*. Geelong: Deakin University Press.

Dumont, J.-P. (1977) 'Review of MacCannell 1976', *Annals of Tourism Research*, 4: 223–5.

Dumont, J.-P. (1988) *The Headman and I: Ambiguity and Ambivalence*. Austin: University of Texas Press.

Errington, F. and Gewertz, D. (1989) 'Tourism and anthropology in a post-modern world', *Oceania*, 60: 37–54.

Evans-Pritchard, D. (1989) 'How "they" see "us": Native American images of tourists', *Annals of Tourism Research*, 16: 89–105.

Fabian, J. (1983) *Time and the Other: How Anthropology Makes its Object*. New York: Columbia University Press.

Favret-Saada, J. (1980) *Deadly Words: Witchcraft in the Bocage*. Cambridge: Cambridge University Press.

Fussell, P. (1980) *Abroad: British Literary Travelling between the Wars*. New York: Oxford University Press.

Geertz, C. (1968) 'Thinking as a moral act: ethical dimensions of anthropological fieldwork in the new states', *Antioch Review*, 139–58.

Geertz, C. (1973) 'Thick description: towards an interpretative theory of culture', in C. Geertz (ed.), *The Interpretation of Cultures*. London: Hutchinson.

Geertz, C. (1980) 'Blurred genres: the refiguration of social thought', *The American Scholar*, 49: 165–79.

Graburn, N. (1983) 'The anthropology of tourism', *Annals of Tourism Research*, 10: 9–33.

Graburn, N. and Jafari, J. (1991) 'Introduction: tourism social science', *Annals of Tourism Research*, 18: 1–11.

Halpern, J. and Halpern, B. (1972) 'The anthropologist as tourist: an incidental ethnography of the impact of tourism in a Dalmatian village', *East European Quarterly*, 7: 149–57.

Hamilton, A. (1982) 'Anthropology in Australia: some notes and a few queries', in G. McCall (ed.), *Anthropology in Australia: Essays to Honour 50 Years of Mankind*. Sydney: Anthropological Society of New South Wales.

Hamilton, A. (1990) 'Fear and desire: Aborigines, Asians and the national imaginary', *Australian Cultural History*, 9: 14–35.

Hatfield, C.R. (1973) 'Fieldwork: towards a model of mutual exploitation', in P.B. Hammond (ed.), *Cultural and Social Anthropology: Introductory Readings in Ethnology*. New York: Macmillan.

Helms, M. (1988) *Ulysses' Sail: an Ethnographic Odyssey of Power, Knowledge and Geographical Distance*. Princeton: Princeton University Press.

Howe, J. and Sherzer, J. (1986) 'Friend hairyfish and friend rattlesnake, or keeping anthropologists in their place', *Man*, 21: 680–96.

Kottak, C. (1983) *Assault on Paradise: Social Change in a Brazilian Village*. New York: Random House.

Krippendorf, J. (1987) *The Holiday Makers: Understanding the Impact of Leisure and Travel*. London: Heinemann.

Leach, E.R. (1984) 'Conclusion: further thoughts on the realm of folly', in E. Bruner (ed.), *Text, Play and Story*. Washington, DC: American Ethnological Society.

Lett, J. (1989) 'Epilogue', in V.L. Smith (ed.), *Hosts and Guests: the Anthropology of Tourism* (2nd edn). Philadelphia: University of Pennsylvania Press.

Lévi-Strauss, C. (1976) *Tristes Tropiques*. Penguin: Harmondsworth.

MacCannell, D. (1976) *The Tourist: a New Theory of the Leisure Class*. New York: Shocken.

Malinowski, B. (1961) *Argonauts of the Western Pacific*. New York: Dutton.

Malinowski, B. (1967) *A Diary in the Strict Sense of the Term*. London: Routledge and Kegan Paul.

Marcus, G. (1980) 'Rhetoric and ethnographic genre in anthropological research', *Current Anthropology*, 21: 507–10.

Marcus, G. and Cushman, D. (1982) 'Ethnographies as texts', *Annual Review of Anthropology*, 11: 25–69.

Marcus, G. and Fischer, M. (1986) *Anthropology as Cultural Critique*. Chicago: University of Chicago Press.

McHugh, P. (1974) *On the Beginnings of Social Inquiry*. London: Routledge.

Mead, M. (1977) *Letters from the Field 1925–75*. New York: Harper and Row.

Mintz, S. (1977) 'Infant, victim and tourist: the anthropologist in the field', *Johns Hopkins Magazine*, 27: 54–60.

Nash, D. (1978) 'Tourism as a form of imperialism', in V.L. Smith (ed.), *Hosts and Guests: the Anthropology of Tourism*. Philadelphia: University of Pennsylvania Press.

Nash, D. and Smith, V.L. (1991) 'Anthropology and tourism', *Annals of Tourism Research*, 18: 12–25.

Nuñez, T. (1978) 'Touristic studies in anthropological perspective', in V.L. Smith (ed.), *Hosts and Guests: the Anthropology of Tourism*. Philadelphia: University of Pennsylvania Press.

Owusu, M. (1978) 'The ethnography of Africa: the usefulness of the useless', *American Anthropologist*, 80: 310–34.

Payne, M.C. (1981) 'Malinowski's style', *Proceedings of the American Philosophical Society*, 125: 416–40.

Peacock, J.L. (1986) *The Anthropological Lens: Harsh Light, Soft Focus*. Cambridge: Cambridge University Press.

Pearce, P. (1982) *The Social Psychology of Tourist Behaviour*. Oxford: Pergamon.

Pi-Sunyer, O. (1981) 'Tourism and anthropology', *Annals of Tourism Research*, 8: 271–84.

Pratt, M.L. (1986) 'Fieldwork in common places', in J. Clifford and G. Marcus (eds), *Writing Culture*. Berkeley: University of California Press.

Redfoot, D. (1988) 'Touristic authenticity, tourist angst and modern reality', *Qualitative Sociology*, 7: 291–309.

Richardson, M. (1975) 'Anthropologist: the myth teller', *American Ethnologist*, 2: 517–33.

Richter, L. (1989) *The Politics of Tourism in Asia*. Honolulu: University of Hawaii Press.

Rojek, C. (1985) *Capitalism and Leisure Theory*. London: Tavistock.

Rosaldo, R. (1986) 'From the door of his tent: the fieldworker and the inquisitor', in J. Clifford and G. Marcus (eds), *Writing Culture*. Berkeley: University of California Press.

Rose, D. (1982) 'Occasions and forms of anthropological experience', in J. Ruby (ed.), *A Crack in the Mirror: Reflexive Perspectives in Anthropology*. Philadelphia: University of Pennsylvania Press.

Said, E. (1978) *Orientalism*. New York: Pantheon.

Smith, V.L. (1989) 'Introduction', in V.L. Smith (ed.), *Hosts and Guests: the Anthropology of Tourism* (2nd edn). Philadelphia: University of Pennsylvania Press.

Strathern, M. (1987) 'Out of context: the persuasive fictions of anthropology', *Current Anthropology*, 28: 251–81.

Sweet, J. (1985) *Dances of the Tewa Pueblo Indians: Expressions of New Life*. Santa Fe: School of American Research Press.

Turnbull, C. (1982) 'Bali's new gods', *Natural History*, January: 26–32.

Turner, L. and Ash, J. (1975) *The Golden Hordes: International Tourism and the Pleasure Periphery*. London: Constable.

Urry, J. (1990) *The Tourist Gaze: Leisure and Travel in Contemporary Society*. London: Sage.

van den Berghe, P.L. (1980) 'Tourism as ethnic relations: a case study of Cuzco, Peru', *Ethnic and Racial Studies*, 3: 375–92.

Wagner, U. (1977) 'Out of time and place: mass tourism and charter trips', *Ethnos*, 42: 38–52.

Webster, S. (1982) 'Fiction and ethnography', *Dialectical Anthropology*, 7: 91–114.

Webster, S. (1983) 'Ethnography as story-telling', *Dialectical Anthropology*, 8: 185–205.

Weightman, B. (1987) 'Third World tour landscapes', *Annals of Tourism Research*, 14: 227–39.

Wheeler, V. (1986) 'Travelers' tales: observations on the travel book and ethnography', *Anthropological Quarterly*, 52: 52–63.

13

The Ethnographer/Tourist in Indonesia

Edward M. Bruner

We have problematized the identity of the native peoples who become the object of the tourist gaze, caught as they are in the paradoxical predicament of encouraging tourism as a route to economic development but realizing at the same time that tourists want to see undeveloped primitive peoples. The more modern the locals become the less interest they have for the occidental tourist. Tourists come from the outside to see the exotic; from the inside, tourism is viewed as modernization. Tourism thrives on difference; why should the tourist travel thousands of miles and spend thousands of dollars to view a Third World culture essentially similar to their own? This necessity for primitiveness may lead the indigenous people to mask their real selves and to devise performances to satisfy the tourist quest for the exotic other (Kirshenblatt-Gimblett and Bruner, 1989). The consequences this predicament may have for the native self have been discussed elsewhere (Bruner, 1991).

We have also problematized the role of the tourist, but where we have done the least in tourism studies is to analyse the identity of those who study tourism, the researchers. We study the voyeurism of the tourist but not the voyeurism of the researcher studying tourists (Walkerdine, 1986). In many fields, including anthropology, we no longer regard the research scientist as a politically detached observer who studies other peoples from a neutral position. In recent years we have become very aware of the multiple ways that our narrative structures, writing practices, academic conventions and ideological stances penetrate our professional practice (Bruner, 1984; 1986; 1989; Clifford and Marcus, 1986; Marcus and Fischer, 1986). We realize that the scientist does not have a fixed monolithic or unified self but is rather a product of a historical era, a disciplinary perspective, a life situation, and that these historical and social factors have a bearing on the production of scientific research. Rather than factor out the personal from the scientific, recent ethnographers have celebrated it (Narayan, 1989; Lavie, 1990; Kondo, 1990).

In this chapter I discuss my experiences serving as a tour guide to Indonesia for affluent American tourists. My focus will be on the identity of the researcher as well as on the tourists. Although the setting is Indonesia, the chapter is more about Americans than Indonesians, and as such is more a contribution to studies of Western culture than to studies of South East Asia. As an ethnographer working as a guide for tourists, I was also led to reflect on the similarities and differences between ethnography and tourism, both Western discursive practices, and these reflections will constitute the concluding thrust of the chapter.

The ethnographer as tour guide

My rationale for becoming a tour guide was to gather data for a comparative study of tourist productions. A key difficulty in studying tourists is methodological: the tourists move so fast through the sites that it is hard to keep up with them. The problem is not one of gaining rapport, for the tourists are accessible, but of finding an opportunity for an extended conversation. It is relatively easy to begin a discussion, but in the middle of a sentence the tour leader announces that the group is moving on to the next site, and your informant has disappeared. Further, tourists become a group in their area of origin, in New York, or Tokyo, or Paris. They travel together, eat their meals together for the duration of the tour, and become a tightly knit social group, not necessarily a cohesive one, but a travelling social unit, sharing the adventures and the trials of a common journey. I felt that the only way for me to enter into tourist discourse would be to join the tour group. As a guide, I would be an insider and I could observe how the tourists actually experienced the sites and the events to which they were exposed. I would be there on the bus with the tourists immediately after a performance to observe their reactions, or I could sit with them at breakfast during a discussion about the itinerary for the day. We have generalizations in the literature about tourist motivations, that they are on a sacred journey (Graburn, 1977), that they are on a quest for their authentic self (MacCannell, 1976), or that tourism is play (Cohen, 1984), but little systematic observation on the tourists' own reactions and interpretations.

Of course, I could have accomplished the same objective by becoming a tourist, but that would have been a prohibitively expensive alternative, especially as my focus of interest was American and European tourists who travel to Third World countries. By becoming a guide, my expenses were paid by the commercial tour agency that hired me, and in addition I received a fee of $200 per participant. I led the Indonesian tour two times, in March 1986 and again in March 1987. On the first tour there were seven tourists and on the second there were 13, so I earned $1400 and $2600. On both tours, however, my wife accompanied me as she always does on ethnological field trips, and we had to pay for her expenses, at cost. As the Indonesia tour, including both air fare and land package, cost about $4200 per person, we actually lost money.

The tourists

As there are many types of tours and tourists (Cohen, 1984), I will describe the nature of my particular Indonesian tour. Briefly, it was an upscale version of what has been called cultural or educational tourism (Mintz, 1977; Graburn, 1983). The agency advertised that their tours were led by 'noted scholars', a reading list had been distributed in advance, and the front page of the tourist brochure for Indonesia presented a biographical sketch of my academic qualifications, stressing that I was an anthropology professor, had conducted three years of field work in Indonesia, and spoke the language. One way to put it was that the tour agency was not only selling Indonesia, it was selling me, at least in my capacity as scholar. Another way to put it was that tourism had coopted ethnography. This was a tour with a tour guide professor and tourist students, ostensibly there to learn. It was comparable, in the advertising and in the tourist view, to the tours organized by universities for their alumni or by museums for their sponsors. Many anthropologists have led such tours but few mention it and even fewer write about it or incorporate the experience into their academic discourse. The participants, however, were very aware of the special nature of their tour. One woman said about another group that they were mere tourists, for they didn't even have their own academic lecturer. Another remarked that he would never go with one of those tour groups that cover all Asia in a few weeks, moving from Hong Kong, to Singapore, to Bangkok and to Bali, for a brief three days in each locality. Our group, it was claimed, by spending three weeks in one country was able to explore Indonesia in depth. In three weeks!

Combining the 1986 and the 1987 populations yields a sociological profile of the tourists. They were older; the average age was about 50. Seven of the 20 were women who had been divorced or widowed and who were travelling alone. Nine were men or women who had previously worked but who were now retired. If, as MacCannell (1976) says, tourists are alienated beings who lead such shallow and inauthentic lives that they have to seek authenticity elsewhere, one would never know it from these tourists. They were well educated: 19 of the 20 had received a college education, and most were from a successful professional or business class, wealthy enough to afford a $4200 three-week vacation. There were physicians, business executives, a lawyer, an engineer, a medical school professor and even a retired PhD in sociology.

I felt comfortable with these affluent tourists in part because of the similarities in our life experiences. Like the tourists, my wife and I were older college-educated professionals, and we too talked about our children. Relationships between persons of similar socio-economic and generational levels may be more comfortable as so much is shared. Personally, I found the tourists to be intelligent, adventuresome and hardy souls. Some had previously organized their own trips, but they preferred the group tour as it took the hassle out of travel, especially in Third World countries. They appreciated that everything was arranged in advance, that no time was lost *en route*, that the accommodations were first class, and that it was a learning experience. Most enjoyed the companionship of others on the group tour, and for many of the single travellers this was a key factor. Some of the older single women were afraid to travel by themselves and were very dependent on the group and on the tour leader. I recorded tourist dreams, and one woman dreamed that she and I were together on the tour bus, that I stopped off at a photography store to buy more film, but I did not return. After a frantic search to find her tour guide, she finally located me in an old church, much to her relief. When I asked what she felt during the dream, the woman replied that she felt terror at being alone and abandoned. Dreams may be read at many levels, of course, but in this dream the manifest content reveals the woman's dependency on the tour group and the emotional force of that dependency.

Many of the tourists had become international travellers at a particular stage in their life-cycle, when they had the leisure time and the money, especially after retirement, or after losing a spouse. One woman told me that her husband, recently retired from a lucrative medical practice, was dragging her all over the world, on one tour after another, as if to make up for the missed vacations during busy working years. Another relatively young woman in her 40s, just divorced, explained that she was going on tours because to live the good life was the best revenge.

Every one of the 20 tourists had been on previous tours, and 10 of the 20 had been on other tours with the same travel agency. All of the tourists, then, were experienced travellers, many went regularly on one or two organized tours a year, and some had been doing so for decades. Tourism was part of their life-style. This was an unexpected finding for me, although it has been reported by others (Foster, 1986). Much of the conversation on tour was about tours: an experience in Zimbabwe, the time the children went along on the trip to East Africa, what happened when the bus broke down in Burma, a tour taken the previous year with Society Expeditions or Abercrombie and Kent, or what it was like when China was just opened to tourism. There was competition within the group as to who had gone to the most exotic places, and who had gone to China first. The conversation reflected and constructed a tourist culture, a subculture of educational tours taken by a leisured class.

I gained some insight into this culture when one day at lunch I asked, who did they show their photographs to when they returned home? The question elicited some uneasiness and a few quiet smiles. What I learned was that they showed their slides to their children, possibly to a close friend or relative, but that in general not many people wanted to see their slides or even to hear about the trip, at least not in any detail. The tourists lacked a home audience, and their most significant others, if I may use that phrase, were tourists like themselves. As this group of others was constituted on tour, as an interest group, there was throughout the three-week period continual animated conversation not so much about Indonesia as about tourism. By the middle of the first week the travellers had consulted one another about where to go on the next tour. What these tourists shared was an interest in tours, and one way to find a meaningful social group to share their interest was to go on another tour.

Or to attend a reunion. In November 1985, before leading the Indonesia tours, I was a guide on a tour to Thailand and Burma sponsored by an organization in Chicago.[1] It was also an educational three-week tour, and the sociological profile of the participants was similar to the profile of the Indonesian tour groups. Some months after our return, the Sullivans,[2] a popular couple on the Thailand-Burma trip, sent us an invitation to come to a tourist reunion on a Sunday at their home in the suburbs of Chicago. The husband was a retired military officer who had a second career as an executive in a bank, the wife owned a women's clothing shop, and as a couple they were intelligent, witty, friendly and fun to be with. Of course, my wife and I were delighted to go, for we had never attended a tourist reunion before. What would it be like? What would we do? More detailed instructions followed, and we learned that in the morning there would be only eight people from the Thailand-Burma tour: the Sullivans, the Bruners, and two other couples. One of the other husbands owned a factory that made electric mowers, and one was a physician. There were at least four additional people from the Chicago area who had been on the tour and who could have been invited, but were not, possibly because all four were single, and of these, two were elderly widows.

The Sullivans told us to bring our slides and the morning was spent viewing each other's photographs. If anyone had a particularly striking photo, others would ask for a copy, but in fact there was considerable similarity in the images, possibly because on tour everyone usually took photographs at the same time, when the bus stopped. There were many romantic images of buffalo in the rice fields, of saffron-robed monks, of smiling Third World children and of Buddhist temples. Another reason for the similarity was the influence of *National Geographic* magazine. While on tour, copies of the *National Geographic* coverage of the country would circulate among the tourists, and this happened on both the Thailand-Burma tour and on the two Indonesia trips. Apparently it was a common practice on educational tours. The Sullivans later informed me that they saved old copies of *National Geographic* – they had a huge stack in the basement – and before each trip would look up the issue of the country to be visited, which provided a model of the kind of images they would seek. The slide show was over by noon, and the reunion took a different turn.

Persons who had travelled with the Sullivans on other tours came at noon for a buffet lunch, and those of us who had been there in the morning joined the larger group. As many of the people were known only to the Sullivans and were strangers to each other, each person was asked to fill out a name tag, and after writing their name, to list the tours taken with the Sullivans. My tag, for example, was 'Ed Bruner, Thailand-Burma', but other tags might list, after the person's name, the East African safari tour, the walking tour in Germany, the English countryside tour, or whatever trips the person had taken with the Sullivans. Thus the mark of one's identity was a name, which was expected, followed by a listing of tours, which shows the importance this group attached to tourism. The walls of the home were covered with photographs grouped together not by theme but by tour, and much of the conversation concerned tours taken or anticipated. A sense of consumerism and consumption pervaded the air, as one person after another told stories of experiences in exotic places.

The centrepiece of the buffet table was quite remarkable, as it contained a number of the souvenirs the Sullivans had purchased on their many trips. There was a cloth from India, a mask from Africa, Chinese pottery, a Bavarian-type Swiss clock, a Masai spear, a German beer mug, Thai temple bells, an Australian boomerang and a Mekonde statue. I was pleased to see this centrepiece, for I had never known what tourists did with all the souvenirs they bought. The display reminded me of Mullaney's (1983: 43) description of a sixteenth-century European wonder-cabinet: 'what comes to reside in a wonder-cabinet are, in the most reified sense of the phrase, strange things: tokens of alien cultures, reduced to the status of sheer objects, stripped of cultural and human contexts.' The objects survive the period and the context that produce them. A wonder-cabinet has absolutely no classificatory principle at work except that the items contained within it are all strange objects, whereas museum exhibits have some unifying theme, such as objects of a particular type or from a certain geographical area of the world. The classificatory principle at work in the centrepiece was that all the objects had been collected on tour, by the Sullivans. Not only the objects in the centrepiece but the guests themselves were classified by tour, which demonstrates the importance of the tour. Each object in the centrepiece served as a reminder of a particular tour, and the object served as the occasion for telling a story about the conditions in which the object had been selected and purchased (Stewart, 1984). It is important to note that the concern was less with the intrinsic quality of the object, such as how it might be used, or with the position of the object in the indigenous culture, but rather with the circumstances involved in the collection of the object by the Sullivans.

These data suggest that the tourists may have more of an experience of the tour group than an experience of Indonesia. It would be too extreme to say that the tourists go to Indonesia as an excuse for joining a tour group. But rather than beginning with a desire to see Indonesia and then deciding that the group tour was a convenient way to go, many individual tourists first decide to go on tour and then select Indonesia. In any case, there is no doubt that the cultural content, the knowledge of Indonesia, is acquired within the context of the tour group, and this is one of the most important things about the entire experience.

Ethnography and tourism

We now ask, what did I learn as a tour guide to Indonesia and what were the difficulties? My double role as a tour guide serving tourists, and as an ethnographer studying them, placed me in an interstitial position between touristic and ethnographic discourse, and I must admit that I had not been aware of the ambiguities of the position in which I had placed myself. As ethnographer I wanted to know how tourists experienced the sites, but as tour guide my task was to structure that experience through my lectures and explanations. My talk mediated their experience and, in a sense, I found myself studying myself. Like the Kaluli shamans who create the meaning they discover (Schieffelin, 1992), I constructed for the tourists the meaning of the sites and then I studied that meaning as if I had discovered it. This is not as unusual in ethnographic research as it may at first appear. Cassirer has noted that when we think we are exploring reality we are merely engaging in a dialogue with our own symbolic systems (Bruner, 1986: 150).

Even more disturbing, during the course of the journey through Indonesia I would slip back and forth between the two discourses, the touristic and the ethnographic, for I could not always keep them straight. At times I experienced myself as pure tourist, gaping in awe at Borobudur, the magnificent eighth-century Buddhist monument in central Java, and at other times I marshalled my reflexive acuity and carefully took notes on tourist behaviour. The same oscillation occurred in my photography. I took photographs of Borobudur that must have been indistinguishable from any tourist snapshot, but then I would turn my camera and photograph the tourists taking photographs of Borobudur. Was I a closet ethnographer on tour, or a closet tourist doing ethnography? Was Sidney Mintz correct, that 'we are all tourists' (1977: 59)? The ambiguity of it all was upsetting.

Having found myself in this predicament, I was led to reflect on the similarities and differences between tourism and ethnography, and particularly to probe more deeply into my own experiences. Early in my career my wife and I had lived in a Toba Batak village in North Sumatra and were adopted into the Simandjuntak clan (Bruner, 1957). I did rather traditional ethnography of rural and urban social organization (Bruner, 1963), and only later in the 1980s did my interests turn to tourism. In the early 1970s, when modern mass tourism was rapidly developing in Bali, I went on a few 'vacations' there with my family, taking time off from anthropological work I was then conducting in Java (Bruner, 1972). We stayed at tourist hotels or beach cottages in Sanur, and from what I recollect, we behaved in ways essentially similar to other tourists in Bali. I thoroughly enjoyed these Balinese family vacations. Thus I have occupied multiple roles in Indonesia, as ethnographer, as tourist, as ethnographer studying tourism, and as tour guide, so I am an appropriate person to write on this topic.

The similarities between tourism and ethnography have been explored with irony and insight by Crick (1985; and Chapter 12 in this volume). Both tourists and ethnographers travel to foreign areas, reside there temporarily, observe native peoples, and return with accounts and stories of their observations. Tourism and ethnography (and colonialism) are relatives (Graburn, 1983), as they arise from the same social formation and are different forms of Western expansion into the Third World. Kirshenblatt-Gimblett (1987: 59) regards 'tourism as a species of ethnographic discourse'. Colonialists frequently yearn for the traditional native culture that they have destroyed, what Rosaldo (1989) calls imperialist nostalgia, but as I have noted elsewhere (Bruner, 1989) it is precisely this traditional culture that ethnographers have usually described and that tourists now come to see. Colonialism, ethnography and tourism have at different periods engaged the mythological 'traditional' culture of primitive people, based upon a gross inequity in power relations. In our contemporary era, tourism seeks to occupy the ethnographic present, the discursive space that colonialism mourns for and that ethnography has recently, and finally, abandoned. As the ethnographic present never existed it has always been reconstructed, formerly in the traditional ethnographic monograph, and now in the standard tourist performance (Lanfant, 1989). This preference for the simulacrum is the essence of contemporary tourism in these post-modern times, where the copy is better than the original (Baudrillard, 1983; Eco, 1986).

It is not, of course, that ethnographers acknowledge the similarity with tourism. 'From the perspective of ethnography, tourism is an illegitimate child, a disgraceful simplification, and an impostor (de Certeau, 1984: 143), and we strive to distinguish ethnography from tourism, for tourism is an assault on our authority and privileged position as ethnographers' (Bruner, 1989: 440). But Mintz, Graburn, Crick, Kirshenblatt-Gimblett and others have begun to highlight the similarities between tourism and ethnography. In the remainder of this chapter I will reverse the focus to highlight the differences. The challenge is to avoid the obvious – that ethnography is science, authentic and work, whereas tourism is commercial, inauthentic and play – and to articulate the differences based upon my own Indonesian field experiences.

Touristic visualization

My most striking insight into the tourist mentality occurred when I was a guide for the second group tour to Indonesia in 1987. In Bali, in addition to the usual tourist itinerary of the *kecak* and *barong* dances, I had arranged for the group to attend an *odalan* or Balinese temple festival, a performance that the Balinese put on for themselves. Such rituals are not on the tour itinerary because they occur at irregular intervals and the time scheduling is unpredictable. A group may arrive at a temple only to find that the festival was over yesterday or will take place next week. Our group arrived on the day of the temple festival, which was fortunate, but we arrived too early, at 10 a.m., and nothing was happening. We took our bus to another nearby site and returned at 11 a.m. only to find that not much had changed. We waited until 11.30 a.m. but there was still not much activity. One of the tourists complained of the heat and suggested to the tour director that we leave. I urged that we wait, noting that the Balinese were resting in the shade whereas the members of our group were walking about in the sun. Just relax, for the ceremony will begin, I assured them.

Shortly after noon, the festival started, and it was spectacular. Elderly Balinese women began dancing in a line around the temple courtyard. Their faces were intense, as if in trance, their finger and body movements slow and delicate. Other women began arriving with pyramids of flowers, fruit and sweets balanced on their heads as offerings to the temple gods. The *pemangku* or priests were sprinkling holy water on kneeling supplicants. The *barong* and *rangda* masks, which look like Chinese dragons, were assembled for a procession. Incense was burning, the *gamelan* was playing, the odours, sounds and colours were coming from everywhere, it was all happening at once, an ethnographer's paradise. At that point, just as the festival was beginning, around 12.30 p.m., the tour director announced that we were leaving for lunch and that everyone should go back to the tour bus.

I protested, and explained that what ethnographers do in these circumstances is to 'hang around', to flow with the events, and to observe. This was a rare opportunity, I said, because such Hindu rituals were only performed in Bali, and an *odalan* is performed at each temple only once a year. Stay, I said, to see this dazzling ceremony. 'But we have seen it', replied one tourist as the group followed the tour leader back to the air-conditioned bus.

'But we have seen it.' These words still haunt me. The touristic mode of experiencing is primarily visual, and to have been there, to have 'seen' it, only requires presence. The tourist 'sees' enough of the Balinese ritual to confirm his prior images derived from the media, from brochures and from *National Geographic*. To 'see' a ritual is comparable to collecting a souvenir to be placed in the centrepiece of a buffet table, a twentieth-century wonder-cabinet. The tourist has 'seen' a strange thing, a token of the exotic, and there is no necessity to go further, to penetrate to any deeper level. To have captured the ceremony in photographs is to have domesticated the exotic, so that it can be brought back home, and the aura of pleasurable mystification remains.

As Clifford (1988) and Geertz (1988) have informed us, if ethnography is anything it is writing, for the final ethnographic product is an account, in words, spoken or written, a lecture, article or monograph. An ethnographer could spend years studying an *odalan*, and many have, as we analyse the time sequence, the placement in space, the ritual symbols, the identity of the social groups involved, and the meaning of it all for the Balinese. For us, being there is just the start of a long process of taking field notes, analysing, writing, revising and presenting. The touristic and ethnographic modes of understanding are totally different.

I had a similar experience with another group in Sulawesi. When we arrived at the hotel I learned that there was to be a large Toradja funeral the next day and suggested at supper that we forget the printed itinerary and go directly to the ritual. One tourist objected that he didn't want to miss anything that was written on the printed schedule, and the group, supported by the local Indonesian guide, decided to follow the set itinerary but to go to the ritual before lunchtime. After a morning of going to dead Toradja 'traditional' villages, where no one lived but where the tourists could buy souvenirs and cloth (and the Indonesian guide could receive his customary commission), we finally arrived at the ceremony in time to see the slaughter of 10 buffalo. At 1 p.m., the group sent a delegate to inform me that they felt it was time to leave, but I managed to keep them there for one and a half hours, better than in Bali. At lunch, we did have a good discussion of animal sacrifice, kinship groupings, and Indonesian beliefs about the supernatural, but I would have rather remained at the ceremony.

That tourism is based on visual perception was reinforced by the contrast between the role of photography in ethnography and in tourism. In my earlier work in Sumatra, I found that I could not do ethnography and photography at the same time. Maybe Karl Heider or Richard Chalfen could do it, but I could not. As ethnographer, I was sensitive to my primary sources of information, my conversations with people and my observations of their behaviour. I had to go along with the flow of the dialogue. As photographer, I went off in a different direction, as I was sensitive to the correct camera angle, to the play of light and shade, to the moment when the elements in the photograph were in the most appropriate arrangement. My objective was a photograph that was aesthetically pleasing as well as ethnographically informative. At a given event or ceremony, I might do both ethnography and photography, but serially, never simultaneously. Each required a different style of concentration and a different play of sensory modes.

On the other hand, tourists observe people and events through the camera lens. Many times I have observed that when tourists come to a new site, their first reaction is to move the camera to the eye, so that they see others through the viewfinder. This is very selective perception, as it places a frame around the object, and it decontextualizes the other (Sontag, 1973; Mulvey, 1975; Barthes, 1981). It removes the surrounding context from view and selects out for emphasis what is contained within the frame, almost as a close-up of life, a well-composed image, to the neglect of the larger environment around the frame. This way of experiencing transforms the native object into images, into frames. The world is seen as a series of framed photographs. It is the ultimate triumph of Polaroid photography, because even without the requisite technology, people and sites are turned into instant images.

Is this emphasis on tourist visualization an overstatement? Not every tourist, of course, carries a camera. If a couple is travelling together, frequently only one person takes the pictures and assumes the photographer's role, although sometimes both may take photographs. Sites require varying degrees of verbal explanation, and indeed there are some verbalizations about every site, in the form of tour guide talk, signs, markers, guidebooks, tourist brochures or even the remarks of other tourists. No site in the Third World is approached naïvely, because there is always some interpretation provided or available before the tourists come to the site. In a sense, every site is pre-interpreted. The tourists 'know' about the site before they arrive, if only because they have selected the site in advance when they purchased the tour, and they do have a prior conception of what they are buying.

Nevertheless, photographic visualization is the dominant mode of touristic perception. As tourists approach the other with camera in hand, they 'see' the Balinese or the Toradja through their viewfinder. The camera held in front of the face of the tourist serves as a mask, a way of enhancing the distance between subject and object, of hiding oneself from the other. The tourist can move in for a close-up but this is accomplished without direct eye-to-eye contact. It is as if what confronts the other is the camera mask (to coin a phrase) of the tourist, which hides his or her real self. Photography is a way of examining the native, a voyeurism, without being personal or committed to the relationship, without seeming to look. Photography provides a role for the tourist in what otherwise might be an awkward encounter. The tourist eye 'sees' through photographic frames.

As a complement to this touristic mode of experiencing, much of the Third World, at least along the main tourist routes, is being transformed as image for the tourist gaze. Native craft demonstrations and performances are being arranged at times of day when the conditions and the light are best for photography. I have observed this phenomenon in Bali, in Java and in East Africa, but I first noticed it as a graduate student during a tour of Monument Valley in the south-west, where Navaho in bright blue and turquoise clothing, riding horses, would herd sheep in the late afternoon, when the sun cast long shadows along the ridges of a sand dune. It made a magnificent photograph, one reproduced many times, and had become a standard part of the tour. The tour leader, in advance, told us exactly where to stand to get the best photographs. Marked photo vantage points along tourist routes are commonplace, but that native life is being rearranged to fit touristic photographic requirements is something else again (Chalfen, 1987: 118). In one of my Indonesian tours, I asked an elderly tourist if he had had a good day, and he replied that it was better than yesterday, as there were more good photographic opportunities. He evaluated the success of his tour by the number of his photographs. Tour agents and entrepreneurs have responded to this need, as native peoples are being given visual but not verbal space in touristic discourse.

Touristic surrender

An executive of a large technology firm on the east coast explained to me that once he boarded the plane for Indonesia he became completely relaxed, because he knew that everything would be done for him by the tour agency, and that everything would be first class. He travelled with this agency, he said, because they really took care of you: there would be no hassles, no concerns, and no necessity to make decisions. I came to understand what he meant. When the group was moving from one island area to another, the instructions were to place your bags outside your hotel room on the day of departure. A bus was waiting to take you to the airport, where you were given your boarding pass. There was no waiting in line, no worry about customs or immigration, passports or tickets. When the plane arrived at its destination, another bus was waiting to take you to the hotel, you were given a key to your new room, and shortly thereafter your bags were delivered. At every step along the way you were told what to do. While on tour you were told when to stay with the group or when there was a period of free time, and in the latter case, you were instructed precisely when to meet back at the bus. The time spent at each site was predetermined by the agency. The main requirement was that you follow instructions, and it was considered bad form to be late or to hold up the group. Almost all of the tourists did as they were told.

This set of practices and the attitudes that accompany it I call 'tourist surrender'. Other writers have described this phenomenon in other terms, suggesting, for example, that tourists become like children (Dann, 1989). What I wish to emphasize here is that the tourists voluntarily surrender control, they let go, and turn over the management of the tour to the agency. They become passive and dependent, and this is what gives them the feeling of relaxation. The *Oxford English Dictionary* defines surrender as 'to give oneself up into the power of another', as a prisoner, and this expresses my meaning in that tourists relinquish power over their actions for the duration of the tour.

I do not, however, accept the model of going on tour as a liminal 'time out' from home, based on the van Gennep, Victor Turner notion of rites of passage, as used by Jafari, as a three-part home–journey–home paradigm. Such paradigms fail to problematize 'home' (Morris, 1988) and from the perspective of my own home university community, with all its turmoil about multi-culturalism, racial and gender issues, it is difficult any more to regard 'home' as a stable beginning or ending. Then too, the journey on the group tour involves an oscillation, from hotel to the bus to the sites, and as I have already mentioned in an earlier section, what the tourists talk about is other tours and tourism more than Indonesia, so that in their conversations on the journey, which are about status and consumerism, they never really left home. What the tourists surrender is not their structural position in a home society but rather control over their journey.

Touristic surrender involves acceptance of the common practices of the group tour, such as the social requirements of group travel and the loss of the ability to set one's own agenda. Surrender makes the details of travel so much easier, but in the bargain, the tourists also surrender control of their relationship with the Indonesian people. Touristic surrender then is just the opposite of the ethnographic stance. Ethnography is a struggle and one never surrenders. An ethnographer is or could be working every waking moment, taking notes, conducting interviews, and continually struggling to understand and to make sense of a different culture. In the field, the constant struggle is against the taken-for-granted, of giving in to native routine, for the greatest danger is in accepting, or surrendering to, native ways to such an extent that one begins to live the native life rather than describing it for a home audience. The enterprise is never completed because even after you leave the field site the hard problems emerge of creating order out of a mélange of discontinuous notes and memories.

Tourism is primarily visual, ethnography verbal. Tourists surrender, ethnographers struggle.

Possibly even more important are two points about which I am still gathering data and am not prepared to discuss at this time, but I will mention them. The first is that tourists, at least those on upscale cultural tourism of the kind I have described, accept no moral or political responsibility for the people they visit or for the accounts of native peoples that they produce, whereas ethnographers these days have to accept full political responsibility for their work. As a tour guide working for a tour agency I found myself fighting the system, and even trying to change it, in ways that I will describe elsewhere.

The second point is that in Bali, for example, which has had at least 70 years of continuous tourism from the late 1920s (Picard, 1990; Boon, 1977; 1990), it is no longer possible to differentiate in Balinese culture between what is touristic and what is ethnographic. There are performances which arise in Balinese life, the province of the ethnographer, but drift into tourism, such as the *barong* drama; and there are dramas such as the frog dance which was created in Batuan in the 1970s explicitly for tourists but which has now been performed in Balinese social life, and hence is now ethnographic. Michel Picard, Hildred Geertz and James Boon are among those exploring these issues. It is not just that Crick and others highlight the similarities between tourism and ethnography as two entirely separate discourses, and I focus on some differences, and that this is a purely scholarly issue, but rather that tourism has influenced the selves and the lives of native people to such an extent that they cannot be entirely sure what is touristic and what ethnographic, between what is performed for outsiders and what for themselves, between what is sacred and what secular (Picard, 1990). If a culture is shaped for 70 years, over multiple generations, to perform for foreigners, as in Bali, and if the evaluations of foreign scholars legitimate some Balinese performances more than others, so that they are emphasized more in Balinese culture, it blurs the boundaries. If a Balinese troupe performs a dance drama in a temple, we call it religion; if in a concert hall in London, we call it art; if in a beach hotel, we call it tourism. But the distinctions between religion, art and tourism are Western categories, not Balinese realities.

Earlier in the chapter, in an ironic tone, I described how I was lecturing to the tourists about Indonesia, thus influencing them, and then studying their reactions to Indonesia, so that in effect I was studying myself. This same process has been operating in Bali and possibly in Toradja (Volkman, 1990), on a more profound cultural level, as Indonesians shape their performances for a foreign audience. Balinese culture, the stuff of ethnography, is itself becoming contaminated with the touristic. The point goes beyond my personal role problem in separating my touristic self from my ethnographic self. The point is that the Balinese and other Indonesian peoples have the same problem, which is indeed a predicament.

Notes

An earlier draft of this chapter was presented at a conference on Tourism and the Change of Life Styles, Instytut Turystyki, Warsaw, Poland, 1988.

1 This was my first experience as a guide. Altogether, I have been a guide on three tours for a total of nine weeks.

2 A pseudonym.

References

Barthes, R. (1981) *Camera Lucida*. New York: Hill and Wang.

Baudrillard, J. (1983) *Simulations*. New York: Semiotext(e).

Boon, J. (1977) *The Anthropological Romance of Bali, 1597–1972: Dynamic Perspectives in Marriage and Caste, Politics and Religion*. New York: Cambridge University Press.

Boon, J. (1990) *Affinities and Extremes: Crisscrossing the Bittersweet Ethnology of East Indies History, Hindu-Balinese Culture, and Indo-European Allure*. Chicago: University of Chicago Press.

Bruner, E.M. (1957) 'The Toba Batak village', in G.W. Skinner (ed.), *Local, Ethnic, and National Loyalties in Village Indonesia: A Symposium*. Southeast Asia Studies, Yale University, and the Institute of Pacific Relations, New York.

Bruner, E.M. (1963) 'Medan: the role of kinship in an Indonesian city', in A. Spoehr (ed.), *Pacific Port Towns and Cities*. Honolulu: Bishop Museum Press. pp. 1–12.

Bruner, E.M. (1972) 'Batak ethnic associations in three Indonesian cities', *Southwestern Journal of Anthropology*, 28(3): 207–29.

Bruner, E.M. (1984) *Text, Play and Story: the Construction and Reconstruction of Self and Society*. 1983 Proceedings, American Ethnological Society. Washington, DC: American Anthropological Association. Reissued 1988, Chicago: Waveland Press.

Bruner, E.M. (1986) 'Ethnography as narrative', in L. Turner and E.M. Bruner (eds), *The Anthropology of Experience*. Urbana: University of Illinois Press.

Bruner, E.M. (1989) 'Of cannibals, tourists, and ethnographers', *Cultural Anthropology*, 4(4): 439–46.

Bruner, E.M. (1991) 'The transformation of self in tourism', *Annals of Tourism Research*, 18(2): 238–50.

Chalfen, R. (1987) *Snapshot: Versions of Life*. Bowling Green: Bowling Green State University Popular Press.

Clifford, J. (1988) *The Predicament of Culture*. Cambridge: Harvard University Press.

Clifford, J. and Marcus, G.E. (1986) *Writing Culture: the Poetics and Politics of Ethnography*. Berkeley: University of California Press.

Cohen, E. (1984) 'The sociology of tourism: approaches, issues, and findings', *Annual Review of Sociology*, 10: 373–92.

Crick, M. (1985) '"Tracing" the anthropological self: quizzical reflections on field work, tourism and the ludic', *Social Analysis*, 17: 71–92.

Dann, G. (1989) *The Tourist as Child: Some Reflections*. Cahiers du Tourisme, Série C, no. 135. Aix-en-Provence: CHET.

de Certeau, M. (1984) *The Practice of Everyday Life*. Berkeley: University of California Press.

Eco, U. (1986) 'Travels in hyperreality', in U. Eco, *Travels in Hyperreality: Essays*. San Diego: Harcourt Brace Jovanovich. pp. 3–58.

Foster, G.M. (1986) 'South Seas cruise: a case study of a short-lived society', *Annals of Tourism Research*, 13: 215–38.

Geertz, C. (1988) *Works and Lives: the Anthropologist as Author*. Stanford: Stanford University Press.

Graburn, N.H.H. (1977) 'Tourism: the sacred journey', in V. Smith (ed.), *Hosts and Guests: the Anthropology of Tourism*. Philadelphia: University of Pennsylvania Press. pp. 17–31.

Graburn, N.H.H. (1983) 'The anthropology of tourism', *Annals of Tourism Research*, 10(1): 9–33.

Kirshenblatt-Gimblett, B. (1987) 'Authenticity and authority in the representation of culture: the poetics and politics of tourist production', in I.-M. Greverus, K. Köstlin and H. Schilling (eds), *Kulturkontakt/Kulturkonflikt: Zur Erfahrung des Fremden*, 26. Deutscher Volkskundekongress in Frankfort. pp. 59–69.

Kirshenblatt-Gimblett, B. and Bruner, E.M. (1989) 'Tourism', in *International Encyclopedia of Communications*, vol. 4. Oxford: Oxford University Press. pp. 249–53.

Kondo, D.K. (1990) *Crafting Selves: Power, Gender, and Discourses of Identity in a Japanese Workplace*. Chicago: University of Chicago Press.

Lanfant, M.-F. (1989) 'International tourism resists the crisis', in A. Olszewska and K. Roberts (eds), *Leisure and Life-Style: a Comparative Analysis of Free Time*. London: Sage.

Lavie, S. (1990) *The Poetics of Military Occupation: Mzeina Allegories of Bedouin Identity under Israeli and Egyptian Rule*. Berkeley: University of California Press.

MacCannell, D. (1976) *The Tourist: a New Theory of the Leisure Class*. New York: Schocken.

Marcus, G.E. and Fischer, M.M.J. (1986) *Anthropology as Cultural Critique*. Chicago: University of Chicago Press.

Mintz, S.M. (1977) 'Infant, victim and tourist: the anthropologist in the field', *Johns Hopkins Magazine*, 27: 54–60.

Morris, M. (1988) 'At Henry Parkes motel'. *Cultural Studies*, 2(1): 1–47.

Mullaney, S. (1983) 'Strange things, gross terms, curious customs: the rehearsal of cultures in the late Renaissance', *Representations*, 3: 40–67.

Mulvey, L. (1975) 'Visual pleasure and narrative cinema', *Screen*, 16(3): 6–18.

Narayan, K. (1989) *Storytellers, Saints, and Scoundrels: Folk Narrative in Hindu Religious Teaching*. Philadelphia: University of Pennsylvania Press.

Picard, M. (1990) '"Cultural tourism" in Bali: cultural performances as tourist attractions', *Indonesia*, 49: 37–74.

Rosaldo, R. (1989) *Culture and Truth: the Remaking of Social Analysis*. Boston: Beacon Press.

Schieffelin, E. (1992) 'Performance and the cultural construction of reality: a New Guinea example', in S. Lavie, K. Narayan and R. Rosaldo (eds), *Creativity in Anthropology*. Ithaca: Cornell University Press.

Sontag, S. (1973) *On Photography*. New York: Delta.

Stewart, S. (1984) *Objects of Desire*. Baltimore: Johns Hopkins University Press.

Volkman, T.A. (1990) 'Visions and revisions: Toradja vulture and the tourist gaze', *American Ethnologist*, 17: 91–110.

Walkerdine, V. (1986) 'Video replay: families, films, and fantasy', in V. Burgin, J. Donald and C. Kaplan (eds), *Formations of Fantasy*. London: Methuen.

Index

Printed in the United Kingdom
by Lightning Source UK Ltd.
113846UKS00001B/78